D1204018

HOW TO INSTRUCT SUCCESSFULLY

How to Instruct
Successfully

Modern Teaching Methods in Adult Education

Thomas F. Staton
Head of Psychology Department, Huntingdon College
Formerly Educational Advisor, Command and Staff College,
Air University

McGRAW-HILL BOOK COMPANY
NEW YORK   ST. LOUIS   SAN FRANCISCO
LONDON   TORONTO   SYDNEY   MEXICO   PANAMA

Preface

THIS BOOK TELLS how to prepare and present a period or a course of instruction. It is intended primarily for those who will be teaching adults but who have not had the benefit of extensive training in education or a great deal of practice in instructing. The basic principles of educational psychology are covered briefly before going into practical methods of teaching procedures.

An instructor's best insurance against embarrassment or failure is thorough preparation for each instructional job. Some people feel uneasy when first faced with the task of teaching a group of adults. This is understandable: no one wants to appear unskillful or inept.

However, if the teacher knows his subject, has planned how he will present it, and has practiced the process of teaching it, he will be able to face his class with assurance and poise. His performance will win the respect and appreciation of those who have come to learn. The instructor-to-be will profit greatly from a conscientious study of the principles and procedures introduced here.

Two themes will be found throughout this book. One is the concept that instruction aims at producing in the learner skills, knowledges and understandings, and attitudes. When a learner acquires or increases a skill, when he knows or understands something which he previously did not, and when he develops an attitude leading to more productive work, his instructor has been successful. This criterion of individual learning is the real measure of instructor success. The acquisition of new skills, understandings, and attitudes is, therefore, stressed in this text as the final standard of measurement of all methods of instruction.

The second theme is the influence of certain psychological factors on how well a person learns from any experience. These factors are believed to be motivation, concentration, reaction, organization, comprehension, and repetition. Accordingly, every method of instruction is discussed in this book in terms of how it may be used to promote the operation of these factors in the students.

Some indispensable elements of an instructional program do not fall under the headings of specific instructional methods; so, included in the text are chapters on evaluating the success of instruction, methods of counseling students to ensure maximum benefit from a program, and suggestions for instructors eager to broaden their qualifications. General chapters on setting up the classroom, organizing a curriculum, and planning the over-all program are provided for the benefit of those responsible for employee training in business, industry, government, and the Armed Forces, as well as those conducting other adult education courses.

This text is intended primarily as a practical "how-to-do-it" manual for instructors in the field, and not as a comprehensive documentation of professional thought on various educational topics. The author has drawn on his twenty years of experience as an instructor, a supervisor of instructors, and a student of educational and psychological literature to write this book in a straightforward and uncomplicated manner. Footnotes are lacking; it is believed that the group for which this book is intended is primarily interested in practical, direct advice on how to instruct. For the benefit of those readers who would like to study a method or topic more extensively, the references listed at the end of each chapter will provide a variety of viewpoints.

THOMAS F. STATON

Contents

HOW TO INSTRUCT SUCCESSFULLY

1

The Nature of Learning

This chapter treats learning as changed behavior. It will consider those aspects of learning which are important in effective teaching.

MOST PSYCHOLOGISTS and teachers think of learning as changed behavior. This practical definition serves to distinguish the process of learning from the act of memorizing by rote. *Learning* facts is one thing: *memorizing* them is quite another. Many training directors fail to appreciate the difference. In the final analysis a personnel training program should create an educational environment in which learning may take place effectively. The success of the program, in fact, will be measured by the degree to which the employee when on the job will think, feel, and act differently about the same situation *after* the experience of training than he did *before* it. If anything has happened educationally, if learning has really taken place, the employee will evidence the fact by an altered approach to his on-the-job task. What was discussed in the training session will make a difference in the employee's on-the-job behavior. When this happens, you have the best evidence that learning has taken place, that the training program has been a success, that your teaching has achieved its goal.

Changed behavior is the logical aim of a training program. When a claims adjuster has completed a program of training in adjustment procedures, you expect him to adjust claims more efficiently—not merely to recite the rule-of-the-book which he has memorized. The aim of teaching better safety techniques to a sheet metal worker, on the other hand, should be greater safety for himself and for those with whom he works. On the job, therefore, the question is not, does he know the rule in the handbook, or can he pass an examination on a safety manual, but, rather, has his behavior been so altered that when he is in the shop hazards are reduced? In personnel training, actions *do* speak louder than words. In fact, they are the most eloquent proof that learning has really taken place.

This idea of changed behavior keeps the emphasis in personnel training exactly where it belongs—on the employee and on his ability to do his job better.

All this does not mean, however, that rules are not important. Quite to the contrary. In many cases knowledge of the rule is indispensable and precedes efficiency of action. Take, for example, teaching your teen-age son to drive your car. In such an instance you would be sure that before the lad took the car on the road, he had fixed firmly in his mind the basic traffic rules and regulations. No driver would be an acceptable driver who did not know the traffic laws and regulations and was not able to apply them instantly to any emergency on city street or open road. Regardless of his skill in operating the car, the rules would naturally come first in learning to drive. But, if he knew both the law and how to manipulate the mechanism safely, then you would presume that he had *really learned* to drive.

As a rule, the weakness is not in not knowing what to do or what ought to be done, but in getting the employee actually to do what he knows to be proper and in keeping with a given situation. He is like the farmer whose county agricultural agent said to him, "Mr. Brown, I can show you how to farm twice as efficiently as you are now doing." Brown looked at him skeptically. "Thanks, Agent," he replied, "but I don't reckon it'd be worth your while. I ain't a-farmin' half as good now as I know how to!"

And right there, in homely illustration, is an insight into human nature that reveals probably the biggest single reason why training programs fail. Our sights get out of line. Knowledge, we feel, is so important that we set our sights upon the goal of getting people to *know* facts instead of motivating them to *use* facts to do a job in a better way.

Knowing the facts is, perhaps, the *starting point* in getting the trainee to change his behavior, but knowledge alone is not enough. The boy may know the rules of safe driving, but this does not guarantee that he will drive safely. Why? A half dozen reasons come to mind:

1. He may not know how the rules apply in actual highway situations.

2. He may never have thought of the rules in connection with what he actually does in driving, but simply as words he has been required to learn by rote.

3. He may know the rules, but disobey them because he does not see that they are really important. That is, he has no *motivation* for applying the rules.

4. He may know very well that the rules are important, but he may prefer the thrill of flouting them.

5. He may simply never give any thought to the rules when he is at the wheel of the car.

6. He may not have the skill to apply the rules to the operation of the car.

Obviously, if his hazardous driving is a result of any of the above causes, merely to urge him to become more familiar with the rules would accomplish nothing. Instead you must change this behavior to conform to the knowledge he already has.

From this illustration we see that learning, in the full sense of the word, probably requires "sublearnings" in at least three areas: (1) *knowledge* or *understanding*, or in simply knowing what to do and how to do do it; (2) *attitude*, or the emotional response of a person toward a particular task; and (3) *skill*, or the ability to coordinate eye, mind, and body into one complex performance whereby the worker is able to do a task easily and proficiently.

In training programs, particularly, aim to have the employee develop all three of these areas: knowledge, attitude, and skill. Also, a word of caution should here be issued. Learning in one of these areas does not necessarily guarantee learning in the other two areas. For example, a supervisor studying human-relations techniques in personnel supervision may develop an intense desire to handle people well (attitude), but he may not have learned the facts about human emotions and motivation. Without this knowledge he cannot handle employees effectively. Or the teacher of a course may have developed a high degree of skill in dealing with his class personnel in the classroom or laboratory, but he may have no desire to employ this skill when actually working with his subordinates. Where such situations occur, one or more of the basic sublearnings has not been acquired. *Learning*, in the broader sense of altering the behavior of the individual when dealing with a specific situation, has not occurred. If the supervisor does not handle people more adeptly and diplomatically than before he took the training course, he has not *learned*, and, for practical purposes, the company's investment in his on-the-job training has been largely wasted.

To be most rewarding, therefore, in terms of the investment of money, time, and effort, training programs must aim specifically to develop all three of the sublearnings in every session of the course. *Knowledge, attitude,* and *skill*—these are absolute essentials in the learning process.

It is not safe to leave learning to chance. Incidental learning is accidental learning. Nor is it safe to assume that the presence of any one of the sublearnings insures the existence of the others. They do not propagate by assumption or by miracle. They must be deliberately developed.

No one involved in personnel training, therefore, can plan too carefully in conditioning the soil in which instruction is to take place, nor can he overestimate the importance of the factors upon which all learning and every successful training program rest, namely, the development of knowledge, attitude, and skill.

Now comes the key question: if this three-sided nature of effective learning is so important in the whole educative process, what methods are available by which you may achieve these results? Obviously, methodology is a matter which this book will discuss carefully in later chapters. Here we will only outline the answer to this question.

Each sublearning is, perhaps, best achieved by a specialized approach. Here is a brief digest of specific methodology that is well suited to each particular sublearning:

1. *Knowledge:* Generally, lectures and reading assignments are the fastest and most economical ways of acquiring knowledge or understanding.

2. *Attitudes:* In developing attitudes the instructor needs to plan his approach carefully, and he needs to direct skillfully the motivation and thinking of the group. Methods of teaching especially well suited to attitude development are the discussion method, the demonstration-performance method, and role-playing.

3. *Skills:* To develop a skill the demonstration-performance method and role-playing techniques are perhaps most useful.

One fact should be plain: in view of the triple aspect of learning, there is no one *best* method of teaching. The goal of learning will dictate the method, and the effective teacher will plan his instructional approach with this principle in mind. In nearly every learning situation, moreover, the instructor will doubtless find that a skillful blending of two or more methods is preferable to the exclusive use of one method.

The principal aim, however, of any training program—the prima-facie evidence that it has succeeded as a *training* program—is the development of *ability to do* on the part of the trainee, and not only the *development* of ability to do but the actual *culmination* of that ability into specific deeds of changed behavior. So meaningful in its more comprehensive sense is the phrase, *ability to do,* —so suggestive is it of the commonly accepted goal of all training —that it might be substituted for "changed behavior" as a description of what should actually result from *all* personnel training.

The big questions are: how can the training program develop in the trainee these skills and abilities? How can it produce the changes in behavior that are necessary in order to justify the whole training program? How can genuine training guarantee greater efficiency on the job?

The answers to these questions will engage most of the remainder of the book. Psychological principles underlie the process of changing behavior patterns, and the psychological implications of effective learning will be discussed in connection with administering an effective personnel training program. Other questions of importance, as these apply to the function of the instructor and his relation to the whole training program, will be answered: How do you prepare for the teaching of a course? How do you plan and present your material? What role does counselling play in trainee instruction? How do you evaluate the effectiveness of your teaching in terms of your own skill as a teacher and the degree to which the material which you have presented has been learned?

These are important questions in the educational aspects of any personnel training program. With these and other pertinent considerations this book will deal.

One important matter demands constant attention in *any* course, by *any* instructor. This is the matter of the educational balance of the whole program. You must be constantly on guard that all three of the sublearnings—knowledge, skill, and attitude— be provided for in all parts of your program.

The author has seen all too many instances in which training periods or even entire programs failed because the instructor succumbed to the temptation of allotting most of the time to one sublearning, neglecting the other two. He may give, for instance, an enthusiastic sales talk concerning the importance of the job, thereby motivating the trainees to do it well, but without giving them the knowledge or developing in them the skills required to accomplish what he so eloquently presented as being desirable and necessary.

The three legs of the tripod of learning must all be of proper length. If one leg be short, or missing altogether, the tripod is useless. Every training program must produce attitudes, cultivate knowledge, and develop skills—all three—and in so far as it lacks any one of these, just so far is it thereby impaired in its effectiveness.

Occasionally, of course, a whole period may be devoted entirely to one or another of the three basic aspects of all training, but in the total program you should be sure that you have done your best to build *all three* legs to full and proper length. For only by so doing will the solidity of the result justify the time, money, and effort invested.

SUMMARY

For purposes of a training program, learning is changed behavior. The changed behavior occurs as a result of three factors which are basic to all learning: (1) *knowledge,* what to do and how to do it; (2) *attitude,* desire or willingness to put into practice what one has learned; and (3) *skill,* the ability to apply on the job that knowledge which has been acquired in the process of training.

Thus, learning is three dimensional, and each of the dimensions has to be properly developed in effective instruction. Learning any one of these three dimensions does not guarantee the automatic development of the other two. The instructor must deliberately aim for each factor separately.

Knowledge usually can be inculcated most expediently by means of reading assignments or lectures. *Attitudes* are cultivated through discussion but may be influenced strongly by other methods. *Skills* are usually best developed through demonstration-performance methods and role-playing.

Keeping a balance among *all three* of these factors is extremely important, and on the maintenance of this balance the success of the instructional program rests.

SUGGESTED READINGS

BRUBACHER, J. S.: *Modern Philosophies of Education,* McGraw-Hill Book Company, Inc., New York, 1950.

BURTON, W. H.: *The Guidance of Learning Activities,* Appleton-Century-Crofts, Inc., New York, 1952.

LINDGREN, H. C.: *Educational Psychology in the Classroom,* John Wiley & Sons, Inc., New York, 1956.

RISK, T. M.: *Principles and Practices of Teaching in Secondary Schools,* American Book Company, New York, 1947.

2

Psychological Factors Underlying Learning

This chapter discusses six psychological factors that influence learning.

THE PSYCHOLOGY OF LEARNING is a complex matter. Psychologists and educators have written a multitude of books on the subject, and no two of these present in all details exactly the same picture.

All agree, however, on a few principles. These principles are the basic laws of effective learning. Again and again it has been seen that the presence of these psychological factors seems to accelerate the learning curve and to make the acquisition of knowledge and the development of skills easier for the learner. Their absence, on the other hand, seems to retard the learning process and to increase the difficulty of teaching the employee.

These psychological factors involved in learning may be regarded as ways in which the trainee's mind must function with relation to a subject for him to acquire easily and effectively the material presented. If instruction is to be successful, then the psychological laws which influence learning must operate toward that end.

This chapter will discuss the psychology of learning from the point of view of the trainee. In later chapters the same principles will be applied to the task of the instructor. The dynamics of learning are as applicable to the instructor as they are to the learner.

9

Motivation

He learns who *wants* to learn. This is the first law of education. You can, perhaps, teach a person against his will; but to do so is like pushing a car uphill with the brakes locked. This desire to learn, educators and psychologists call *motivation*.

Motivation involves two things: (1) knowing what is to be learned and (2) understanding why the learning of it is desirable. Given both of these elements of motivation, the process of learning is likely to get off to a good start.

To appreciate the value of motivation, reflect upon your own experience. Perhaps you accompanied a friend to a lecture on a subject in which you had utterly no interest and in which, furthermore, you saw no possibility of any value accruing to yourself or to your work. You sat, however, listening deferentially, but without enthusiasm or interest, to all that was said. As you reflect upon that experience, how much was your behavior changed as a result of it? Probably not at all.

Now, contrast this experience with another one. You have an opportunity for advancement. It means increased status, a raise in pay, better hours, and improved working conditions. The supervisor calls together a group of potential candidates for the position. You are one of them. The lecture begins. This time you are far from apathetic. You listen intently. To get every word, to act upon it judiciously, means your future. In this situation there is no doubt of your interest—nor of your motivation. This is a lecture, like the other one you attended, but what a difference—in your reaction. That you are motivated, there is not the slightest doubt. For in this instance you really *want* to learn.

Most psychologists feel that some form of motivation is, perhaps, the most important single element in efficient learning. It is the springboard that launches you into a condition in which other factors of the learning process may begin to operate and that ultimately will combine to produce learning.

Concentration

Concentration focuses the full power of your attention on a particular learning situation. Motivation, of course, helps in this focusing process; but the high-energy nature of concentration is important. Do not confuse, for example, the mere paying of attention with the much more intense matter of concentration. To do so is to miss the whole point and to misunderstand the unique character of concentration.

Concentration produces results. There is a great deal of difference, for example, between the amount of learning a person will acquire in a training period when he merely pays attention and that which he will acquire when he turns the white heat of his concentration on the material being presented by the instructor. When you devote every iota of mental energy you can muster to the learning of one particular matter, then you are really learning.

Unfortunately, the relationship between learning and attention is not simply in direct ratio. Fifty per cent attention does not result in fifty per cent learning, and so forth. Rather, the curve of learning sags low for most of the mere-attention period, but rises sharply at the extreme limit of attention, which is concentration. Where nominal attention ceases and concentration begins, there the learning curve shoots steeply upward, and thereafter, the more intense the concentration the more rapid and effective the learning.

Look at the graphs in Fig. 1. They will demonstrate the unique character of the learning curve in relation to the factors of attention and concentration. The whole educative process would be simplified if the direct line relationship of Graph A were true. Graph B, however, more probably depicts the real nature of the learning process. Note how the learning curve lags for most of the distance and then zooms upward at the extreme limits of mental application. This means that for rapid, effective learning, concentration is necessary.

In the absence of concentration, material entering the mind has a tendency to impress itself but vaguely on the consciousness. The impression may be clear enough for the person to understand generally what is being seen or heard, but not forceful enough to make a lasting and vivid impression. Everyone has had the experience of reading a page, word by word, without retaining the haziest impression of what he has read. This condition results most

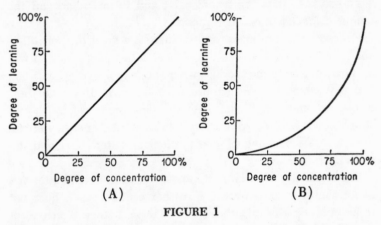

FIGURE 1

frequently from lack of concentration, and it illustrates the importance of this factor in the whole process of learning.

Reaction

You get out of a situation exactly what you put into it. This old adage is true for learning as it is true for most other areas of living. Watch an infielder catch a ball. His mind and his muscles work in harmony, like a precision instrument. He sizes up the situation; he considers what is best to be done at any split second; he identifies what is coming and where it is coming from; he stretches himself to intercept the ball in the right place at the right instant.

In the learning process action is also basic and required. You cannot learn by being a sponge. No one ever acquired knowledge or skill by merely vegetating—by soaking himself in an educational environment. Whether listening to a lecture, watching a demonstration, or engaging in any other form of learning activity, the trainee must spring into mental activity to a degree comparable to that of the infielder catching the ball. He needs mental agility, alertness, calculation, and stretching to catch the facts and ideas as they are batted to him by the instructor.

If the trainee's mind simply sits passively, merely watching what is going on without trying to intercept ideas, the important matters of the training session will whiz by him like hits going by an infielder who simply stands and watches, passively and without interest, as the balls go sailing by.

People learn only as a result of their own effort. You cannot really teach a trainee anything. In the last analysis, you can only show him how to learn. And yet in this fact lies the unique function of the instructor.

His is the responsibility of stimulating the learner, of presenting the material so clearly, so challengingly, and with such coherent organization that the trainee will be aided in acquiring the facts and becoming proficient in the skills. At best the instructor can only assist. The hard and inflexible truth remains: learning in the last analysis is that which every man must acquire by his own efforts. In a very real sense it is "Operation Bootstrap." Every man ultimately must educate himself.

Organization

The difference between a stained glass window and a basketful of colored glass may be nothing more than a matter of organization. It is the way the pieces are put together that makes the difference. So is it in learning. The difference between learning and bewilderment may be only the difference between the way facts and ideas are perceived and arranged in his mind by the trainee.

The purpose of the training session, therefore, is to aid the trainee to piece together the bits of information and the procedures for skill development into a logical and meaningful whole. When a training session does this, it has accomplished much in the direction of making learning a creative and purposeful experience.

A few facts well presented, an aim clearly seen, are better than a tangled maze of data whirling in disorganized educational chaos. Do not be too concerned about the mere dispensing of knowledge, per se; but be greatly concerned about whether the knowledge that is dispensed has a logical relation to a larger, organized, and totally integrated whole.

This, however, is to be said: as the ability to take a group of unrelated data, to look at a complex situation, to hear a tangled maze of reports, and to compose from these disparate elements a meaningful picture is the mark of a top executive or a skilled teacher, so is it also the mark of an adept trainee to be able to take unrelated facts and skills and to convert them into a job-efficiency approach. Executive, teacher, and learner alike employ organizational techniques as a convenient means of problem solving. Organization converts the raw materials of learning into a constructive approach toward meeting an educational goal.

In the jargon of business and industry, the comprehending of the organizational pattern is variously phrased. Getting the theme, the drift, the big picture are merely different ways of saying the same thing—that the person has comprehended the organization of the whole in terms of its discrete parts.

Comprehension

Comprehension means, literally, to take hold of with the mind. It is, therefore, grasping mentally those significances, meanings, implications, and applications that make a situation understandable to the learner. To see what a thing means, to grasp its significance, is the goal and summit of all learning. Comprehension is the keystone which holds the arch of the sublearnings in place. Without it, skills, knowledge, and attitudes are worthless, and personnel training is vain.

Comprehension takes many forms. Sometimes it comes slowly, almost imperceptibly, like the gradual brightening of the dawn.

As you grope your way through a problem, first one fact becomes understandable, then another, and another, until the whole glows meaningfully and clear.

At other times you suddenly behold the answer clearly, totally, like a flash of lightning, illuminating the entire situation. Such a flash is called *insight*, and is a form of comprehension.

Generally, however, comprehension dawns slowly. Through motivation, concentration, and reaction you develop a body of facts, ideas, or skills; through organization you fit them together into a logical pattern; and, as you study the matrix of data thus created, you gradually begin to comprehend the significance and implications of the whole matter. To be complete in the fullest sense of the term, however, learning must go one step further.

Comprehension, in the ultimate sense of the term, requires not only that you understand but that you be able to *apply*, appropriately and effectively, the material you have understood. Most training directors have seen men who have learned everything about a job and yet somehow seem unable to *do* the job effectively. Question them about the work and they will answer correctly; name any specific skill, and they can perform it. But ask them to do the *whole* job as a complete, integrated task and their ability crumbles. What is it that they lack? The chances are that these men lack the cement of comprehension to bind together the bits and pieces of job skill and knowledge into a solid *ability to do*. They have not learned how to *apply* what they so well know. Application, therefore, is the golden key to the temple of success in personnel training.

Comprehension is dynamic. At its best it may be creative. It results from deliberate thought and imagination. If you *really* comprehend, then you are ready to answer decisively such questions as: What is the central idea of this paragraph (topic, chapter, discussion)? What do these facts mean? What do they imply? When should one use this particular skill; for what types of job application is it best suited?

Something, you see, must happen in the awareness of the

trainee over and beyond the mere acquisition of facts or the development of skills. He must seek an application in terms of his on-the-job behavior. He must use the skills and knowledge which he has acquired. Ultimately *his behavior must change*. This is the critical test of learning, the real test of comprehension.

Thomas Watson, president of IBM, gave to the business world its most important word. You will see it on executives' desks, in offices, in the shop—in fact, wherever men work. It is the dynamic command, *Think!*

For the trainee that is the final word in comprehension. Think! What is the meaning of this attitude in terms of better production? *Think!* What does the employment of this skill mean in terms of easier, less fatiguing, more economical work? *Think!* What does the content of this training period mean in terms of your own efficiency and perhaps eventual promotion?

Thinking through an assignment or the content of a training period to a point of complete comprehension—to that point where your mind *really grasps* the significance of it all—is real mental work, but the value of the results richly repays the outlay of effort.

Repetition

Now that you have scaled the heights of comprehension, you ought not to let your achievement slip from your grasp because you have abandoned the ramparts. Yet this is always the danger. The imps of forgetfulness will take over unless you are alert and active against them.

Forgetting is the curse of learning. Yet to forget is human. Everybody forgets. Research shows that the day after the members of a class study a subject or hear a lecture they will have forgotten much of what they knew at the close of the period of learning. A week later they will have forgotten more; and as time passes they will forget, although at a reduced rate, more and more of their original fund of learning. But they will never forget completely all that they have learned. The curve of forgetting is represented as a sharply descending and then gradually flattening, asymptotic line, with the greatest forgetfulness taking place soon after the cessation of learning.

The foil to forgetting is repetition. Repeat an operation or a fact and you will increase your ability to remember it; you will strengthen your skill in performing it. Review a set of facts and your likelihood of remembering them increases greatly. Continue the repetition at stated intervals—at first more frequently, every day, for example, or every few days—then at gradually less frequent intervals, and the possibility of your forgetting the material almost ceases to exist.

Thoughtful repetition undergirds and reinforces the temple of learning. But the act of repetition must be thoughtful and purposeful. Mere unthinking duplication avails nothing. Automatism is different from purposive reiteration.

Take a typist, for example. She may type a letter over and over without actually noticing its thought content. Obviously blind repetition produces no learning. To be effective, therefore, as a learning procedure, repetition must be accompanied by concentration and active mental reaction to the subject matter being repeated.

And so, we have come to the last of the six psychological factors which strongly influence learning. Other authors may suggest different factors, or give different names to some of those we have discussed above. But one cardinal fact remains: psychologists and educators generally agree that he who studies will learn faster, will learn more, if he incorporates within his study these six basic approaches to learning. And he who teaches will be the better teacher if in his teaching is an indication that he pilots his class by means of these six lamps of learning.

SUMMARY

Six psychological factors strongly influence learning. These are:

Motivation—the willingness to learn. Motivation results largely from two subfactors: (1) a clear understanding of what is to be learned and

(2) a clear understanding of the reasons why the learning of it is important.

Concentration—the focusing of the full power of your attention upon a particular learning situation. You should be careful not to confuse the mere paying of attention with dynamic concentration. Learning accelerates as concentration intensifies.

Reaction—when you wake up, live, and *think*, in a learning situation, that is reaction. It means getting into the game and contributing something on your part to help yourself to learn.

Organization—this is putting the pieces together into a meaningful mosaic.

Comprehension—the ultimate step in the learning process. It is the perception of meanings and implications of material studied, and understanding the application of what is learned. A learner should study for comprehension, not mere memory.

Repetition—the greatest preservative of learning known to man. Repetition is the antidote for forgetting, but it must be thoughtful and purposeful.

To consciously incorporate these six basic psychological factors into any learning, studying, or teaching situation makes that a more promising situation so far as the achievement of skills, the creation of salutary attitudes, and the acquisition of knowledge are concerned.

SUGGESTED READINGS

BERNARD, H. W.: *Psychology of Learning and Teaching*, McGraw-Hill Book Company, Inc., New York, 1954.

BURTON, W. H.: *The Guidance of Learning Activities*, Appleton-Century-Crofts, Inc., New York, 1952.

BUXTON, C. E.: *College Teaching: A Psychologist's View*, Harcourt, Brace and Company, Inc., New York, 1956.

FRANDSEN, A. N.: *How Children Learn: An Educational Psychology*, McGraw-Hill Book Company, Inc., New York, 1957.

JUSTMAN, J., and W. H. MAIS: *College Teaching, Its Practice and Potential*, Harper & Brothers, New York, 1956.

NICHOLS, R. G., and C. A. STEVENS: *Are You Listening?* McGraw-Hill Book Company, Inc., New York, 1957.

3

Applying the Principles of Learning

This chapter explains the application of certain educational and psychological principles to the personnel training program. It suggests ways in which the instructor can apply these principles by means of specific techniques.

OF THEORETICAL PRINCIPLES we are likely to ask, what does it all mean? What's the use of all this? I'd like to know what good this stuff will do *me*.

In a practical-minded world, such comments are natural. Personnel training, so we think, must deal with meaningful, practical, immediately applicable facts. And ultimately this is so.

But all facts are not always immediately applicable. Every *practical* fact results from a long history of hard thinking and clear understanding. There is, in other words, a *reason* why things are so. And we have found from expensive experience that when an employee knows the reasons for what he is doing, when he is "filled in" on the background, and when he sees his own work in the fullness and entirety of its significance to the whole operation of which he is a part, it then makes more sense to him. He *does* his job better because he *understands* it better.

The ability to show the relation between principles and their application is one mark of a skilled instructor. Take an example. High school algebra and plane geometry are rather remote academic matters for most of us in personnel training. We left these subjects behind us long ago to pursue more practical matters. The equation $a^2 + b^2 = h^2$ is for most of us who studied it a ghostly reminder of an old Greek, Pythagoras, who stoutly asserted something about the square of the hypotenuse being equal to the sum of the squares of the other two sides of a right triangle.

Now this academic babbling seems far removed from the demands of the workaday world. Many a carpenter and garageman may never have heard of old Pythagoras. Yet they cannot effectively do their common everyday tasks without his aid. For a carpenter to figure the length of a rafter to support a roof of a certain height and pitch over a floor of a certain width demands a working knowledge of the theorem of Pythagoras. To see the relevance of Pythagoras to the solving of a practical problem makes what formerly seemed remote and useless knowledge thrillingly alive and useful.

Just so, the laws governing the circumference of a circle may seem to belong to the far away and long ago; yet, $c = \pi d$ is necessary to tell a garageman by how much smaller or larger tires than those already on your car, and prescribed by the manufacturer, would falsify the readings on your speedometer and odometer.

You, perhaps, never thought of these facts as being relevant beyond the point where they were needed to pass a high school mathematics test.

The Nature of Learning

Most of the subjects that we studied in school were included in the curriculum on the assumption that in one way or another they would be useful in later life. One reason for studying government, for example, was that we might better understand the platform of a political party and cast our vote more intelligently. But all too frequently while we were studying it we did not see the larger relationship of the particular subject studied to the larger life situation. Somewhere along the line the emphasis became misplaced, and we were taught facts for facts' sake. The facts, rather, should have been taught as relevant and necessary for successfully meeting the problems of the everyday world. If so taught, they would have been easier to learn because they would have had an immediacy and an urgency about them that otherwise they lost.

When a training program teaches facts for facts' sake only, it fails. The only reason for teaching anything in a training program is that the trainee may find it has everyday application to his job, whereby he may do it better and do it more intelligently. An instructor can measure the effectiveness of his instruction by the degree to which the trainee can do something he could not do before, or by the degree to which he can perform the same operation more effectively than ever before.

This *improvement in ability to do* is the only criterion which will in the end justify a training program. It is the only ground on which employee training of any kind can be defended. Ultimately, personnel training must give account of its reason for being from a dollars-and-cents standpoint.

Looked at candidly, a training program has no excuse for being except that it saves the company money or increases the efficiency of the company personnel, or both.

If a welder as a result of special training can do a more efficient job because he is better able to judge temperature or because he knows more readily the different welding characteristics of various metals, he is more valuable on the job than the workman who must learn these facts by the costly and time-consuming trial-and-error method.

The facts themselves are always subordinate to the more efficient work which results from knowledge of them on the part of the employee. Yet, often, an efficient job cannot be done without the more remote and sometimes downright theoretical fact. Ultimately, however, the better job—the money-saving, time-economizing approach—is the acid test of the worth of any personnel training program.

Take a practical example of the kind of training that brings dollars-and-cents results. You are preparing a training program in sales psychology for salesclerks. The problem is to emphasize the effect of the customer's mind set, or susceptibility to suggestion to sales of related items. A customer who has bought a pink dress, for example, is a better-than-average prospect for buying accessories. The salesperson, knowing this fact, ought also to know exactly what to *do* to take advantage of the sales potential in the situation most effectively. Having sold the customer a pink dress, the salesclerk should not, however, begin to talk about gloves and shoes in general. She should talk rather about *pink* accessories, or suggest colors that go with *pink* specifically. In other words the salesclerk will do well to capitalize upon the *pink* mind set of the customer. To do so may well result in other sales in addition to the pink dress.

The effective instructor is the one who recognizes the applicability of the facts and principles that he is teaching to the job that his trainees have to do on the production line. It is a part of the teaching process to make the transfer for the student from the material on the blackboard to the everyday demands of the employee's job. Teaching should stimulate those who are being taught to make, on their own initiative, new and wider applications of the knowledge that they have acquired.

In the example just cited, the instructor has done an effective job of teaching if, during the group discussion, one of the employees volunteers, "While she's thinking about her new pink dress, you could also talk about the fact that by getting a vivid belt and accessories to match she can have another whole new costume built around the pink dress—a sort of two-in-one approach."

When trainees offer such suggestions on their own initiative, when they begin to think of the training in terms of what they can do with it on the job, that is a sure sign that a desirable learning process is taking place. It may not be too much to suggest that the instructor may gauge his own success as a teacher by the way in which his trainees on their own initiative carry out the ideas which he has presented and apply them to other job situations than those he has suggested.

Personnel training is always best when it relates the trainee and his job to each other in terms of applicability of the facts being taught. In job training theoretical knowledge, or a facts-for-facts'-sake approach, should always be carefully scrutinized in terms of practical application to the occupational demands of the trainee. Definitions and statements of principles are justified as abstract materials only when they stimulate and improve on-the-job behavior. In short, personnel training which boosts sales, promotes better occupational performance, or aids worker efficiency is probably good personnel training procedure.

Even in demonstration or role-playing, training may sometimes go awry. Whenever the instructor devotes more thought to the words and facts themselves than to what those words and facts mean in terms of job performance, at that point his instruction goes off tangentially from its real center of relevant and productive usefulness.

Let's see what this means in terms of an actual training program. An instructor was attempting to show trainees the proper way to solder connections. As a skilled workman, the instructor knew every step of the process perfectly. He had prepared carefully for his lecture-demonstration presentation. As every instructor should, he knew far more about the subject of soldering than he needed to know to make a successful lecture-demonstration presentation to the group before him. Educationally this was desirable. A teacher should usually know many times as much about his subject as his students, if he is to seem to have mastered it. In this case the instructor knew, for example, that solder was an amalgam; that flux was necessary because, otherwise, the metal would oxidize, causing a poor joint; that "sweating" a joint was in reality making use of the principle of capillary action, and many other technical facts about solder and soldering. And all these facts were, perhaps, important and necessary for the *instructor* to know. It was just such knowledge that, in fact, qualified him to be an instructor. But such knowledge is treacherous, and unless deftly handled such facts might easily cause an instructor's downfall with respect to his *teaching* function. In his presentation he may become lost in his own maze of factual data. He may fail to organize the *essential* facts into a logical, lucid lecture. The trainees, in consequence, trying to follow his too scholarly presentation, likewise will become bewildered amid the welter of what seem to them irrelevant data. They will miss the important, practical points. They will not see clearly the *simple* procedures which they should understand thoroughly in order to do their own elementary soldering jobs better.

Of course, if you know your subject thoroughly, you will naturally be interested in every minute aspect of it. Such an attitude is normal and praiseworthy. But when you are preparing your training presentation, be especially careful to organize your knowledge so that *what to do* and *how to do it* stand out boldly and unmistakably for those who are attempting to learn. Do not burden your hapless trainees with abstruse technicalities or a mass of minutiae which they cannot grasp and to which they see no value. Give them only those essential facts which they need to do the job that they are expected to do. And in presenting those facts emphasize that they are essential and important for the improved job performance which as trainees they are expected to achieve.

One secret in aiming instruction in the direction of producing a skill, an attitude, an understanding is to use plenty of concrete, specific, realistic examples. Illustrate and apply directly to the job situation the principle you are attempting to teach. Have at least one illustration of a practical application for every major fact or principle presented. If that fact or principle is crucial to the whole operation, emphasize its importance by using two or three illustrations to drive home the importance of its critical worth.

In teaching, examples are time-consuming. If you omitted the illustrative material you could cover more ground. The object, however, in personnel training is not comprehensive coverage. It is to give primarily that knowledge that will increase the trainee's skillfulness—to improve his ability to perform a specific task. By far it is better to give him that selective knowledge which will teach him a few skills well, or to assist him in improving the skills he does have, than to deluge him with facts, tempting him to dabble aimlessly in many areas.

Applying the Psychology of Learning

Teaching, therefore, involves two things: (1) the *material* taught, (2) the *people* who are taught.

So far in this chapter we have talked about only the first of these. Now we come to the human aspect of teaching. In Chapter 2 we discussed the psychological principles that underlie all learning. In the remainder of this chapter we shall explore ways in which the instructor can utilize these principles in helping the trainee to learn more effectively. Subsequent chapters of the book will describe particular methods of instruction. With respect to methods, however, it is important for the instructor to grasp and to remember this cardinal fact:

Every step of every method is merely a device by which the instructor attempts to utilize those principles of educational psychology which help to promote learning.

To be successful, every instructional activity should, therefore, embrace six principal steps:

1. Motivation of the trainee;
2. Maintaining complete attention;
3. Promoting mental activity (thinking);
4. Creating a clear picture of the material to be learned;
5. Developing comprehension of the significance, the implications, and the practical application of the material being presented;
6. Repetition of the five preceding steps until learning has taken place.

These are the fundamental steps that lead to success in any training program. They embody certain basic principles in the psychology of learning that cannot be ignored if training is to occur effectively. By means of these six steps the instructor leads the trainee to achieve skills, attitudes, and knowledge; and in the last analysis such achievement is *learning*.

MOTIVATION

The beginning point in all instruction is to create in the trainee a desire to learn. He must want what the program has to offer. This desire for training must frequently be sparked by some inducement whereby the trainee sees value in what he is asked to learn. This seeing of value in learning is called *motivation*.

The wise instructor will recognize that two elements are essential to all motivation:

1. The spelling out, clearly and explicitly, of what the trainee is expected to learn—and why he is expected to learn it;

2. The creation of a sense of urgency in the trainee to possess the skills and the knowledge which the training program will offer.

These two prerequisites for motivation seem at first sight to be relatively simple goals and easy to achieve. Consider what the training program aims to do, however, in terms of trainee needs, and you will realize that the task of motivation is not so easy as it at first appears.

Motivation is not only a matter of a few introductory remarks. Rather, most instructors who motivate their groups successfully find that they must devote several hours of conscientious work to the problem of stating clearly and accurately the aims of their program in terms of the trainee's abilities and his needs. Nor is motivation a matter of the first session only; it is rather a continuous process going on throughout the whole progress of training.

If the program, however, is to succeed ultimately, this motivation must be done early and be done well. It is one of the most difficult phases of the whole teaching process, but to learn to do it adeptly and to perfect one's motivational techniques and skills in terms of group needs is to display one of the best evidences of the master teacher. In terms of final results it repays many times over the effort, the thought, the planning, and the care that it requires.

"Well begun is half done." The adage is eminently true in personnel training. The other half must be diplomatically handled during the rest of the period of training.

Let's see at close range what motivation really means. Consider that you are preparing a training program for foremen and supervisors in human relations techniques and procedures. In trying to put the objectives of your program into words, you state: "This program proposes to develop an understanding of the basic psychological needs of human beings and to formulate some methodology for the meeting of these needs through the application of certain psychological techniques."

That statement of your objective is perhaps accurate—but how stuffy! How dull and unattractive, how remote from the vital, everyday problems of a group of foremen and supervisors. They need to have this academic jargon translated. It must be put into terms which they can understand. The wording of the objective must reflect an appreciation on the part of the instructor of the on-the-job problems and needs which these men face. The instructor must see, in short, a foreman or a supervisor dealing with another human being. He must appreciate *from the foreman's standpoint* the problems and the needs which supervisory personnel as a group face, and he must state the objectives of the course in terms of these problems and needs.

How to do this? Be specific. Be concrete, and above all, be down to earth. In your own mind think about the goals and purposes of your courses in any way you please; but when you put your thoughts into words for an employee group, choose words that state your ideas in terms of their needs, their problems, their work, and their occupational demands.

Let us, therefore, restate the objective of the course in terms of specific job demands and personnel needs: "This course will show you how you can use certain principles of psychology in handling problems that come up on the job. It will tell you what to do, for example, when Frank and Joe can't get along together and continually hold up the work because of their personal fights, or when Bill is so sore about his failure to get a raise that he isn't turning in a full day's work."

There! The goals in that statement are clear and unmistakable. The harassed supervisor or foreman will go for a course of this kind. It is designed to relieve some of his headaches; it purports to help him solve some of his problems. He will be motivated (in layman's language we say, he will be anxious . . .) to get started and to find out how an application of "certain principles of psychology" to the job situation can assist him. The motivation is built into the statement of the purposes of the course. It will arise from the fact that the statement points out precisely what he will learn and the usefulness of this knowledge in making his work less onerous; and it says it in simple, understandable, down-to-earth language.

While the first session of the course must deliberately include a motivational approach, motivation cannot stop there. It must continue throughout the course. The instructor must always be alert for an opportunity to capitalize upon the many occasions which will afford a chance for a motivational appeal to the trainees.

While motivation is essential, it should be handled casually. The best motivation is that which develops naturally from the context of the teaching. It arises out of opportunities which many times cannot be planned, but which the alert and tactful instructor recognizes *as opportunities* for motivating the trainees.

HOLDING THE COMPLETE ATTENTION OF A GROUP

Having motivated the trainees the instructor now must capture and hold their attention. To this end, instructional periods must be carefully planned. An alert, attentive group can get much more

from instruction than one that is only partially interested or
nominally deferential, as was pointed out in Chapter 2. A good instructor does not merely hope his trainees will give his subject
their complete attention. He plans his instruction to provide for
attention-holding activities.

To arrest and hold the attention of the group, the instructor
has recourse to several channels of approach:

1. *Humor.* Every successful instructor has a stock of humorous
illustrations or witty expressions that he can call upon when instruction threatens to get dull. A word of warning, however.
Do not tell a joke merely for the joke's sake; it lessens the dignity
of your period. But a funny story that makes a point, or an alertness that seizes upon chances to sprinkle a touch of humor judiciously through an instructional period will work wonders in holding the class's attention. A good example of this extemporaneous
humor occurred when a strip of paper covering the instructor's
chart inadvertently fell off before he was ready to reveal the
chart to the trainees. The instructor gazed down sadly at the
cover sheet lying on the floor. He looked up at his audience, shook
his head resignedly, and said in a droll voice, "Awfully hard to
keep a secret around this place!"

2. *On-the-job Application.* Get your teaching down out of the
clouds. Let what you say and what you do be a down-to-earth
experience for your training group. Point out again and again just
how the material you are presenting applies to the more efficient
handling of the actual job situation.

An instructor should learn early in his teaching experience that
you cannot *tell* a trainee that something is important. He'll not
believe you—at least, not more than once. The instructor who
merely cries repeatedly, "Now, this is important!" largely wastes
his effort. Don't tell them it's important; *show* them!

Point out exactly when, where, and how an idea is important
and applicable on the job. If you can make the trainee see that the
idea is invaluable, that with it he has an edge over other workers,

without it he is handicapped in his work and at a disadvantage—
if you can do this effectively, you will have no trouble in holding
the trainee's attention and interest.

3. *Enthusiasm.* When you are fired with enthusiasm, your enthusiasm is contagious. It spreads. Every teacher should be a
salesman par excellence. He sells ideas. But if a salesman is not
sold on his goods himself, he cannot sell others. Neither can a
halfhearted teacher, who presents his material in a desultory
manner, fire his students with enthusiasm. Psychologically something must happen to you before it will happen to others. First,
you must see the relevance of your lesson to the trainee's job.
You must be convinced that the lesson you are presenting is
really important for the group that you are teaching. If you take
the trouble to figure out exactly what your material means to those
whom you teach, it will help you to develop some enthusiasm in
presenting it to them. In a very real sense, therefore, you should
go into your training session exclaiming, "Man, what an idea!
They've got to see it. This has tremendous possibilities. They've
simply *got* to see it!"

Keep your own fire blazing, and you will kindle a kindred blaze
in the minds and hearts of your group.

4. *Audiovisual Aids.* No amount of lecturing can take the place
of the moment when the young doctor sits in the operating arena
and actually *sees* the professor of surgery perform the operation.
At that moment the whole meaning of being a doctor leaps to life.
A hundred pages of medical text, a term's lectures suddenly become embodied in an operation that is before the young doctor's
very eyes.

So, likewise, when the instructor is actually showing the trainee
certain how-to-do-it techniques with the machinery, or other
materials which the employee will be using on the job, the
trainee's attention and interest usually stay at a very high level.
In those periods where words are the principal means of communication between instructor and trainee, an effective instructor
will inject pictures, diagrams, models, or other eye-catching mate-

rial into his teaching to help in keeping the group's attention. Visual aids will be discussed at greater length in Chapter 10.

5. *Group Participation.* Some instructors think they must do all the talking. This is a mistake. Sometimes you may be amazed at what excellent ideas your trainees have. And it keeps them awake, if they talk occasionally.

Interrupt your discussion or lecture from time to time to call upon someone in the group for his opinion or for the answer to a question. By so doing you keep everybody alert. They react to the necessity of keeping up with what is going on. And, incidentally, seldom do you realize, when you are doing *all* the talking, how humdrum and monotonous the droning voice from the front of the room may be. Try taping your actual class lecture sometime. Then dispassionately listen to the recording a couple of days later. You'll hear what the group heard—and it may be for you a startling and blood-curdling revelation.

One of the primal steps, therefore, in the psychology of learning is certainly getting the attention of the group. We have suggested several techniques toward that end. As you teach you may discover others. You will also find ways to combine the above attention-getting procedures and methods.

One fact is certain: lose your listener's attention and you lose your learner. Resourceful, inventive thinking to devise ways to keep the learner with you will return high dividends in learning on the part of the trainees, but without the trainee's attention you accomplish nothing.

PROMOTING MENTAL ACTIVITY

Not only should the instructor arrest attention, he should also spur activity on the part of the trainee. In one way or another the instructor must find methods by which he engages the mind of the trainee in wrestling with the idea that he is presenting.

Every successful instructor attempts to spark a *reaction* in the minds of his trainees. He seeks to involve *their* minds actively in the ideas *he* is presenting.

One fact ought to be crystal clear to every instructor: what you say or do for your group is not nearly so important as what you can get them to say or do. It's trainee activity that counts. In education this is called *participation*, and it is a vital link in the learning process. It is eminently true, you learn to do *by doing*.

There are many ways of inducing participation on the part of the trainee. Here are some:

1. *Set Up a Tryout Situation.* This is the conventional laboratory approach. Give the trainee an opportunity to try out in practice those principles and procedures which you have discussed in the training session. This is an application of the learn-to-do-by-doing technique.

2. *Require Notes.* This imposes a dual obligation. You are involved in this requirement as well as the trainee. When a trainee takes notes he must follow attentively the words of the instructor. He must think actively, organize clearly, and express communicatively what the lecturer has said. He must separate that which is central from that which is peripheral; he must distinguish between the principle and the *application* of the principle.

The instructor also must create order from the chaos of his own thinking. He must see clearly what he is attempting to do, and express it in the most logical, orderly manner. One of the greatest compliments a trainee can pay a teacher is, "It is easy to get a clear set of notes from your instruction." Boiling down the instructor's ideas to the few words that can be recorded in a notebook while instruction is going on is one of the very finest forms of mental reaction and trainee participation.

3. *Ask Questions.* Asking your trainees questions helps to stimulate mental activity. It also helps to hold their attention. Come, therefore, to your training period with some definite questions in mind to ask at appropriate times.

Learn also the technique of asking questions. And the first step in this technique is: take your time. Ask a question. Then pause for a few moments. Finally, ask someone to answer the question.

Pausing before calling for an answer almost guarantees that

everyone has been mentally reacting to the question, each has been trying to formulate the answer. Although only one person may actually voice the response, the minds of the whole group have been busy thinking about it. And, after all, what you are *really* striving for is the mental reaction primarily, not the vocalization which merely articulates it.

4. *Say It Strikingly.* A startling statement will wake up sleepy minds. Phrase an old idea in a new way and people will begin to think. The unconventional will shock them. It will set them to figuring out what the statement means or how it may be true.

Say, for example, to a group of supervisors: "A person with pride doesn't dare to be impolite." On first hearing this statement they are bewildered. They react with the thought, "That's ridiculous." Then comes the afterthought—a rephrasing, as it were, of your original sentence: "A proud person doesn't dare not to be polite." Ah, that throws new light on the idea. He doesn't *dare to take the chance* of being impolite. Why? Suddenly they realize that rudeness will elicit the contempt that the *proud* person does not covet from his associates. By the time your trainees have followed this thought pattern they will have done plenty of thinking. With one terse statement you will have stabbed their flagging attention wide awake.

5. *Let Someone Else Talk.* Getting trainees to suggest, to explain, to further the ideas you have introduced is another way of promoting reaction within the group. Instead of compelling the group to listen to you all the time, let someone else talk. The explanations may not be as good as those you would have given, but the mental activity you induce within the group often outweighs this deficiency. Try being a guide for a while. Discussion of situations by trainees, talking together about what to do and how to do it, with the instructor sitting on the sidelines merely guiding things, achieves a high degree of learning activity. It also affects attitudes more, perhaps, than a lecture would have done. In succeeding chapters we shall talk about discussion methods at greater length.

Let your trainees participate as much as possible. This may be mental or physical participation, but whenever, wherever you can keep the trainee busy, at that point you are perhaps doing your best instructing. The lesson plan as a device for teaching will be described in full in Chapter 4. Here you will find detailed suggestions as to different ways of building trainee activity into your program of instruction.

CREATING A CLEAR PICTURE

In Chapter 2 we saw that if the trainee is to learn effectively, he must be able to see the over-all plan of what he is studying. To this end you can assist learning on the part of the trainee if you will find ways to provide him with the over-all picture so that into the total pattern he can fit the pieces of information as they come to him during the progress of the course. He will thus be able to construct intelligently throughout the course the larger educational picture. Recall, for example, how much easier it is to put together a jigsaw puzzle after you have a clear idea of what the finished picture will be. To change the figure somewhat, when you start out on a journey, you are more likely to arrive if you know where you are going.

A popular plan among successful instructors is known as the "whole-part-whole" sequence of instruction. To begin with, give the students a *preview* of what is going to be covered in a unit of instruction. Then spell out the whole unit carefully, emphasizing the *details*. Finally, when you have finished detailing the operation, give a *summary* so that the trainee may look back upon the matter again, as a whole, before leaving it.

This method is sometimes popularly described as the "You-tell-'em-what-you're-going-to-tell-'em; then-tell-'em; finally, tell-'em-what-you've-told-'em" method. In principle, this basic procedure is a safe one to follow. This book, for example, is based on the whole-part-whole principle. The preface and table of contents give the over-all preview of the subject. Also, at the beginning of each chapter the preview technique is carried even further by giving you in a brief paragraph a statement of what the chapter will cover. The chapter that you are now reading was structured in just this way. Immediately following the chapter heading, "Applying the Principles of Learning," was a brief preview statement. Now you are reading the details of the chapter. At the end of the chapter you will find a summary, giving in condensed form a recapitulation of the contents of the chapter. This is perhaps the best example of the whole-part-whole method: preview, details, and summary.

1. *Outline.* One method of giving the overview is for the instructor to pass around at the first meeting of the group an outline of what the instruction will cover. If the subject matter is somewhat complicated with many different angles and phases, the outline should be drawn in greater detail. List each of the major points that you will cover during the course. Clearly indicate, in terms of relative importance, under each of the main points the subheadings. The subheads will show the trainee the more detailed aspects of the topic and prepare him to give relative weights to the various matters as they arise within the framework of the course. The outline as an aid to clear organization and a tool of teaching will be discussed more fully in Chapter 6.

2. *Summary.* Perhaps you recall in your own school career being somewhat bewildered at times as to the exact relationship between what the teacher was explaining at the moment and the general topic of the discussion. At this point, let us hope that the instructor paused and summarized what he had been saying in terms of the broad overview. You suddenly realized that what you had thought unrelated was, clearly enough, part of a larger and entirely integrated body of knowledge.

The more complex the presentation, the more important is it that you summarize from time to time, giving a brief recapitulation of what you have done up to a certain point and a brief prediction of things to come. Sometimes these need not be more than a sentence or two. In this way, however, you keep your hearer from getting lost. He may have lapsed into inattention and lost you some way back. With a summary you can usually rescue him from his wandering in the wilderness, bring him back into line, and keep him with you.

Certainly at the end of each session you will want to summarize. You are, in fact, closing a chapter of instruction. This final tying together of what has transpired presents to the trainee a package of essential fact and principal details. It helps him fix in his mind the important materials covered during the period, and permits him to leave the training session feeling that he has firmly within his grasp the substance of the session.

COMPREHENSION AND APPLICATION

The devices mentioned thus far have been instructor-centered. The instructor is responsible for the outline; the instructor presents the summary. These are channels *provided by the instructor* whereby the learning process may operate. The best evidence that this learning process has been operating is seen in the fact of comprehension. And this is a *trainee-centered* activity.

Comprehension. Comprehension results in a deep behavior change on the part of the trainee. At the outset of this chapter, the position was taken that the remembering of facts per se was not the objective of a training program. Rather, a training program is aimed at developing in the trainee the ability to perform certain operations more effectively as a result of knowing certain facts or through the application of an auxiliary body of knowledge.

Facts and skills *as an end in themselves* are of little value. Facts and skills as a means of getting a job done more efficiently or more expertly are very important. Note, however, that when they are used *as a means*—rather than *as an end*—in other words, when they become learning *tools,* then they become very important. It is their utilization that is important. When employees can take certain facts and combine these with discrete skills and, by application of both to a specific work situation, do a given job more expertly, more efficiently, more skillfully, then they give commanding evidence of the fact that something very deep and integral has taken place in terms of the whole learning process. The trainee has *laid hold of*—for that is the literal, the basic, the root meaning of *comprehend*—that which transcends knowledge or skill as an end in itself. He knows how to do new things or how to do old things better as a result of the knowledge that he has received or the skills that he has developed. This is learning brought to flower. This is comprehension in the most significant sense of the term.

Application. Let us look at comprehension somewhat more intimately. Two engineers receive the same brochure describing the qualities of a particular alloy. Both read the brochure and understand the facts equally well. But one engineer sees the *application* of these facts, while the other engineer merely learns the facts. The first engineer perceives that certain specifications of the metal indicate that it is invaluable in solving a knotty technical problem causing a bottleneck in his research and ultimately in production itself. Now he sees a relationship between fact and problem, between knowledge and a specific need for that knowledge. The ability to perceive the relevancy of learned facts to particular problems confronting the worker is the essence of comprehension and is called *application*. Knowledge alone is not enough. Knowing what to do with what you know—this is to *apply* one's learning.

Application is the final step in the process of learning. It is the summit of all education. Everything else the instructor does is merely build-up to make sure this particular level is reached, for here is the goal of learning—the skills, understanding, attitudes which comprise the ability to do.

How can an instructor be sure that his trainees follow through to the point of comprehension, and beyond that to an application of the facts? How can he induce them to cease revering the fact for its own sake and knowledge for the mere sake of knowing more things? There are five principal steps that are necessary:

1. State clearly the fact or idea you want the trainee to learn.

2. Explain what the idea means in terms of job context.

3. Discuss it so that it is well fixed in the minds of the trainees. You may invite further discussion or comment from the group.

4. Give one or more examples, depending on the importance of the matter, of ways in which this information may be applicable to actual on-the-job situations.

5. Ask the group to contribute additional examples, illustrating exactly how this information or that skill or attitude may be applicable to several on-the-job situations.

For example, you are teaching foremen ways of enlisting group spirit and loyalty on the part of their employees. "Cultivating a feeling of belonging to a group," you remark, "is one of the best ways to develop group spirit and loyalty. When a person feels that he is important as a part of the group, he will also feel more united to such a group." And you proceed to talk about the importance of developing a sense of group loyalty in lower-echelon personnel. But while you talk, you want your foremen to *comprehend* the significance of belonging, not merely to remember whatever words you may have said about "belonging." Do not leave the subject, therefore, without having said words to this effect: "I want you to think of some of the benefits that would accrue to *you* as supervisors and foremen if all your men had a tight sense of belonging to your particular outfit. What are some of those benefits? Let's hear them."

You are, of course, at this point employing a technique of motivation, and you are also using a method of enlisting group participation. After several benefits have been suggested by the supervisors themselves, you might ask, "What are some of the ways, then, in which you might develop in your crew a sense of belonging? Let's pool our thoughts so that everyone can benefit from everyone else's ideas."

When your trainees are able to make the *application* of your ideas to practical, on-the-job situations, you know that they have *comprehended* what you have attempted to teach them.

In terms of comprehension the instructor should always remember that the important fact is not how much material the trainee has covered but how genuinely he has comprehended the principles of application of that material to the job which he is actually doing.

The more complex the idea, the longer the time, generally, that comprehension requires. The mind is not like a photographic plate. You cannot expose it once to a set of new ideas and expect it to retain much of the impression. Rather is it like firm clay, which resists the initial impression but if repeatedly impressed, will sooner or later take the mark of imprint upon it.

REPETITION

So with learning, every successful instructor learns that *repetition* is the key to effective teaching.

Repetition, however, demands resourcefulness. You must not be like a record stuck in a groove. Repeating again and again the same or even different words will bore your class and kill their interest. Employing a little ingenuity, you can make the principle of repetition your most effective teaching aid. If you are awake as an instructor you will realize that opportunities to employ the *principle* of repetition in concrete situations are legion.

Posters and other visual aids, for instance, judiciously displayed will remind the trainees of ideas discussed in the training session. A cartoon or a picture on a bulletin board may recall a thousand words. From time to time announce a test. At the time of the announcement hint that the test will cover the material found in the notes taken in class. Repetition suddenly becomes an urgent necessity for every member of the group. Use the technique of asking questions in class to afford an opportunity for a brief review. Let your questions be relevant to the material you have covered in earlier sessions. Give a little time for searching of notes to find the answer before you call on someone to reply to your query. Those few, brief seconds are psychologically very important. They afford time for a brief, intensive scanning of notes, and this is a form of repetition. All these techniques do one thing: they help to fix in the minds of your trainees by means of repetition the ideas that you have already presented in class.

To provide opportunities for review and to structure the classroom situation so that your trainees will take advantage of a review opportunity is to show the marks of a successful teacher.

Another way of securing repetition is to employ to that end the occasion of returning a test. After you have graded the papers and handed them back to the trainees, take a few minutes to review the correct answers. This helps to fix them in the trainees' minds.

An important consideration in getting people to remember what you have covered in class is the principle of *distributed practice*. Perhaps the idea of distributed practice can best be expressed by an example. If you have a fifty-minute session with trainees each day, you might spend the first ten minutes reviewing yesterday's lesson, the next thirty minutes on today's lesson, and the last ten minutes reviewing a lesson you had a week ago. If your training program does not consist of regular daily lessons, you could apply this principle to the form the lessons do take. For example, if you give a man individual instruction in welding for a few minutes whenever you both have time, you might occasionally use the time to have him go through a process you taught him several days ago. In the long run, the people you are instructing are likely to learn more through these reviews (which constitute distributed practice) than by spending every session of instruction exclusively on new material.

SUMMARY

As far as training programs are concerned, learning is acquiring the ability to do things or to do them better. This means that instructors should always direct their instruction toward the job the trainees will be doing. If instructors follow this policy faithfully, it will be easy for them to *motivate* trainees because trainees will understand just what it is they are supposed to be learning and why it is important for them to learn it. To be most effective, the instructor must hold the *concentrated* attention of his class. Illustrations, applications, humor, enthusiasm, and questions will help him do this. He must get the trainees' minds to *react*. Questions, problem situations, discussions, case studies, tryout situations, and encouragement of taking of notes are ways of getting mental activity from the group.

Trainees must see the *organization*, the over-all picture of the subject they are studying, not merely memorize the facts and parts without any clear idea of how they work together. The whole-part-whole scheme of instruction is a good way for the instructor to accomplish this organization in trainees' minds. Handing out outlines which trainees fill in as the period goes along can also be helpful. To be sure that trainees *comprehend* what is being taught, use plenty of practical illustrations and applications, and get trainees to suggest more. If they see how to apply what you have been teaching, the chances are they comprehend it. Finally, do not depend on one going-over to fix things in trainees' minds. It takes *repetition*. Use reviews, tests, posters, summaries, and questions to get trainees to think over things they studied earlier.

SUGGESTED READINGS

ALEXANDER, W. M., and P. M. HALVERSON: *Effective Teaching in Secondary Schools*, Rinehart & Company, Inc., New York, 1957.

BURTON, W. H.: *The Guidance of Learning Activities*. Appleton-Century-Crofts, Inc., New York, 1952.

FRANDSEN, A. N.: *How Children Learn: An Educational Psychology*. McGraw-Hill Book Company, Inc., New York, 1957.

4

Planning for Instruction

This chapter demonstrates how to start with the general purpose of a training program and design a course of instruction which is tailored to achieve that purpose. It illustrates in detail how to produce an integrated course of instruction instead of a miscellaneous collection of lessons.

WHEN A NEW COMPANY is being set up, or a new business established, one of the first things its organizers do is to divide the functions of the business into various departments of activity—production, personnel, sales, and so on. The same basic process is followed when a program of training is being developed. As soon as the general scope of the training is determined, it is convenient to begin dividing the subject matter of the course into parts comprising homogeneous material. If this division is done unwisely, the course of instruction can be changed from one big whole to many separate, miniature courses, producing a training course analogous to a bunch of cords, each dangling by itself, not connected with the others. A better plan is to interweave the separate themes of the training course, keeping each theme a separate entity for purposes of convenience and preparation, but interrelating them to form one strong training course, as separate cords are woven together to form a rope.

Assembling the subject matter of a course into units and interweaving the units to form one integrated course is sometimes called the "unit method" of organization. Each unit is composed of all the material which the course contains on one subject. A training course for supervisors, for instance, might cover the topics of company policy, work supervision, human relations, and management. Under the unit plan of course organization, each of these topics might constitute one unit of the total course. Each would be developed to afford adequate treatment of its particular topic, but throughout the course each would also be tied to the others by showing how all four topics are interdependent and influence each other.

The effectiveness of the unit method of construction depends largely on how skillfully the interrelation of the different units is shown. Showing supervisor trainees, for example, the effect of principles of human relations on company policies, the way management functions apply to the work the supervisors are responsible for, and a hundred other such interrelations will help them to perceive all the things they learn as one systematic, organized body of helpful information, rather than a collection of unrelated details.

You probably studied something about the Federal Reserve System of banking when you were taking American history in school. The chances are that if you have any memory at all of the Federal Reserve System you recall merely a few disconnected ideas and facts regarding it. Your spotty memory of it is partly due to the fact that you probably never studied it as one unified topic but in bits and pieces scattered throughout the whole of American history. A unit of study would have presented all the data relating to the system as one integrated unit. At the same time, the unit would have brought out the effect the Federal Reserve System had on other aspects of American history and the circumstances of history which caused the system to develop as it did. A course in American history organized around the main themes of our national history could be called a "unit-oriented" course.

Planning a Unit-oriented Course

The process of building any good training program starts with the determination of the exact objective of the course. It continues with the identification of each subject or topic which must be covered to achieve this objective. Then these individual subjects must be fitted together to form the course.

To illustrate the unit process of developing a course, we shall use the example already mentioned of a training course for supervisors. The same principles and procedures apply in the development of a systematic supervisor-conducted, on-the-job training program or an apprentice training program. The supervisor training course is used here for purposes of illustration because, as a more highly formalized type of training program, it involves a higher degree of internal organization and integration of instruction procedures and materials. The Sample Course Plan shows the result of the steps of analysis and synthesis mentioned above and discussed in more detail later.

SAMPLE COURSE PLAN

Supervisor Training Course

OBJECTIVE

To develop within certain, selected personnel the capabilities required to direct the activities of a group of employees in such manner as to evoke their best efforts, highest accomplishment, and cooperative attitude

SCOPE

1. To give the trainees a knowledge of company policies, rules, and regulations as these apply to employees for whom the supervisors are responsible
2. To develop personal competence and skill in being able themselves to do, if necessary, the work they supervise
3. To define supervisory-level functions of management and to develop ability in exercising these functions
4. To develop the ability to inspire workers to demonstrate their best efforts and attitudes toward their work
5. To create an interest in supervision and a desire to do it well

COURSE ORGANIZATION (UNIT PLAN)

1. Administrative policies
2. Work familiarization

3. Management functions
4. Human relations

COORDINATION

Each instructor will show the interrelationship of units by referring to material which is being presented in other units which is pertinent to the material that he may be discussing. (*Example:* A lecturer on management function of *control* refers to the administrative policy [1] of work-flow charts. He reminds the trainees that learning to prepare these charts is a part of their work-familiarization [2] training and that deficiencies in human relations [3] both cause and result from lack of *control.*)

Each conference period, regardless of the unit, is built around topics which require consideration of each of the four major unit subjects. To permit synchronization of instruction, periods from each unit are presented each day, rather than completing one unit before taking up another.

[1] Note interrelationship; see item 1 under "Course Organization."
[2] Note interrelationship; see item 2 under "Course Organization."
[3] Note interrelationship; see item 4 under "Course Organization."

As has already been suggested, the first step in constructing any training program is to determine its exact objective, what you want it to do, and more particularly what you want trainees to be able to do as a result of taking it. For a supervisors' training course the first objective that occurs to you might be, "Make better supervisors." This is fine as far as it goes, but it does not go far enough. It is as if a golf coach were to ask, "What do you want my instruction to do for you?" The answer, "Improve my game" would be perfectly true and accurate, but not nearly so helpful to the pro as a more definite reply such as, "I want to get more distance on my iron shots and to correct a tendency to slice with my woods."

So dig deeper into the question of what ability, attitude, or knowledge you (or the president, the vice-president, or whoever) want the course to produce. What are the specific things your supervisors need to know, or to be able to do better, in order to be better supervisors? What determines whether a supervisor does a good job or a bad one?

The quality of the supervisor's work is perhaps best measured by the quality and quantity of the work done by the people he supervises and by the attitude that prevails among them. A meaningful over-all objective of the supervisors' training course, therefore, might run something like this: "To help supervisors maintain high production and morale within their sections." Obviously the exact wording might be altered for many reasons. If the emphasis is to be on improvement over what has been done in the past, "attain better" could be substituted for "maintain high." If this is a preparatory class for employees who have not yet served as supervisors, the objective might be better stated: "To develop within selected personnel the capability to direct the activities of a group of employees in such a manner as to produce their best efforts, the highest accomplishment, and a cooperative attitude."

When the exact over-all course objective has been determined, the next question to consider in constructing this illustrative training course for supervisors might logically be, "What are the specific knowledges, attitudes, and skills which will produce in supervisors this desired ability?" A conference of company officials, department heads, or others of sound judgment should probably be called to determine these attributes, for this is an absolutely vital step in the construction of your program. In fact, at this point is determined the direction your training program will take. If an important knowledge, attitude, or skill is overlooked here, your course will be incomplete. If little, incidental knowledges and skills are given exaggerated importance here, your training course can become sterile, an unfruitful emphasis upon trivia. So enlist the best brains available, and talk the matter over long enough to get this basic breakdown of your course into the major components *right*. Hold as a target this criterion: to identify every major separate skill or knowledge family required by the job, but to let no trivia creep in.

In the supervisors' training course, the different skill, knowledge, and attitude families might turn out to be something like these (shown under "Scope" in the Sample Course Plan):

1. Knowledge of company policies, rules, and regulations as they apply to employees for whom supervisors are responsible

2. Personal competence and skill in doing the work they supervise

3. Knowledge of supervisory functions of management, and ability to exercise them

4. Ability to inspire workers to their best efforts and attitudes

5. Interest in supervision and a desire to do it well

Each of the first four requisites for supervisors might be developed as units of instruction. The fifth one (supervisory attitude) obviously could not be, but can result from the nature of the personnel selected to attend such a training course and as a side product of the other four. It is undesirable to depend on side learnings as a means of achieving major aims, but some things can be taught better as adjuncts to something else than as entities within themselves. You cannot teach trainees proper attitudes by having them learn a set of rules pertaining to attitudes. You may cultivate in them these attitudes by helping them develop skills in human relations which will keep them interested in the subject. Keep the attitude aspect of your instruction as a major goal, to be planned and worked for throughout all your units.

The five subject areas identified under "Scope" in the supervisors' Sample Course Plan are not true objectives as now stated, but merely designations of areas of skill, attitude, or knowledge. If the first four areas are to be developed as units of instruction, the next step is to determine the real objective of each of these areas or units and to ascertain what particular abilities or knowledges supervisors are expected to develop in each area as a result of the training program.

Let us pause and summarize what we have done up to this point. We have determined the over-all objective of the training course. We have determined the scope of the course, i.e., what knowledges, abilities, and attitudes must be developed to achieve the over-all course objective, and we have grouped these knowledges, attitudes, and abilities into units. Now we shall develop one of these units, as a sample, in more detail.

Developing a Unit of Instruction

For purposes of illustration, the fourth area, "Ability to inspire workers to their best efforts and attitudes," will be developed here as a unit of instruction. "Human Relations for Supervisors" would seem to be a suitable name for the concept and probable content of this fourth knowledge-skill family identified in the analysis of the course.

Next we need to identify for this unit an over-all objective which will guide the development of necessary specific objectives and learning outcomes. The process previously described of identifying the over-all objective of the training course and using it as a guide in breaking the total subject matter into areas or units is now repeated on the unit level, and the exact objective of the unit is determined.

The Sample Unit Plan which follows illustrates a convenient form for recording the results of systematic unit planning.

SAMPLE UNIT PLAN

Supervisor Training Course

UNIT 4—HUMAN RELATIONS FOR SUPERVISORS

Over-all Objective. To enable supervisors to obtain better work from their subordinates by developing in the supervisors more skill in meeting the psychological needs of people in work situations

Specific Objectives

1. Understanding of the basic psychological needs of people which may be partially satisfied in the work situation
2. Appreciation of the personal advantages accruing to the supervisor and the company through workers' finding satisfaction of their psychological needs in the work situation

3. Skill in handling personnel and the situations which arise on the job in such a manner as to afford workers maximum satisfaction of their psychological needs through the work situation

4. Ability to handle unusual situations in a manner conducive to the development and maintenance of good human relations in the section

5. Knowledge of certain proved techniques in supervision which tend to promote superior human relations in a section

Unit Outline

1. "Employee Satisfaction and Supervisor Achievement" (lecture: 20 minutes' duration). Emphasize relation between employee satisfaction and employee effort, and between employee effort and supervisor success, demonstrating with illustrations.

2. "Cases in Supervisor-Employee Relations" (conference: 30 minutes). Study and discussion of cases where supervisor-employee relations were crucial to the resolution of the situation. These cases should provide motivation for the unit as a whole.

3. "Basic Psychological Needs of People" (lecture-discussion: 70 minutes). The nature and effect of basic psychological needs and how they can be gratified on the job. Trainees will be encouraged to volunteer experiences, ideas, interpretations, and comments on illustrative problems.

4. "Principles of Supervision" (lecture: 50 minutes). Basic principles and techniques of handling people in supervisory relationships.

5. "Laboratory Exercise in Handling Employee Human Relations Problems" (role-playing exercise, analysis, and discussion of simulated employee human relations problems: 3 hours). Trainees will alternate in roles of supervisors, employees, analysts, and observers. Last thirty minutes will be a conference designed to identify specific guiding principles or ideas which can be inferred from the exercise.

6. Test (30 minutes). Multiple-choice test on facts and principles brought out in the unit.

The over-all objective of this unit might be determined to be, "To develop in supervisors a high level of skill in human relations to the end that they will be able to inspire workers to their best efforts and attitudes." This might be stated more succinctly: "To improve the human-relations skills of supervisors," or more elaborately: "To enable supervisors to obtain better work from their subordinates by developing in the supervisors more skill in meeting the psychological needs of people in work situations." The main idea is to derive an objective which actually states what you want these supervisors to be able to do as a result of studying this unit of work, and says it in such a form that the stated objective will serve as a guide to everyone working on the project—guide them in knowing how to resolve questions or what to do in particular situations.

The statement of the over-all unit objective should make that objective a clear, sharply defined knowledge, ability, skill, or attitude to be striven for. Spend enough time, thought, and discussion on its wording to be sure that it states exactly what you really want the unit to accomplish. Fuzzy wording at this point will almost certainly predestine fuzzy instruction; the instructor will be proceeding with only a vague idea of what his instruction is supposed to accomplish, instead of knowing what clearly identified student abilities are to be developed. It is virtually as difficult to build a sound, crisply effective program of training on inaccurate, incomplete, or indefinitely expressed objectives as it is to organize a company wisely and well without a clear knowledge of what its functions (just another word for objectives) will be.

Objectives are the targets at which a program aims. If they are the wrong targets, not the ones that really need to be hit, or if they are foggily obscured behind a mist of ill-chosen words, the score is bound to be low, no matter how good the shooting. Throughout the whole field of education it has been found that hours spent polishing objectives into accurate form, and insuring that the objectives stated are the ones really needed, pay perhaps the biggest dividends of any hours spent on an instructional program.

Having identified the general purpose of the unit and what it is to accomplish, through formulating its objective, you are now in a position to analyze the unit's general subject area further, to ascertain what specific objectives must be achieved to accomplish the big one. In the human relations unit of the

Supervisor Training Course a representative list of specific objectives might be those stated in the Sample Unit Plan:

1. Understanding the basic psychological needs of people which may be partially satisfied in the work situation

2. Appreciation of the personal advantages accruing to the supervisor and the company through workers' finding satisfaction of their psychological needs in the work situation

3. Skill in handling personnel and the situations which arise on the job in such a manner as to afford workers maximum achievement of their psychological needs through the work situation

4. Ability to handle unusual situations in a manner conducive to the development and maintenance of good human relations in the section

5. Knowledge of certain proved techniques in supervision which tend to promote superior human relations in a section

Now we have determined the over-all, general objective of the human relations unit and also its specific objectives. Next we get into the actual content—the facts, principles, concepts, exercises, and activities which are to compose the subject matter of the unit. Until now, you will recall if you think closely over what has been done, we have only identified the objectives to be achieved. Nothing has been said about what topics should be covered to accomplish the objectives, or what the actual down-to-brass-tacks facts and figures are which should be taught. In the unit plan of organizing instruction, these bits of actual subject matter and skills are called "learning outcomes." Pursuing our rope analogy a bit further, these are the actual fibers, not the substrands into which they will be woven or twisted or the whole rope which the substrands make up. In identifying the learning outcomes required to achieve each objective, we get right down to the basic fibers, the actual subject matter to be taught in the course.

For purposes of illustration, we shall take from the Sample Unit Plan specific objective No. 1, "Understanding of the basic psychological needs of people which may be partially satisfied in the work situation." We shall identify the learning outcomes encompassed by this objective and construct a lesson plan to accomplish this objective and teach its learning outcomes.

Psychologists have identified a number of basic psychological needs. Most of these fit into four categories—recognition, opportunity, belonging, and security. In one way or another, a

DIAGRAM OF THE ORGANIZATION OF A COURSE

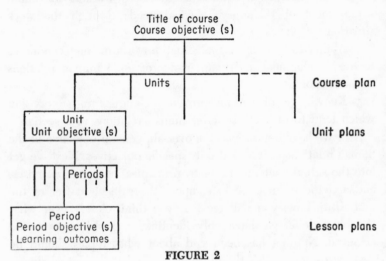

FIGURE 2

person's work situation may assist or interfere with his satisfaction of each of these psychological needs, and so to achieve this specific objective it may be necessary for trainees to acquire the following concepts, or learning outcomes:

1. People's pride and self-respect make them want recognition, i.e., to be thought of as individuals, to be known, to be complimented, and to get attention.

2. People generally dislike being under restrictions. They want the opportunity to think, talk, and do as seems best to them. The more opportunity they have to exercise their initiative, the more enthusiastic and loyal they are likely to be.

3. Man is by nature a gregarious creature. He wants to feel he is a part of any organization he works for, not that he is merely attached to it. He needs a feeling of belonging on his job.

4. Every normal person wants security. Absolute security cannot be obtained, but promoting certain feelings of security on the job will result in better production and better worker morale.

Every specific objective in a unit must be broken down into the learning outcomes necessary to achieve it, as we have done here. When this has been done, a plan must be devised for teaching each learning outcome. The instructor must determine what he should do and what he must motivate the members of the training class to do to achieve these learning outcomes. This plan, which is the actual blueprint of a specific period of instruction, is called a "lesson plan" and is discussed later in the chapter. Lesson plans combine into units; units combine to form the course.

After lesson plans have been prepared for each period in a unit, they must be examined as a group to see if they actually cover the objectives and full scope of the unit. Of course, each one was designed to help achieve one or more aspects of the objectives and to provide coverage of some phase of the scope. But in their actual preparation, individual lesson plans sometimes take unanticipated directions, and the final results may not be precisely what was intended when the scope and objectives for the periods were originally specified. So, examine all the lesson plans in the light of the unit objectives and scope, and see if the requirements of the unit are really met by the lessons as finally developed.

If these requirements have not been met, elaborate the lesson plans as necessary to cover any aspects of the unit which have been overlooked, adding new periods if necessary. If material which is not germane to the unit has been included in the lessons, cut it out.

Having assured yourself that your lessons as planned actually meet the specifications of the unit, covering all necessary aspects, neither overlapping undesirably nor containing irrelevant material, consider how they can best be fitted together to form the unit. Which lesson should come first? It should be one which does not presuppose knowledge to be acquired subsequently and at the same time one which will catch the interest of trainees and motivate them for the unit. Which one comes naturally after the lead-off lesson? Does it need minor tailoring to fit neatly and logically after its predecessor? If so, plan the modifications needed. Painstakingly examine each remaining lesson, as to both its proper order in the unit and its fit into the niche finally selected for it, until your unit is completely organized. Then follow exactly the same process in fitting the separate units together to form the whole course. Conscientiously following this plan will go far toward guaranteeing that you will emerge with a complete, tightly organized course which will accomplish its objectives.

Choosing an Instructional Method

When a unit has been identified, its objective established, and its general scope and content determined, the question arises of how the unit can best be taught. How can the scope and content best be covered to achieve the objective?

As was pointed out in Chapter 1, the objective of a training program is almost always to produce some *ability to do*. This ability to do ordinarily requires skills, knowledge, and attitudes. Skills, knowledge, and attitudes are developed through the operation of the psychological factors of motivation, concentration, reaction, organization, comprehension, and repetition. Choosing instructional methods for a unit, then, becomes a matter of determining how trainees can be led through the steps of learning which will best develop the skills, knowledge, and attitudes required for the particular ability which the objective calls for.

Four general methods of instruction are commonly used in

training programs. They are the lecture, the demonstration-performance, the group discussion, and role-playing. All are supplemented by reading and problem assignments, and all are used with greater or lesser variations from their pure form. Thus, the lecture method may be interspersed with questions and answers, or with recitation. The group discussion may take the form of analyzing a problem or studying an example, or case, and so on through innumerable combinations, variations, and permutations. Most training-course objectives can best be met by using one, a combination, or a variation of these four general methods, each of which will be discussed in detail in subsequent chapters.

Knowledge, skills, and attitudes related to the subject area of a unit will all usually be required to achieve unit objectives. To insure that none of the necessary learnings are overlooked, a committee of instructors or an instructor with two or three other persons knowledgeable in the unit subject area should determine the method to be used in teaching each portion of the unit. This should be done at the same time the objective, scope, and content of the unit are planned.

As in many educational matters, there is no formula for selecting methods to be used in a unit or specific period. A general guide is:

1. Introduce the unit and develop trainees' knowledge and understanding of the subject by one or more lectures.

2. Use role-playing or demonstration-performance methods to develop skills and give trainees a feel for the subject.

3. Hold group discussions to analyze problems, stimulate thinking, and develop attitudes on the subject being studied.

4. Accompany the above methods with appropriate reading assignments and problems or written exercises.

It is reasonable to suppose that most units will require use of at least two or three of the major training methods to achieve their objectives most fully. In planning a unit the committee should keep in mind the necessity of providing trainees with learning experiences in all three areas—skill, knowledge, and attitude—and specify methods of conducting the periods of the unit which will produce trainees developed in each of the three areas.

Planning the Component Parts of a Unit: Lesson Plans

In this and subsequent chapters on specific methods of instruction it will be assumed that the course planning committee provides the individual instructor with a lesson title, objective, method, and some indication of the scope and direction the period is expected to take. The instructor will then begin to study these directions for his period, gather material, and subsequently develop more refined or specific objectives and learning outcomes as he works out the details of his period.

The lesson plan may be constructed for one fifteen-minute period, or it may cover all the objectives in a unit and be broken at convenient places to fit the time schedule of the training course. The length of the lesson makes no difference in the construction of the plan; the procedures, principles, and content are the same. The lesson plan is frequently referred to, and with considerable accuracy, as the blueprint of a period of instruction. It shows the location, scope, dimensions, material, building procedures, and finished product of the period. It is the scheme referred to in Chapter 3 whereby ways of calling into play all the psychological processes which affect learning are planned for a period, so that the instructor enters the classroom with a clearly defined course of action laid out. In that course of action he has provided for motivation, organization, visual aids, and the other things that will help him get his points across, and has drawn up a plan which brings in each of these factors at the appropriate place.

For purposes of illustration, we shall examine a lesson plan for one specific objective of the human relations unit—understanding the basic psychological needs of people which may be partially satisfied in the work situation (specific objective No. 1, or No. 3 of the Unit Outline, in the Sample Unit Plan).

This Sample Lesson Plan (Table 1) will serve as an example for constructing lesson plans for each element of instruction, large or small, that is to be taught. Every period of instruction should be planned in a similar manner, and the instructor should carry that lesson plan, in written form, into the classroom. A lesson plan in your mind is generally no lesson plan at all. It is nebulous, wishful thinking until it has met and passed the test of being put down in written words so it can be checked, re-checked, and cross-checked for adequacy and completeness, and used as a guide in conducting the lesson.

It is meticulous, monotonous work to make out a lesson plan, and some inexperienced instructional and supervisory personnel are extremely reluctant to do the work necessary to produce one in writing. However, a poll of experienced instructors will reveal that very few of them would go into a class without a written lesson plan any more than they would start to build a house without blueprints.

The three columns of the Sample Lesson Plan are an important feature. The column on the left keeps the continuity straight; that is, it keeps the outline of the material to be covered in sys-tematic order and shows the interrelations of different elements of the instructional program. The middle column keeps the in-structor reminded of the activities he should engage in to get the learning outcomes across. The right-hand column reminds him that, in the last analysis, it is what *the trainees* do that determines whether or how much they learn. It keeps him alert to the fact that he must handle his presentation in a manner which produces the *trainee activity* which he provided for in constructing the lesson plan.

Do not try to short-cut the lesson plan by abbreviating it or leaving off one of the columns. It is, when you finally stand before your class of trainees, more than a blueprint; it is the actual edifice of your period, and every room has to be complete and unified into an organic whole to make your period an effective learning experience.

TABLE 1. SAMPLE LESSON PLAN

Course	Supervisor Training Course
Unit	4, Human Relations for Supervisors
Lesson	Basic Psychological Needs of People
Time	8:30 a.m., Tuesday, January 16, 19—
Instructor	E. F. Dunlap
Lesson objective	To develop in the trainees an understanding of the basic psychological needs of people which may be partially satisfied in the work situation
References	T. F. Staton, *Human Relations for Supervisors*, Educational Aids, 2208 Woodley Road, Montgomery, Ala., 1957
Instructional aids	Blackboard and chalk Slide projector, screen, and slides
Student assignment	None
Length of period	70 minutes
Plan for conducting the period..	The instructor will give a short introduction to the period, identifying the basic psychological needs of people, explaining their significance, and posing practical questions as to their relation to worker morale and production. He will then elaborate on each psychological need and will ask the class members to cite instances where this need was shown by an employee, explain what was done, and discuss the result. Major factors comprising each of the basic psychological needs, if not brought out by class members, will be identified by the instructor.

58

Introduction to subject

Body of lesson

Learning outcome	Instructor activity	Trainee activity
Understanding the nature, operation, and significance to supervisors of the basic psychological needs of people	Discusses the concept of psychological need Identifies the basic psychological needs Asks for illustration of the relation of such needs to what people do Shows slide on effect of satisfying psychological needs	Relate what is being said to their own lives and experience Cite illustrations Comment on meaning of slide
People want *recognition*: as individuals of good work, loyalty of their importance of what they have to say	Explains that recognition involves acknowledging the personal dignity, importance, and worth of the individual (cites example) Asks for good or poor examples from the experience of the class Leads analysis and discussion of examples Shows illustrative slides at appropriate points	Take notes and mentally relate example to own experience Recall examples Interpret and generalize from the examples

59

TABLE 1. SAMPLE LESSON PLAN (*Continued*)

| Learning outcome | Body of lesson | |
	Instructor activity	Trainee activity
People want *opportunity*: to do things their own way to exercise initiative to advance, better themselves to assume responsibility to earn credit for themselves	Outlines the various dimensions encompassed in "opportunity" Shows its relation to freedom of action, initiative, getting ahead, being able to get credit for things done Shows slide to illustrate over-control Calls on class for elaboration of significance of opportunity in American culture Invites suggestions as to ways in which workers can be given more satisfying opportunities	Take notes and begin broadening their original concept of opportunity Through discussion of own experiences gain increased perception of importance of opportunity to Americans and relate it to needs of employees
People want to *belong*: feel they know the ropes feel they are contributing something to the organization know what is going on be accepted by the group know and be known by other workers	Explains concept of gregariousness and its implications for situations where cooperative work is required Asks trainees to suggest ways workers may be denied the sense of belonging that they need in their work Points out, or asks class for, ways to promote feelings of belonging	Take notes Search memories for own feeling of need to belong (as child, adolescent) Perceive significance of hitherto unrecognized symptoms of need for belonging in fellow workers Cite such cases and offer comments on how to handle

60

People need to *feel secure:*
against unexpected change
that they can depend on the boss's honesty, fairness, backing
against criticism without help

Asks someone in class to volunteer to explain meaning of psychological maturity

Invites supplemental elaborations from other trainees (may call on individuals)

Completes explanation, covering any points not yet covered

Asks group to develop a plan of section management which would make optimum provisions for section members' psychological security

Mentally formulate explanations in expectation of being called on

Supplement own ideas with notes on comments by other trainees and instructor

Work to develop a plan usable in an organization to increase psychological security of members

Summary

Summary of principles and applications developed during period, by instructor or members of class

Review

Lesson of one week ago reviewed by reference to its lesson plan and discussion of crucial points

When you begin to construct lesson plans, you are likely to find that after you write the first two or three items in the columns you tend to fall into a routine of listing the learning outcome, putting "Explains . . ." or "Asks for suggestions from the class . . ." in the Instructor Activity column, and in the Trainee Activity column, "Listens," "Takes notes," or "Offers suggestions." Contrast such routine entries with the constant variety in the entries given in these columns of the Sample Lesson Plan. That variety is one of the reasons for constructing a lesson plan. If the instructor goes to the class with only a mental lesson plan, his questions and handling of the period quickly become the weary routine of a few stereotyped treatments of each subject. No instructor can think on his feet fast enough to keep in his period the interest and variety that he can *plan* into it, working at leisure with all the resources at hand to get information about his period. Remember, too, the higher the level of trainee interest that is maintained, the more the trainees will learn from the period. It takes conscious effort to build interest into the lesson plan, and it will not be built into the period if it is not in the lesson plan.

A written lesson plan, particularly when backed up by good unit and course planning, provides perfect opportunity for the instructor to double-check his projected instruction to determine whether he has built into it all the steps of motivation, concentration, reaction, organization, comprehension, and repetition and directed his efforts toward achieving the skills, knowledges, and attitudes which every element of instruction *must* achieve to be worth while. Look down the three columns after you draft your lesson plan. See if you have generously provided for all necessary psychological factors leading to learning. Be certain you have built up to thorough accomplishment of the three aspects of learning necessary to produce the *ability to do*. If you have not, rework your plans for the period to get the steps and final outcomes in there.

We have now traced the development of a program of instruction from its original conception to the final blueprint for a particular period. From the over-all course objective the principal subject areas are determined. From these subject areas, units of instruction and unit objectives are derived. Within the units, the specific objectives necessary to fulfill the over-all unit objective are determined, and from specific unit objectives the content of the unit is outlined. Then a lesson plan is prepared for teaching each period of a unit.

When each unit has been developed in the manner of the sample one on "Human Relations for Supervisors," when a lesson plan has been made for each period as for the sample period on "Basic Psychological Needs of People," the basic work of course preparation is complete. The finishing remains, the weaving together of the periods, tailoring each to show its relation to kindred subjects in other portions of the course as has been described. This requires that each individual instructor constantly relate his instruction to the over-all unit and course objectives and to other related instruction in the course. This completes the course preparation; your instruction is now a unified program, not a mélange of periods.

SUMMARY

An instructional program starts with the over-all objective to be achieved as a result of training. This over-all objective breaks down into different aspects of the training subject which must be covered to achieve the over-all objective. Each of these aspects or phases of the over-all subject is commonly called a "unit," because it is one unified phase of the larger course. The instructor should put the knowledges and skills required for mastery of each of these subject areas into the form of objectives which, when achieved, lead to realization of the over-all objective of the course. At this point, if you, as the instructor, have followed the unit plan, you have identified the course and its over-all objective, the units which compose the course, and the objectives of these units. The next step is to determine the specific things which must be learned to achieve the unit objectives and design a plan for learning them. This final plan of instruction is called a "lesson plan."

A lesson plan starts with a heading and introduction which identify the course, unit, and topic (if smaller than a unit). Usually the lesson plan will be for one or two periods. Then in order come the objective, the readings the instructor found helpful in preparing the lesson, information about instructional aids, and a summary of just what will be done in the period.

The body of the lesson plan consists of three vertical columns. In the left-hand column are listed the learning outcomes to be achieved during the period. In the middle column are described the activities in which the instructor will engage to achieve these learning outcomes. In the right-hand column are the trainee activities which the instructor has planned for the class. Care should be taken to provide an interesting variety in the instructor activities to prevent monotony and loss of interest. Extraordinary care must be taken to insure that a variety of mentally stimulating trainee activities throughout the period are planned to insure mental reaction which is vital to learning.

Inexperienced instructors are sometimes impatient of the work involved in making out a lesson plan. Generally, the more experienced the instructor and the more accurate his self-evaluation, the more he regards a written lesson plan as an absolute prerequisite to his periods of instruction.

The last step in preparing the course is weaving the periods into units and the units into one unified course. The lessons are checked and modified as necessary to provide for full achievement of the unit objectives and to fit them into a logical order. Finally, the units themselves are similarly studied, modified as necessary, and fitted together to meet the over-all course plan and objectives. If the unit plan of organization has been followed closely, this is a relatively simple matter of instructors' keeping their individual periods in a clear relation to the course objectives and to other periods.

SUGGESTED READINGS

ALEXANDER, W. M., and P. M. HALVERSON: *Effective Teaching in Secondary Schools*, Rinehart & Company, Inc., New York, 1957.

BURTON, W. H.: *The Guidance of Learning Activities*, Appleton-Century-Crofts, Inc., New York, 1952.

RISK, T. M.: *Principles and Practices of Teaching in Secondary Schools*, American Book Company, New York, 1947.

UMSTATTD, J. G.: *Secondary School Teaching*, Ginn & Company, Boston, 1953.

5

The Lecture Method

This chapter discusses the advantages and limitations of the lecture method of instruction, and gives steps to follow in gathering material for a lecture and preparing to present the material in lecture form.

A LECTURE HAS BEEN DEFINED as a process by which facts are transmitted from the notebook of the instructor to the notebook of the student without passing through the mind of either. Although unfortunately this is often true, it does not have to be so. A properly planned lecture is a fine instructional device adaptable to teaching almost any subject or to supplementing other methods in teaching. Indeed, there are few circumstances where any other method of instruction can be used to its fullest potential without being supplemented by some amount of lecture. For instance, the explanation portion of the demonstration-performance method influences largely the effectiveness of the demonstration, and the introductory briefing in the group discussion sets the tone of the discussion. The lecture method, on the other hand, can frequently be used without assistance from other teaching methods to achieve the best learning outcomes possible on a subject.

Paradoxically, the lecture method is one of the hardest methods to use effectively, and yet it is usually difficult to convince a would-be lecturer that this is a particularly hard method to use. This is because the nature of lecturing tends to conceal its faults. An instructor putting on a demonstration cannot fail to recognize his shortcoming when he is *not* doing the things he is telling his trainees he is showing them how to do. The instructor leading a group discussion is miserably conscious of it if he cannot get the trainees in his group to talk or cannot keep them on the subject.

On the other hand, the lecturer merely stands up and talks. He knows his subject, he has been talking all his life, so he talks about his subject for the prescribed number of minutes, and sits down with the feeling that his lecture has been a success because he has covered all the material he planned to cover. Would that this were true! Too often it is not. The lecturer has covered his subject, but if he has not carried his listeners through the six psychological steps resulting in effective learning, he almost certainly has not produced in them the desired skills, knowledges, or attitudes, and so his lecture has been a failure. But he does not *know* that he did not achieve the desired learning outcomes and can only evaluate his lecture by how well he seemed to himself to talk.

Most poor lectures, and most failure on the part of lecturers to recognize defects in their lectures, are due to one thing: *lack of a lesson plan.* An outline of the talk becomes part of a lecture plan—the center column—but is by no means all of it. Most poor lecturers stop in their preparation when they have outlined their lecture. They would be better lecturers if they started with their period objective, determined the specific learning outcomes trainees should achieve in the period, outlined their lecture to start trainees toward the learning outcomes, and then planned for trainee activities to insure the accomplishment of the factors in learning which lead to achievement of the learning outcomes. This chapter will discuss some general considerations regarding the lecture method, then present a guide to planning a lecture which is oriented to learning outcomes and learner activities, rather than being oriented to the outline of a talk.

Despite its difficulty as an instructional medium, the lecture method is so valuable that most training programs will use it to a considerable degree. It is unrivaled as a means of introducing a new subject to a group of trainees, sketching out for them a field they will be studying later in detail, orienting them to the policies, rules, and expectations of the company, acquainting them with principles and concepts, and illustrating the application of these principles and concepts in their immediate working situation. It is a means whereby an instructor can spend hours gathering bits of needed information from here, there, and yonder, and then present in a few minutes' time the information he spent hours gathering, saving each of the trainees hours of hunting down the information for himself. It can be used to instruct any number of trainees at once, the number being limited only by the size of the room available or the efficiency of the public address system. One instructor, consuming the time for only one preparation of a period, can handle a group which might require the preparation and period time of a dozen instructors if another method were used.

Weaknesses in the lecture method of instruction are, in fact, usually weaknesses in the *lecturer*, notably in his failure to plan a period, not in the lecture method. If the lecturer is enthusiastic, his lecture generally will motivate an audience, not put it to sleep. If he is challenging, his lecture will stimulate thought in the minds of his hearers, not stupefy them. If he is logical and clear, his lectures will educate his listeners, not pass automatically to their notes. Naturally, there are some types of instruction in which the lecture alone cannot do the job in the best possible fashion. A lecture cannot make a description of how to tie a square knot as vivid as a lecture supplementing a demonstration can make it, nor can it describe the interplay of hostile personalities as vividly as a role-playing exercise with an accompanying interpretation.

Fortunately, the difficulty in using the lecture method lies largely in the unfamiliarity of most people with basic principles of good lecturing. Almost any person of average verbal fluency and intelligence can develop himself into a competent lecturer by assiduous practice in preparing and rehearsing lectures, following a clear-cut set of steps; that is, if he has anything to say in the first place.

The remainder of this chapter will be devoted to suggesting ways of gathering the data an instructor must have as a foundation for his lecture, procedures for building from the accumulated material a learning-producing lecture, and principles for preparing to present it. As discussed in Chapter 4, it is assumed that the instructor will be given a period objective, method, and some indication of the scope of his subject when he is assigned the period. This being the case, he is prepared to begin active gathering of material for his lecture as soon as he has familiarized himself with his period assignment.

Gathering Material for a Lecture

In demonstration-performance instruction, role-playing, and group discussions, the material to be considered is usually already available in a compact package, or it is to be drawn from the minds of the participants according to some sort of outline as the period progresses. In the lecture method, however, you, the instructor, may be assigned to "tell those trainees about so-and-so," and you have to take it from there. Often there will be no organized body of knowledge on the subject which would make your job merely one of saying in your own words what an author already has written. Where a complete treatment of your subject area is available in writing, it is likely to be written for a different type of audience from the one you will be addressing or be too long, too short, too complex, or approached from a different point of view from that demanded by your particular training situation. At any rate, the way things are said in writing is seldom the most effective way of saying them orally, so it is usually not wise for a lecturer merely to paraphrase a written article. Usually a lecture will be better if you take the trouble to look over several possible sources of information about your subject, taking pertinent ideas and facts from each and weaving a body of material that exactly fits your needs and your audience.

If you are given some printed material and told to lecture from it, you have no problem in gathering material. Read your material and you can go directly to the next phase of preparation, that is, tailoring your lecture to people.

For purposes of discussion here, we will assume you are *not* given a neat package of written material and told to present it in lecture form. We will assume you are given the topic and perhaps a few miscellaneous references or manuals and told to work up a lecture. This is a harder kind of assignment, but can be simplified by a systematic approach.

At least three types of resources should be explored when you are gathering information for a lecture. The first is your own mind. Sit down in a quiet place, with paper and pencil and *think*. Ask yourself the question, "What things ought to be covered in a lecture to this group on this subject?" Write down the general topics that should be covered as they occur to you, and then list the subtopics which belong under the general topics. At this stage of the game you should not be too selective. If a topic seems to belong in the lecture, write it down without examining it too closely to see if it really is important. Perhaps your lecture assignment is to tell a group of employees about safety procedures, regulations, and precautions in the factory. Try to recall all the safety measures the factory requires. Rack your brain for reasons why the different safety measures are important. Think of any suggestions you can call to mind that, if followed, would make workers in the factory safer. Put every idea down on paper as it comes to your mind.

After a reasonable attempt at formulating your own ideas of what ought to be in your safety lecture, start reading. Read all company memoranda, instructions, or handbooks available on the subject of industrial safety. If time permits, see if the local public library has additional books, pamphlets, or magazine articles on the subject. Make notes on anything you come across that was not included in your own brain-child list. The reason for making your own list first is that reading the writings of others tends to get your thinking in a rut. Doing the creative thinking first gives a chance of coming up with a fresh, effective approach that might not come after you have got into the habit of thinking like everyone else on the subject. The writings, on the other hand, will still be there for you to go to when you have thought the problem through for yourself.

Maybe something you read will suggest some idea to you that is not in the written material itself and that you had not thought of. By all means put it down. At this point you are trying to learn all you can, get all the ideas you can, about safety in your factory. You are like a miner in the pit digging out ore; you are just getting it out, the refining will come later.

Having done your own thinking about the subject and your reading about it, next talk to some of the people you think might know something about it. Ask foremen for ideas on how the number of accidents could be reduced. Make notes of any suggestions they have for cutting down accidents, whether they would be impractical because of other considerations or not. Particularly, make detailed notes of any accidents, near accidents, or potential accidents *avoided* by safety measures and any failure of personnel to observe safety measures which might have caused accidents if this had not been detected and corrected. Do your best to get these people who work on the firing line to recall and recount all the instances of such things they have heard of or experienced. Live illustrations are one of the things that make a good lecture. People with personal experience in the field are the best source of such illustrations. Get all you can out of them.

In the process of thinking, reading, and interviewing, you have done more than merely accumulate a collection of notes about safety in your factory. You have acquired a feel for the whole subject of safety—things that are being done, the reasons for them, things that need to be done, how to go about doing some of them, the problems encountered in putting over a safety campaign, and how people react to the whole idea of factory safety. You have gained some perspective on the subject. You have a mass of facts and ideas at your finger tips and in your mind.

A word of warning here: You will give a poor lecture if you

assume that your preparation is almost done at this stage. It is not. It is at most half done. There are two distinct phases in preparing a lecture. One is accumulating the subject material to be taught, the other is putting it in such form that people will learn it most effectively. Either is perfectly useless without the other. If you keep this concept clearly in mind, you are likely to perform the second phase of your preparation well.

Tailoring Your Lecture to P-E-O-P-L-E

An instructor teaches two things: subject matter and people. Both must be provided for in the preparation. The phase of gathering the subject matter has just been described. Here is a step-by-step guide which shows you how to work over your mass of material and erect from it a strong, sound, successful lecture. When you have prepared your lecture according to this guide, you will find that constructing the lesson plan for your period is easy; you have in your mind the ideas necessary to complete the three columns of the plan and provide you with a sound blueprint to guide you in conducting your period.

This whole guide is based on the central idea that your lecture is for people and must be constructed with them in mind. It is an effective, usable formula for carrying class members through the six psychological factors of learning which help them do their jobs better through developing appropriate skills, knowledges, or attitudes. To make the steps simple to remember, each step is built around one key word whose first letter corresponds to one of the letters of the word *people*. Getting these key words in mind and remembering them will be easy if you associate each with its corresponding letter in *people*. These basic steps in preparing the material of a lecture for presentation are:

P inpoint your exact purpose.
E xamine your audience.
O rient your talk to their knowledges and interests.
P artition your material into a few briefly worded ideas.
L imit your material to what your audience can take in readily.
E xamples! Use lots of them, illustrating every point.

And here is how you can prepare your lecture in terms of P-E-O-P-L-E. Follow these steps accurately and you can use the lecture method with skill, with competence, and with very good results.

PINPOINT YOUR EXACT PURPOSE

This involves a detailed study of the over-all objective of the period assigned until the real purpose of the period is clearly perceived. It also involves breaking the objective into sublearnings to be achieved (the learning outcomes of the lesson plan). These learning outcomes provide detailed guidance in selecting material to be included in your lecture.

For purposes of illustration we shall follow through on the lecture on safety. You have been given your subject, "Safety First!" In a general way this establishes the scope of your talk, but it does not establish the specific purpose of it. As discussed at length in Chapter 4, this is where many lecturers predestine their lectures to failure before they even step up to the podium. They fail to pinpoint *exactly* what they want to accomplish as a result of their lecture, they merely talk about a subject rather than saying things calculated to bring about an exact desired result. Their audiences are not motivated to learn, because to be motivated to learn something, people have to understand what they are supposed to be doing—to know the objective of their study.

If the subject of your lecture is "Safety First!" your exact purpose, or objective, might be any one of several. It could be to interest a group of supervisors in supporting a program of safety education. It could be to get workers to obey company regulations pertaining to safety precautions. It could be to persuade employees to abstain from certain dangerous practices, or to adopt certain practices which will make for greater safety. The important things are (1) to pinpoint your purpose in terms of what you want your listeners to do as a result of hearing you and (2) to select from the mass of material you have gathered that which seems best calculated to get them to do it. If your purpose is to interest foremen in supporting a company safety drive, do not waste time covering the details of company safety regulations. These may be important, but they belong somewhere else. Try to do everything and you wind up doing nothing. Concentrate on facts and ideas that will persuade foremen to support the safety program, if that is the objective.

If your objective, on the other hand, is to get employees to abstain from certain dangerous practices, do not dilute your effectiveness by talking about the various organizations that try to promote industrial safety or by giving statistics about man-hours lost per year in the United States from industrial accidents. Pick your material with an eye to convincing them that the practices under consideration are dangerous, showing them how they can most easily avoid these practices and perhaps giving them a few statistics on how many people have sustained injuries from these dangerous practices.

Sometimes your purpose will be to create a certain attitude, not to show people how to perform some specific act. Your objective might be to convince workers that observing safety precautions is important to them. If you can create that attitude, you believe you will have a foundation on which to accomplish later "do this" types of objectives. Citing company regulations, with penalties for violations, might help develop this attitude. It might also promote antagonism toward the company. Some statistics on the smaller number of injuries in a group that consciously aimed at safety compared with one that did not might produce the attitude and avoid the undesirable side attitude.

To summarize, start building your lecture to achieve a specific result and to achieve your exact period objective. Design every part of it to achieve one or more of the specific learning outcomes which must be achieved to accomplish the objective. Aim it like a rifle to hit each specific target; do not blast off like a sawed-off shotgun to blanket an area. You want to accomplish certain audience results, create certain attitudes, develop certain abilities, and get trainees to act in a certain way. Pick exactly what you want to accomplish, and aim everything in your lecture to accomplish these learning outcomes. Here the three columns of the lesson plan prove their worth. See that the ones on instructor activity and trainee activity always add up to the appropriate learning outcome in the left column.

EXAMINE YOUR AUDIENCE

How much do these people know about the subject on which you are going to lecture? It is important to determine the extent of their knowledge, for there is no use in telling them things they already know or in presenting complicated ideas which they cannot understand because they lack the basic knowledge needed to handle the more advanced concepts. If you do this, your listeners will completely lack motivation, interest, organization, and comprehension. Are these the people who will be *doing* the thing you ultimately want done as a result of your talk, or will their primary job be to *get others* to do it? If they will be doing it, you can concentrate on convincing them of its importance and getting them to understand how to do it. If they will be getting others to do it, it will take both of these learning outcomes, plus the additional one of understanding how to produce the first two in other people.

You will probably have the advantage of talking to a relatively homogeneous group of people. Their position in the company puts them in a group to hear your lecture, so probably all will be salesmen, all department heads, all typists, all machine tenders, or the like. You can capitalize on this fact in your lecture. Visualize the audience you will be lecturing to. Will it be composed of brash youngsters, relatively uneducated people, top-level executives, women with homes and family responsibilities? Identify what things your listeners will have in common. It will pay you to spend some time on this. Perhaps you should make a composite picture of your typical listener by estimating the answers to the following questions about your audience: Age? Sex? Educational level? Boss or worker? Highly skilled or semiskilled? Degree of loyalty to company? Cooperativeness? Probable feeling about the subject you are talking on? Write a description of your average listener.

If you stop to think about it, you will realize that a talk designed to achieve exactly the same purpose might be entirely different if you prepared it for two groups who differed greatly. To make this intelligent adjustment of your talk to your audience, you must have a clear idea of the nature of your audience. Successful lecturers say that they seldom give a lecture in the same form twice unless they are addressing two groups indistinguishable in composition, attitude, and purpose. And how can a lecturer show his audience how the material being taught is important to *them* unless he knows just who they are and what their purpose is in attending the lecture?

ORIENT YOUR TALK TO THEIR KNOWLEDGES AND INTERESTS

In effect, a lecturer proposes to take his listeners with him on a tour through a storehouse of facts and ideas. To keep them with him, he has to tell them about things they are interested in, in a way they can understand. Good lecturers spend considerable time figuring approaches that will make the greatest appeal to a particular audience (based on the analysis of the audience just described). Would an approach emphasizing the number of man-hours the company lost and how much industrial accidents cost the company be a good approach? That depends on the audience. If it is composed of semiskilled workers, probably not. They are unlikely to realize fully that in the long run what hurts the company hurts them and will probably take an "I couldn't care less!" attitude toward a recitation of the company's lost-time woes. The same approach might be highly effective if the presentation is to the company's board of directors, whom management is attempting to sell on an expensive program of safety education for workers. If this approach were used in talking to the workers, they would fall out of the lecturer's tour; they would be physically in the room but mentally miles away because they would not be interested in the lecturer's explanations on his tour. The board of directors, however, would stay right with him, interested and taking it all in. To orient your talk to your listeners, then, you *organize* the material in terms of their *motivation,* and also in terms of their *comprehension* of the subject. Only by doing this can you insure the mental *reaction* necessary for your listeners to achieve new or improved comprehension.

On the other hand, if during your safety talk to the board of directors you get to talking about the danger of standing between the letha and the morda of the canxit while reefling the alts, even your most enthusiastic exposition of how elbows are likely to be clipped by the oakler will not take them far along the route over which you are trying to lead them. They simply will not know what you are talking about. Being interested in company profits, a few might stay with you for a little while, but people tend to resent lecturers' assuming that they know things they really do not know. It is an indirect reflection on a listener's intelligence or education for a speaker to talk as if everyone should certainly know the words and expressions he is using, when the listener really does not know them at all. He resents the slight and becomes uncooperative.

So work hard to determine the best appeal to your particular audience. Are they mostly young unmarried girls? The chances are that they will be more impressed by the danger of a badly scarred face than of a mere fractured skull. Ask yourself, "What aspect of this subject will appeal to this particular group of people?" Of course, you cannot omit essential material just because it is not fascinating, but try to find an angle, an approach, an appeal that will make it interesting, adapting it to fit each particular group to whom you lecture.

PARTITION YOUR TALK INTO A FEW BRIEFLY WORDED IDEAS

This is a step in organizing material for presentation where many lecturers go astray. They talk about their subject as a whole, or they meander vaguely from one topic to another and back again, following the path of their wandering fancy or the inspiration of the moment as to when they talk about what. At the end of a talk so haphazardly arranged, listeners are apt to be like the report given of Columbus after his first voyage of discovery, "He didn't know where he was going when he started, he didn't know where he was when he got there, and when he returned he didn't know where he had been." Listeners cannot get the sense of a lecture that rambles along with no perceptible pattern, following no organizational plan that they can see. They soon become discouraged and stop trying. This illogical wandering cannot occur if you are following a well-written lesson plan.

An opposite extreme from this foggy mass of words and ideas in scrambled confusion is the practice of dividing a lecture into innumerable points which the lecturer diligently makes. He says, "And another point . . . ," until it would take a memory expert who is also fast at shorthand even to remember them, much less relate them to each other and to the subject. Sometimes these points are expressed in such long, rambling sentences that the listener is unable to sift the real point from the mass of words in which it is buried. This is another sort of pseudo-organization which cannot take place if the lecturer is following a written lesson outline as given in Chapter 4.

But you have to cut a cake into pieces before it can be eaten very satisfactorily. Similarly, unless a lecture is unusually short and simple, it needs to be partitioned into clear and simple sections for your audience to take it in. (Think how difficult it would be to grasp the procedures outlined in this chapter if it were not broken into sections, each one keynoted by a short, summary-type heading.)

You cannot paragraph a speech as this chapter is paragraphed, but you can partition it into homogeneous groups of ideas and give a short, easily understood title to each section. (This is basically a process of *outlining* your lecture.) Your lecture to factory workers on safety might break down into sections something like these:

1. The average worker in your job loses _____ hours per year through on-the-job injuries.

2. The most common injuries are _____, _____, and _____.

3. Most of the injuries are caused by _____, _____, _____, and _____.

4. They could have been prevented by (a), (b), and (c) steps.

5. Here is what we ask you to do: (a), (b), (c).

6. If you will do these things, your chances of being injured will drop as follows: (a) you will have X/X as many cuts, (b) you will have X/X as many bruises, . . .

LIMIT YOUR MATERIAL

Confine your material to what your audience can take in readily. Remember that the objective of your lecture is not to cover material but to produce better job performance. Better job performance requires that trainees not merely *hear*, or even just *remember*, material presented to them, but also *comprehend* it. And the amount of material the average person can comprehend in one period is strictly limited.

It is seldom wise to have more than a half-dozen main ideas in a lecture. Unless your audience is unusually alert and able, it cannot take in more than that many major concepts in an hour. A lecturer can cover material a great deal faster than an audience can take it in. Design your lecture in such a manner that you follow each important fact or idea with a bit of discussion of the fact, or an explanation of the idea. This gives your listeners the opportunity to mull over the point in their minds and to comprehend its complications, and multiplies by many times the chances of their remembering it.

If you speed from one point to another, stating each one without elaborating on it and without allowing the needed sink-in time, you are likely to achieve the same result you get when you hold a flat pan under a water faucet and turn the faucet on full blast. A lot of water comes out of the faucet and hits the pan, all right, but it splatters right out, and when you remove the pan, you have in it much less water than you would have had if you had run the water into it slowly and gently. Material presented too rapidly in a lecture tends to be dashed out of the minds of listeners in just the same manner.

You will achieve best results, the most learning from your listeners, if you learn to identify accurately the portions of your material most essential to the objective you are trying to achieve (the learning outcomes of your lesson plan) and concentrate on putting these essential points across in a manner which will hold the interest of your listeners.

Illustrate them with real-life examples. Eliminate the mass of other material it might be good for the audience to know, unless you are certain you can get it in without crowding or hurrying your handling of the essential points.

People tend to get bored with details, but they are not bored with having obviously important facts and ideas explained fully. So leave out the boring trivia, but develop the really important ideas fully. Remember, it is not how much you cover that counts, but how much your listeners take in. If you try to cover too much, they will actually understand and remember less than if you had covered a smaller amount.

These is no exact formula for computing how much material can be profitably included in a lecture period. Trying to hold your material to a half-dozen main points which you support well and clearly is about the best rule of thumb available.

EXAMPLES! USE LOTS OF THEM, ILLUSTRATING EVERY POINT

This one step promotes several of the psychological causes of learning. It *motivates* listeners by showing them how the topic under study has occurred in real-life situations, it holds their *concentration* because they can imagine themselves in the situation being illustrated, it promotes *reaction* by stimulating thoughts such as "How would I handle a situation like that?" and it promotes *comprehension* of material through showing its application to actual jobs.

Here is where you use the anecdotes, examples, reminiscences, experiences, and tales of the foremen and others to whom you talked in the process of gathering your lecture material. If you think back on your own experience listening to lecturers, you will doubtless recall how you became more interested, more attentive, when they began to tell of something that happened to someone—"A man was rolling carriages of boxes onto a freight elevator in a factory in Chicago last year, and as he approached the elevator shaft one morning, he . . ."

Exploit this tendency of people to be interested in people, what they did and what happened to them, by having one or more incidents to illustrate every main point you make. Make the stories as real as possible, telling where, when, and to whom (omitting the actual name but identifying by job) the thing happened. Not only will your audience follow you more closely, but they will be much more impressed with what you say if you show its application by examples from life. They are more likely to do what you recommend if you can cite a convincing case of what happened to someone who didn't. If you can get an illustration with some humor in it, so much the better.

An old Chinese proverb said, "One picture is worth a thousand words." Anecdotes and examples are verbal pictures making a dead or abstract subject take on the appearance of real life. Sometimes it requires considerable time on the part of the lecturer to find examples that make his points clearly, but the time is well spent. It does much to make the difference between a lecture that merely covers the subject and one that actually achieves in the listeners the results desired.

Rehearsal

When you have gathered your material, tailored it to fit P-E-O-P-L-E, and prepared a blueprint of your period in the form of a lesson plan, you have one thing more to do before you actually present your lecture. Rehearse it before a mirror or to some other instructor who will listen with the idea of suggesting ways in which you might improve it.

An unusually brilliant speaker gave one of his most outstanding lectures one day on the subject "How to Prepare a Speech." When he had finished, a member of his audience asked him, "Doctor, is rehearsing a speech *really* necessary if you know your subject thoroughly?" The lecturer responded, "Sir, the talk I just gave I have given fourteen times in the past year. Last night I rehearsed it in front of my mirror at home for three hours. Does that answer your question?"

Thomas A. Edison said, "Genius is 1 per cent inspiration and 99 per cent perspiration." So is developing a good lecture. It does not require a person of exceptional ability to prepare and deliver a fine lecture (or any other type of speech). It does require a person willing to invest enough time in gathering material, willing to work hard enough at tailoring his talk to P-E-O-P-L-E, and willing to rehearse it until he can say it clearly and well.

SUMMARY

The lecture is an unusually flexible and valuable method of instruction, but its effective use requires an unusual amount of skillful preparation. The first phase in preparation consists in gathering the material to be presented. The instructor should first try to think the subject through in his own mind as thoroughly as possible, then read up on it, then interview people who have worked in areas related to the subject to get their ideas and experiences. With this mass of information, ideas, and examples he is ready to construct a lesson plan, and begin building his actual lecture.

The key to building a successful lecture lies in tailoring it to P-E-O-P-L-E, which involves:

P inpointing the exact objective(s) to be achieved
E xamining the audience to see what sort of people the lecture will be given to
O rienting the material to audience knowledges and interests

P artitioning it into groups of homogeneous ideas (a form of outlining the lecture)

L imiting the amount of material included to that which the audience can readily take in, and

E xamples! Plenty of them!

Then rehearse it until the words come smoothly.

SUGGESTED READINGS

BAIRD, A. C., and F. H. KNOWER: *General Speech: An Introduction,*
McGraw-Hill Book Company, Inc., New York, 1957.

BUXTON, C. E.: *College Teaching: A Psychologist's View,* Harcourt,
Brace and Company, Inc., New York, 1956.

JUSTMAN, J., and W. H. MAIS: *College Teaching: Its Practice and Potential,* Harper & Brothers, New York, 1956.

MUEHL, W.: *The Road to Persuasion,* Oxford University Press, New
York, 1956.

SANDFORD, W. P., and W. H. YEAGER: *Practical Business Speaking,*
McGraw-Hill Book Company, Inc., New York, 1952.

6

The Demonstration-Performance Method

This chapter explains what the demonstration-performance method of instruction is, when it is most profitably used, and the steps in preparing a period of instruction to be presented by the demonstration-performance method.

THE DEMONSTRATION-PERFORMANCE method of instruction is perhaps the simplest and most natural of all instructional methods. It is the first method of instruction man ever used, as when a cave man added wood to a fire and his son watched and imitated him.

The demonstration method is probably best adapted to teaching manual skills, where physical movement and the handling of things are to be learned, or to teaching routine processes. There are at least two types of demonstration, the more formal demonstration when an instructor stands before a group of trainees and says, "Now, if you will please observe me, I shall demonstrate the preferred method of assembling this electric drill," and the informal method, when a foreman stops by where a man is working and says, "You'll wear yourself out reaching over there to drill that hole, man. See, if you give this a quarter-turn, . . ."

The informal demonstration is the easier and may be the more effective method under some circumstances, but it has serious limitations. It is time-consuming and may permit much waste of materials and man-hours before it covers all that the trainee needs to know. But it is invaluable for *individual* coaching on points that one person has not learned well.

The formal method requires much more planning and pre-arranging on the part of the instructor, but is likely to result in better prepared trainees than relying on the informal method of giving coaching only when the foreman notices that it is needed. For this reason it is worth while for many companies who have employees performing detailed mechanical or other manual or procedural work to design formal training programs for new employees. The cost in time and money is less than catch-as-catch-can coaching of individuals on the job because it gets workers to a higher stage of production more quickly and minimizes the amount of material they spoil in learning.

It has been emphasized that *any* form of instruction begins with determining an over-all objective, that is, deciding exactly what a person is supposed to be able to do as a result of the instruction. The next step in planning the program is determining exactly what special skills, abilities, and knowledges (learning outcomes) must be mastered in order to achieve the over-all objective. Then, as shown in the section on lesson planning in Chapter 4, the instructor's activity is designed to help the trainee master each of the special skills, abilities, and knowledges.

Preparing Demonstration-Performance Periods of Instruction

Let us take the example we have already mentioned, assembling an electric drill, as the subject of training for a newly employed group of workers who will do this job for a company which is adding electric drills to its line. We shall trace the steps involved in developing a training period based on the demonstration-performance method of instruction, and identify the psychological factors in learning which various steps promote.

DETERMINE THE OBJECTIVE OF THE PERIOD

This is always the first step. Exactly what the objective is depends on a variety of factors, such as whether the complete assembly is to be accomplished by each worker, but it might be something like: "To enable trainees to assemble electric handdrills from completely machined parts and ready-assembled electrical components." This objective provides the basic guidance for the instructor as to what goes into the period. Understanding precisely what the objective is helps trainees to be motivated to learn and aids them in organizing what they learn into a usable body of knowledge.

DETERMINE THE LEARNING OUTCOMES NECESSARY
TO ACHIEVE THE OBJECTIVE

Construct the left-hand column of your lesson plan. These learning outcomes establish guides for the instructor activities and trainee activities of the period. Decide what particular skills and knowledges are required to assemble the parts of a drill. These necessary skills and knowledges will be the specific learning outcomes which must be achieved in order to attain the over-all objective of the demonstration. A partial list of such learning outcomes in this sample case might be:

1. Knowledge of the basic components of a drill and their relation to each other (how the chuck attaches to the drive shaft, how the drive shaft fits in the bearings, how the switch attaches, etc.)

2. Ability to do simple soldering of small copper wire connections

3. Ability to distinguish between ball and needle bearings and install each

4. Ability to make firm nonsoldered connections by means of screw caps

5. Ability to identify placement of insulated wires which will and will not expose them to friction or interfere with the operation of moving parts

6. Development of manual dexterity to make such placements of wires

7. Sufficient knowledge of wiring and assembly of small electric motors to permit visual inspection of electrical components before

installing them in drills, recognizing such defects as missing brush or faulty attachment of switch wire

8. Knowledge of the order of assembly that can be accomplished fastest

9. Knowledge of the layout of component parts which will permit selecting each one and moving it where it is needed with least time and effort

A good way to compose such a list of learning outcomes is to lay out the pieces of a drill just as your trainees will have them, put the drill together, and make running notes of what you have to be able to do to assemble it. One convenient thing about the demonstration method: Even if you should overlook listing one skill as a learning outcome, if you actually use that skill in showing your trainees how to put the drill together, and they imitate you and get the job done, you may achieve your over-all objective anyway.

This fact probably causes you to think, "If that is so, why go to all the bother of listing learning outcomes in the first place? Just show them the whole process of putting the drill together until they know it by heart and let 'em go!" You can do it that way. In the 1940s, though, when American industry was having to give workers two weeks' training and then depend on them to do jobs that had in the past required one to four years' apprenticeship, it was found that the simple "show 'em and let 'em go" system was uneconomical. Just as a person learns to play a good game of golf faster by being taught systematically than by picking up the skill himself through knocking a ball around, it was found that trainees learned their assembly or other jobs much faster and better if the people teaching them knew each particular learning that had to be mastered and explained it to them instead of throwing the book of the whole job at them without breaking it down into sections that they could assimilate easily.

If one step in the learning procedure has not been identified by name and skill, the whole program will not be wrecked, but if there are many such oversights, the demonstration will not teach trainees as fast or as well as it otherwise might. It is well worth striving hard to identify all the things that have to be learned to do the over-all job and to teach trainees each one of them systematically.

SELECT AND ASSEMBLE THE EQUIPMENT FOR YOUR DEMONSTRATION

What are you going to use for your demonstration? If the demonstration concerns a small object like the electric drill, an actual drill will be all right if you have only a half-dozen or so trainees in a class. If you are showing them how to assemble a bigger thing, with bigger pieces, the actual object may be all right for a class of a hundred or more. If you have a large number of trainees, however, and are working with tiny parts, you may find it better to use a bigger-than-life model for your demonstration so everyone can see the pieces and what you are doing with them. Such models are time-consuming and expensive to construct, even when dummied up out of balsa wood, and unless you are going to use one a great deal, it may be more practical simply to teach your trainees in smaller groups.

You may be able to handle a larger group if you supplement your putting together of the actual small parts with a large picture or diagram showing each part you are working with, pointing to the appropriate part in the picture as you assemble each tiny part of the actual implement you are working on. Your own judgment will tell you how many people can really see your hands and the parts as you assemble them. Remember, *it is not a demonstration if your trainees cannot see your movements and the pieces you are working with,* for they cannot comprehend what you are teaching if they cannot see what you are doing and their only reaction will be bewilderment.

REHEARSE THE DEMONSTRATION UNTIL YOU CAN DO IT ACCURATELY AND AUTOMATICALLY

While you are actually putting on the demonstration, you will need to be concentrating on telling your trainees what you are doing and what they are to remember. The movements you make and the multitude of things you do should be so familiar to you that you do not have to keep part of your mind on what to do next and how to do it. All that should have been taken care of—reduced to a process as automatic as steering your car and shifting gears—before you get to the demonstration session itself.

In the last-minute preparation for rehearsals, after the learning outcomes have been determined, the instructor should decide what learning outcomes he wants to elaborate most in his demonstration. Sometimes this pattern of emphasis will change after the first rehearsal, because it may be found that something the instructor planned to emphasize was really quite clear and simple and required little explanation. Similarly, it will sometimes be found that a certain procedure is hard to put into words and harder yet to do in such a way that an audience can see it clearly. Special pains and time should be spent on such tricky points, and they should be located and practiced *before* the actual demonstration.

This means that when the instructor is rehearsing his demonstration he should rehearse his explanations, too. *Say the explanations aloud exactly as if the class were present.* It is surprising how often an explanation that seems perfectly clear as one thinks it over gets him tongue-tied, confused, and hopelessly mixed up when he tries to put it into actual words. The only way to be sure it will not happen to *you* is to have the explanations that accompany your demonstration rehearsed so that they have *proved* themselves to be as smooth and clear as the manual operations of the demonstration.

By the time the rehearsals are completed, then, the instructor has a well-thought-out pattern of explanations that point up the major steps of the demonstration and make the whole process clear.

An outline of the demonstration—exactly how you decide to perform it and how you will explain it—constitutes the center column, "Instructor Activity," of your lesson plan.

This step of preparation is also the logical place to prepare the right-hand column of your lesson plan, "Trainee Activity." Of course, you will want trainees to be watching you, observing what you do, listening to explanations, and taking notes throughout your demonstration. You might make a note of that at the beginning of the column. But careful study of your demonstration will usually reveal that there are difficult points or important ideas which you want trainees to note in some special way. Perhaps they should be given a moment to write an explanation in their own words at one point. Make a note to that effect in the "Trainee Activity" column, and provide time for it. Perhaps each should handle and inspect one item which requires tricky manipulation. Perhaps they should copy something verbatim. Right here the instructor should cudgel his brain, asking himself, "What can I have the trainees do throughout the demonstration that will help them learn more than they can by just watching, listening, and taking notes?" Put the answers in the right-hand column!

PREPARE THE "HANDOUT" AND/OR EXPLANATION WITH WHICH YOU WILL START THE DEMONSTRATION

Having determined the precise learning outcomes you want to accomplish and having familiarized yourself thoroughly with how to assemble that drill (think how embarrassing it would be if you got the drill almost assembled and found you had to disassemble it because the switch wire had to be soldered on *before* the motor was installed), you are ready to plan the activities and materials which you will use in support of your demonstration.

Perhaps you want the trainees to come to your training period with some idea of what they will be learning. In that case, the day before the session you may want to issue to them an outline of what you plan to do during the period. The outline might consist of the learning outcomes you want to achieve, listed in the order that you will get to them in the period, and with space between them for the trainees to make notes during the period. After looking over the outline, they will come to the training session with a moderately good over-all picture of what they are to learn, thus fulfilling the *organization* requirement in the psychology of learning. This handout and the notes they take will help them in the *repetition* step, too, because when in doubt they can check these notes and the handout to remind themselves what to do next. Taking the notes will help get the mental *reaction* you are after, and help hold their *concentration*, too. Seeing the whole picture of what they are going to be learning may help them to be *motivated* to learn, and studying their own step-by-step notes on how and when to do what may help them *comprehend* the whole business.

If you do not want to issue such a handout (or perhaps even if you do), you should certainly give some lead-off explanation (introduction to subject) of the whole process you are going to teach. Do not merely say, "I'm going to show you how to put a drill together. Watch what I do." Your trainees will learn much more from the session if you do some preliminary explaining to get their minds set on what you are trying to show them before you get into the real meat of the session.

In this preliminary explanation you should:

1. Fix firmly in your trainees' minds what you want them to learn from the session and why it is necessary for them to learn it (increasing their motivation to learn).

2. Let them know the general pattern you are following in teaching them, so that they will know how to follow you (further clarifying the organization for them).

3. Tell them what you want them to be doing while you are going through the demonstration (to maintain reaction, concentration, and comprehension).

Your explanation should motivate the trainees, tell them what they are supposed to learn, and indicate why they need to learn it. It may also give them the over-all picture, the organization, of the period.

It might go something like this:

> During this period I am going to show you how to assemble an electric drill, which will be your job for the next few

months. By the end of the period you may not be able to establish any speed records in getting one together, but if you've watched closely and made notes on what I tell you, you will be able to put one together so it will work. Now, each major operation I do in putting this drill together I will name for you as I go along, and I'd like you to make notes of them in the order in which they come. (NOTE: These operations may come very close to being your specific learning outcomes for the period. However, do not read aloud the learning outcomes for the period in the hope of giving trainees a good preview of the period. They cannot take in these learning outcomes that fast, and you will only be wasting time.) I'll explain how I do each step, but on the first go-round you'd better not try to make notes on these "hows." If you do, you'll miss much of what I am trying to show you. Just get the major steps on the first run-through, and then we will go over it more slowly and you can get down the details. Then, from those directions you have recorded, and your memory of what I did, you'll be able to go to your table and put drills together!

Naturally, your explanation and language will be adapted to the level of the workers you are training. This introduction might be appropriate to a group of girls who had not worked previously on small-implement assembly. For experienced assembly people you would cut it down in length and pitch it higher in level to suit their experience.

Conducting Your Demonstration

To show the application of the demonstration-performance method to a procedural job, in contrast to an assembly job, we shall shift here to a demonstration of making up a purchase order requisition. If there are more than a half-dozen or so persons in the training class, the instructor will do well to have an enlarged reproduction of the purchase order form on the wall where trainees can see exactly what he points to and thereby locate it easily on their own work copies of the form. Go slowly through the whole process of filling out the requisition, explaining each step as you go—how the requisition number is determined, how the responsibility area is located, and so on. If the preliminary preparation described in the preceding section was done well, putting on the actual demonstration is the simplest and easiest part of the whole process.

There are a few things the instructor should watch in his demonstration, however. If they can see well, it is unlikely he will have trouble holding trainees' attention; they usually are thoroughly engrossed in a demonstration. But it is easy to confuse some of them by using in your explanation of a process expressions unfamiliar to them. As an example, in office talk "WO" may be commonly used in place of the words "work order," but do not use it in your demonstration!

Even with carefully prepared explanations, the instructor may brush by a procedure or point in the explanation with someone not understanding it. Therefore, he should keep his eyes and mind constantly alert for the furrowed brow, the lost expression, or the tense restlessness that signals a trainee who has lost the trail. When such a lost trainee is identified, stop the demonstration and go back to where his confusion started and bring him up to date. If he is so slow that he constantly hinders the whole class, a real lost ball in the high weeds, it may pay to tell him to try to follow and that he will receive any needed help and explanations after the class period is over.

Pausing in an explanation to ask someone to explain in his own words what you have just gone over or to ask a question about the subject helps to keep your audience alert and thinking (promoting concentration and reaction) and is a good way to pull an inattentive trainee back into the session. Asking the class if anyone has any questions can help locate trainees who are not getting the ideas and will show the instructor where he needs to spend more time and care on his demonstration or explanation to insure comprehension.

Usually it is a good idea to encourage trainees to take notes during a demonstration. Taking notes not only will promote mental activity and attention, as well as help trainees remember what the instructor said and did, but also will provide an easy way for the instructor to check on how accurately and clearly he is putting his ideas across. If he has made the main points of his demonstration and explanation stand out clearly, as discussed in the foregoing section on rehearsal of a demonstration, this will show up in the trainees' outlines. The instructor can get a very clear idea of whether he is directing trainees' attention toward the proper things and whether he is sufficiently emphasizing the main points.

Finally, as the demonstration and accompanying explanations are completed, it is wise for the instructor to summarize what he has done and said, rapidly running over his main points again (*repetition*). This summary need not take more than a minute or two and not only gives trainees a chance to fill blank spots in their notes but also helps them see the process which has been demonstrated as a unified sequence of actions (*organization*) rather than a series of unrelated steps. This process promotes *comprehension*.

LET THE TRAINEE DO THE JOB UNDER CLOSE SUPERVISION

It is usually not a good idea to let trainees go ahead without supervision and try to fill out their work forms or assemble their models while you are giving this first walk-through. The army had a name for the way to chaperone them through their first few trials; they called it "by the numbers." Do not let the trainees try to fill out their forms or assemble their models while you are concentrating on what *you* are doing. They will learn too many wrong ways of doing things. Hold them off until you can pace them through one operation. *S l o w l y* walk around and see that everyone is getting it right, then take them *s l o w l y* through the next operation, and so on. This is the performance portion of the demonstration-performance method. Trainees are usually eager to try to do the job themselves, and *motivation, concentration,* and *reaction* are likely to be high. They are obviously getting the *repetition* factor of learning, too. But the instructor should check to see that the *organization* and *comprehension* factors are not overlooked through trainees' attention to the mechanics of what they are doing.

CALL ON ONE OF THE TRAINEES TO DEMONSTRATE AND EXPLAIN THE PROCEDURE

As a variation to this, you may have one trainee perform the demonstration and another explain what is being done. If the demonstration is of a very simple skill or process, it may not pay to spend much time on the *why* of doing it a certain way or examining the explanation given of the performance. However, if the trainee doing the demonstration makes an error, or the narrator explaining the process overlooks an important point, it may be worth while for the instructor or another trainee to criticize or analyze the demonstration and suggest ways in which the performance could have been improved.

Another variation on having one trainee demonstrate and explain the procedure to the class is to use the buddy system of practice. This consists in pairing off all trainees, then having one watch the other do the job and try to give him suggestions which will enable him to do it faster or better. Then they swap positions, and the demonstrator becomes the observer. This technique has great value if properly used. It provides individual coaching for every trainee (although admittedly the coaching is not of expert quality), and observing with the responsibility of helping the partner improve promotes the keenest sort of mental activity and learning on the part of each trainee in his role of observer.

To be most effective, however, the job of the observer should be held strictly to helping the demonstrator do the job better and not allowed to degenerate into an effort to pick flaws in the other man's job. This means that observers should not report short-comings of the demonstrators to the instructor, but should concentrate on trying to get their partners to develop the highest possible competence on the job. If the instructor makes it clear that he holds each member of a buddy team as responsible for the performance of the other member as for his own, it will do much to make the teams real mutual-aid societies instead of throat-cutting rivals.

DECREASE THE INTENSITY OF SUPERVISION AS TRAINEES LEARN THEIR JOBS

When a trainee leaves the training program, he should be able to perform his job with only a reasonable amount of guidance and supervision. This means that he should have been growing out from under close supervision during the latter part of his training so he will not flounder when he goes out on his own.

KEEP ON-THE-JOB DEMONSTRATION-PERFORMANCE INSTRUCTION SYMPATHETIC AND CONSTRUCTIVE

At the beginning of this chapter we noted that we could give informal instruction by the demonstration-performance method, as well as the more formal training program. This instruction falls under the heading of supervision, on-the-job training, or sometimes, regrettably, bawling out. Foremen, supervisors, and others responsible for improving the performance of workers on the job will find that they get best results if they keep the *training* aspects of their work as sharply separated as possible from their *disciplinary* or critical responsibilities. A worker will be more likely to follow the suggestions for improving his work given him by his boss if the boss's attitude when he gives the suggestions indicates that he is trying to help the worker, not trying to find fault with him. The way the boss goes about giving this on-the-job training will have a great effect on how successful he is. If his approach to the worker is "You're not doing that right, *I'll* show you how," he will meet with resentment and resistance and will accomplish little. On the other hand, if his approach is "Let me show you a trick I stumbled on for doing that. . . . You might find it helps you along," the chances are the worker will appreciate the suggestions. The chances are also much better that, when the boss's back is turned, the worker will actually try to make his suggestions work. Using courtesy and tact in on-the-job instruction is not pampering workers; it is handling them in the way that gets best results for the boss.

SUMMARY

The demonstration-performance method is most useful in teaching manual skills and simple manual-mental skills or processes such as filling out routine forms. For best results, planning for demonstration-performance instruction must include establishing the objective of the program and determining the required specific learning outcomes, choosing the equipment for the demonstration, rehearsing the demonstration and explanation, and preparing an introduction to the demonstration proper. When these things are done well, the demonstration itself is easy, but the instructor should watch to see that everyone is keeping up with the demonstration and explanation. After showing the class how the job is done and explaining it, the instructor should let the trainees try it themselves, checking each step of the process as they do. As the trainees demonstrate ability to do their jobs better, the instructor should give them more freedom and responsibility and less supervision. When they are full-fledged workers, the demonstration-performance training will be continued by foremen, supervisors, or others; this on-the-job training will get best results if so handled that workers take it as suggestions to help them, not criticisms for doing things wrong.

SUGGESTED READINGS

CALHOON, R. P., and C. A. KIRKPATRICK: *Influencing Employee Behavior*, McGraw-Hill Book Company, Inc., New York, 1956.

DOANE, R. C.: "Demonstration: Before, During and After," *Industrial Arts and Vocational Education*, vol. 43, pp. 15–16, January, 1954.

NAIL, O. P.: "Use Demonstrations in Teaching," *Agricultural Education Magazine*, vol. 26, p. 68, September, 1953.

7

The Group Discussion Method

This chapter shows how the group discussion method of instruction can be used in a training course to capitalize on the body of knowledge possessed by trainees. It tells how to get a class discussion started, how to hold it on the road so it will contribute most to the training program, and how to end it in the most advantageous manner.

DOES YOUR SUBJECT demand understanding and reasoning, as contrasted to physical skill or mere memory, for best results?

Would you like to use the knowledge and experience your class members already possess to help you develop their knowledge further?

Is it practical to handle your trainees in groups of no more than fifteen? (Considerably smaller groups might be preferable in most cases.)

If your answer to all three of the above questions is "Yes," you will probably find it advantageous to use group discussion as a primary or supplemental method of instruction. The more complex the understandings and reasoning procedures required in the work for which your instruction is preparing trainees, the less trainees can do their jobs by formula, the more you will find discussion helpful as an instructional medium. More than perhaps any other single method, discussion stimulates every person in the group to do constructive, creative thinking on a subject, contributing the benefits of his personal experience and ingenuity to a common pool for the benefit of all. Demonstrations, lectures, and role-playing all are more effective if supplemented by thorough group discussion of what was said or done.

There are at least three major forms of group discussion—directed discussion, conference, and seminar—different enough in preparation, conduct, or result to justify their separate consideration. All have so much in common, however, that this chapter will, first of all, explain the major principles and procedures of the discussion method generally, and subsequently relate their application to the different types of discussion.

Preparing a Discussion Period

Good discussions do not just happen. To insure a solid, learning-producing session, much more is required than merely getting a group of trainees together and announcing, for example, that today we are going to talk about how to handle first aid emergencies when crews are working in rural areas. The purpose of a discussion is not merely to talk about a subject. Its objective is for trainees to achieve specific learning outcomes through thinking and discussing a subject, pooling their knowledge of it, and applying constructive imagination to it.

This requires careful planning. As in other methods of instruction, the "Learning Outcomes" column of the lesson plan is the guide on which the period depends. But in the discussion method, the column "Trainee Activity" carries the principal action of the period, and the column "Instructor Activity" is concerned only with the guidance the instructor exercises to keep trainee activity energetic and well directed.

Here are a number of things an instructor should do to prepare for a group discussion of a topic in a training program. Following these steps of preparation will do much to insure that the lesson plan is well thought out, and to set up a discussion period with maximum likelihood of achieving the period objective.

READ UP ON THE SUBJECT TO BE DISCUSSED

First of all, read up on the subject to be covered by the discussion as thoroughly as time and circumstances permit. Supplement this reading by discussing the topic with other knowledgeable people in as great detail and at as great length as is feasible. It is desirable, where possible, to have a trial run of the discussion, using a small group of instructors or supervisors to represent the trainees. Since this is often impossible, an instructor's talking through the subject with others is suggested as a practical, convenient substitute.

Perhaps in no other form of instruction is such comprehensive knowledge of the whole subject area required of the instructor as in the discussion. The reason is that in lectures, demonstrations, and performances, the instructor can confine the attention of the class to the ideas *he* puts on the floor. There is a minimum of opportunity for maverick angles or ideas which give a new and unexpected slant on the subject. The instructor discusses the angles he is prepared to discuss, spends his time answering those questions he feels most competent to answer, and dismisses the class with his material covered.

It does not work that way in a discussion. Here the trainees are the source from which the period's information and ideas must be largely drawn. And it takes a thorough knowledge of the whole subject area for the instructor to keep a group well bunched along a predesigned trail, recognizing when the thinking is straying from the line and bringing it back without antagonizing the group, showing the relevance of meaningful but obscure contributions of an astute but somewhat incoherent discussant, and keeping the group always moving toward the learning outcomes—all without seeming to dominate them. It takes a much more thorough knowledge of the subject to do this than merely to talk your own way to the desired end, permitting the group to follow you.

SEPARATE YOUR TRAINEES INTO LIKE GROUPS

Put your trainees into as like groups as possible. One of the criteria of the success of a discussion is how well everyone participates. You will not get the desired evenness of participation if your group is composed of one segment of trainees who have had several years' varied experience in the area being discussed and another segment to whom the whole field is new, unexplored, and slightly intimidating. So if you will have more than one discussion group, make an effort to put the more experienced in one section and the less experienced in the other. This gives all an equal chance to talk without seeming on the one hand to display their ignorance or on the other to be pompous in their superior knowledge. The argument that the less experienced will learn more from the experienced is misleading: If it were sound, the logical thing would be to let the inexperienced listen to a well-prepared instructor and eliminate the discussion entirely. Naturally, where numbers and circumstances do not permit the formation of homogeneous groups, it will not be practical to follow this principle. It is usually a desirable thing to do wherever circumstances permit.

The value of the discussion method lies in its potential for stimulating individual thinking and expression from its members, not from its capability of pouring the sacred word into untutored ears. So groups should be small enough for everyone to have an opportunity to participate frequently in the discussion. Trainees will learn more that way. The exact size of your groups is not too important. Generally, eight to twelve in a group give good results. As few as five, plus the instructor, may be successful, and as many as fifteen may possibly be assigned to a group, although a group of this size is undesirable because the opportunity for individual participation is extremely limited. The reticent member is likely to be left out of the discussion and, consequently, out of the most valuable of the learning experiences.

FORMULATE THE OBJECTIVES OF THE DISCUSSION

This is done as described in Chapter 4. Be sure your objectives penetrate to the heart of things and specify what you really want. This means that the objectives should avoid such statements "To discuss ways . . ." or "To think about . . ." in favor of more functionally oriented statements such as "To enable trainees to assist the customer in finding . . ."

IDENTIFY THE DESIRED LEARNING OUTCOMES

Make a list of the answers to these questions: "What things do our trainees have to know to be able to do the things specified in the objectives? Which of these things should we teach them in this discussion period?" These things will constitute your desired learning outcomes. Refer to Chapter 4 again for further guidance in wording a learning outcome in such a manner that it becomes a helpful guide to you in planning your period. It will help you to state the learning outcome in functional forms of ability to do, as you did the objectives, but this is not always practical. Sometimes there are bits of fact, or important ideas, that it is necessary for trainees to learn and remember, but it is hard to pin down any one thing they will do or do better as a result of knowing them. Therefore, list a knowledge or fact (as contrasted with an ability to do) as a learning outcome rather than omit it, but remember, you increase the chances of your program to produce good results when you are able to state a high percentage of your learning outcomes in the form of abilities to do.

FORMULATE THE EXACT SUBJECT OF THE DISCUSSION

Formulate the question, situation, problem, idea, case, or proposition which will be the subject of the discussion. In your own mind you will probably start with the memory of a situation or case, or a single sentence such as was mentioned earlier in the chapter: "How can we best handle first aid emergencies occurring among crews working in rural areas?" But this is not a form suitable for presentation to a group for discussion—unless the purpose of the group is to cultivate skill in preparing discussion topics rather than skill in dealing with first aid emergencies. If presented in the form of this simple question, the group must inevitably spend much of the allotted time arriving at answers to such questions as, "Do they mean how we can best give them first aid at the truck?" or "Should we think in terms of rigging the truck so that an injured man could be carried to the hospital in it?" or "Should we get into the subject of how much first aid training men on a line crew should get?" This may not be bad. Such a broad study of the whole topic may be what you are after; maybe the company does not know the answers and wants to get some from experienced crewmen. This would be a seminar discussion, where there are no established answers and the purpose is to try to use the group's combined experience and brainpower to find some.

More frequently, however, the discussion will be for the purpose of helping the discussants (especially if they are trainees) to learn and understand already known answers. In such an instance, it is merely wasting the company's money and the group's time to have them wandering around looking for the precise section of the subject they are to explore and the approach they are expected to take. The key is: *Describe the subject you want the group to discuss in sufficient detail that all their time can be spent in discussing it, without wasting time hunting through a big, nebulous area for the specific topic they are expected to study.*

A statement of the discussion topic which would satisfy this criterion might be:

> Ninety per cent of accidents in line crews occurring in rural areas consist of falls, cuts, burns, or shock, or some combination of these. The seriousness of injuries resulting from these accidents is influenced heavily by the judgment, skill, and promptness with which they are treated. A standard procedure insuring best and quickest handling of injured

men, one that is well understood by everyone and can be put into effect immediately and efficiently whenever such an emergency arises, is needed. A safety committee has developed such a standing procedure to be used in event of injuries. You are requested to study this plan, and attend a group discussion of the procedure at 8:30 A.M., Wednesday, January 23, in the locker room. The purpose of the discussion will be to

1. Familiarize you with the procedure, how it works, and your part in it

2. Determine how crews can be persuaded to learn and follow the plan

3. Examine the plan to see if it can be improved upon and, if so, suggest such improvements

DISTRIBUTE THE APPROPRIATE INFORMATION IN ADVANCE

Get the topic, together with any appropriate handouts or reading assignments, to the discussants long enough in advance of the meeting for them to have opportunity to study and think on the subject *before* the meeting. How long this should be depends on circumstances. Less than twenty-four hours probably allows too little time for preparation. More than three or four days runs the risk that the whole thing will be forgotten.

PREPARE AN AGENDA

This is the lesson plan, under a special name commonly used in connection with group discussions. It consists of the standard lesson plan supplemented by an outline of the subject to be discussed and an indication of the order in which subpoints of the subject should be discussed to best achieve the desired learning outcomes. It should always be reinforced with a number of thought-provoking questions, or subproblems, to be posed at the beginning of the discussion, and from time to time through it. These questions and problems give discussants direction and stimulation and help get the minds of the group working promptly and constructively. They are also excellent devices for shifting the discussion from one topic to another or recalling it to the subject when it is straying.

Prepare a generous list of such questions—questions which require explanations as answers rather than those which can be answered with a flat "yes" or "no" or a very short statement. Cluster a few of these penetrating questions around the opening idea on your agenda and two or three others at the beginning of each new or major point you plan to cover, to help you shift the attention of the group to your next item and start their minds off on the new track.

PREPARE A LESSON PLAN FROM YOUR AGENDA

One experienced discussion leader has said that the success or failure of a discussion period is already predestined when the instructor enters the discussion room by the amount and quality of preparation he has done beforehand. This is an exaggeration, since the best-planned discussion can be spoiled by maldirection or a number of other factors, but it does give needed emphasis to the importance of the instructor's entering a discussion period with as complete a lesson plan as is required for any other type of instruction, including all the steps enumerated above. The lesson plan is the complete blueprint of the parts to be played by the instructor and the discussants, and the relations of those parts to each other. It shows how the agenda leads to learning outcomes and hence to objectives. It gives system and perspective to a period which without this safeguard can easily degenerate into a mere bull session. The aforesaid special steps in preparing a discussion can only *supplement,* but do not *replace,* the fundamental step of preparing a lesson plan.

READY THE PLACE FOR THE DISCUSSION

The arrangement of furniture in the room can have considerable effect on the success of a discussion period. The most desirable arrangement is for all discussants to sit around a table, so that everyone can see everyone else. If a suitable table is not available, simply arrange chairs in a circle facing each other and let the discussants sit in a hollow circle. The discussion will probably be unsatisfactory if conducted with discussants seated in rows as in a lecture hall, because part of the essence of discussion (as contrasted to reading or writing) is the personal touch involved in face-to-face communication. Try to secure a table of a size which will permit everyone to sit comfortably around it, with ample space for notes, papers, and elbows.

Aside from the necessity for discussants to be able to look each other in the eye without undue contortions, the requirements for a discussion room are no different from those for any other classroom. A blackboard is well-nigh essential, for reasons which will be seen later. Light, ventilation, comfortable chairs—all are desirable in about the same degree as in a lecture room.

Be sure you have ample space around *your* chair for your lesson plan and agenda, as well as the list of questions you have handy. It is also a good idea to bring along any supplementary material to which you might find it convenient to refer during the discussion. Table space, or at least an adjacent chair, to accommodate such books or papers will be helpful. Have plenty of blank note paper and pencils handy. You may find it preferable to require discussants to bring such materials for themselves, or you may prefer to have the materials at their places when they arrive.

Like any other method of instruction, the ultimate function of the different steps in conducting a discussion of any kind is to guide trainees through the psychological processes producing effective learning. As in the lecture or other methods, the group must first be *motivated*. In some ways this is even more important in the discussion method than in others because the group itself, not the instructor or selected members, must generate the energy and momentum to carry the period along. *Concentration*, getting everyone's attention and energy focused on the problem, is necessary, and of course *reaction*, the mental activity of the trainees, is the very life-blood of discussion. To prevent digression and rambling, *organization* of the topic, and of the discussion as a whole, must be clear to everyone. The objective of the discussion is to *comprehend* the significance of the topic discussed, and *repetition* is helpful in fixing in the mind any material studied, regardless of the method of study used. With the basic psychological causes of learning in mind, we shall now consider the specific techniques of conducting a discussion to achieve them.

Starting a Discussion along Profitable Lines

SKETCH OUT THE DISCUSSION TOPIC IN YOUR OWN WORDS

This is usually necessary even though everyone has received a handout on the topic. When the participants sit down, their minds are likely still to be on what they had for lunch, what they are going to have for lunch, what they did last night, what they are going to do tonight—in fact, on anything at all except the case they are supposed to study or the problem they are to discuss. They have to start thinking, reasoning, talking, and learning about that case or problem. Your talking gently leads their mental processes to focus on the assigned discussion topic and gets them in the mood to consider the problem at hand; it promotes motivation, through identifying the objective of the period, and concentration, through getting trainees' minds on the subject. It presents the over-all organization of the subject, making it easier to keep the discussion on the track.

ASK A THOUGHT-PROVOKING QUESTION

When you finish your orientation talk on the area the discussion is to cover, it is a good idea to leave a clue to start someone else talking. The question is this clue. Make it one that cannot be answered conclusively with a word or a sentence. This compels reaction on the part of the trainees; it starts them thinking, gets the ball rolling. Do not ask, "Do you think that is a good idea?" Someone says "Yes" and you are right back where you started. If the questions you prepared while formulating your agenda do not get the discussion moving as you wish, you might try outlining an opinion of your own and asking, "Tom, how about telling us how your ideas fit with those I just outlined?" (Note the difference between this question and asking, "Tom, what do you think of that idea?") It is hard for Tom to give a pat answer, such as, "I think it's fine," to the question as recommended. It requires some thought and explaining to answer. This initial question can point the discussion in the direction you want it to go or can lead it astray. So see that the question will start people thinking along the lines of the problem.

PRESENT A LIFELIKE ILLUSTRATION AND INVITE COMMENTS

Sketch out a situation or illustration relating to the topic and ask, "What would you do in a case like that?" This either can take the place of the thought-provoking questions just mentioned or can supplement them. Generally, the colder the group and the less eager they are to discuss the topic at hand, the more helpful it is to have a real-situation introduction to start them thinking and talking. Using a couple of extra questions or examples serves as additional priming to get the discussion operating in case it fizzles out after the first example. There is no better way of motivating your discussants than through presenting them with lifelike situations whose successful handling depends on knowledge of the subject under discussion.

This use of lifelike situations is sometimes called the case-study method of instruction. Fundamentally, the case-study method is the group discussion method, using *cases* as the subjects for discussion. The case-study method ordinarily implies extensive analysis and interpretation of a case selected to demonstrate the learning outcomes of the period. A modified case-study method, however, may be used by assembling a number of short cases, each illustrating a single learning outcome and each to be discussed only briefly. Such brief cases are excellent devices to start a cold group talking. People tend to talk much more readily when discussing what other people should have done than when discussing more abstract topics.

Keeping the Discussion Moving Successfully

JUSTIFY OR USE EACH CONTRIBUTION IF POSSIBLE

Try to find some justification or use for each contribution of a participant. In group dynamics language this is called "permissiveness." The idea is that everyone will feel much freer to give out his ideas if he finds they seem to be appreciated and that he is not ridiculed or ignored if his contribution does not fit in with what most people are thinking. You can use this, in reverse, as a gag for the person who talks too much. Acknowledge his orations with grunts and immediately ask someone else a question. This is a drastic procedure, recommended only after kindness has failed, for sometimes it scares everybody in the group *except* the over-talkative one.

KEEP THE DISCUSSION ON THE TRACK

This is easier said than done, but here are some techniques that will help:

1. Watch the agenda, your *organization* of the period, to spot where the discussion is straying from it. Do not be a slave to it, ruthlessly cutting off discussion of any idea you do not have on your list, but pay it healthy respect. If you did your planning job well, *most* of the things the group *needs* to discuss are on that agenda. It is all right to let a few irrelevant points be discussed as long as plenty of time is left for the pertinent ones, but generally, when you see the discussion straying from the agenda, it is a good idea to start watching for opportunities to bring it back tactfully to its proper subject.

2. Have a recorder, or secretary of the group, outline the discussion on the blackboard. This is highly valuable in practically all discussions. It is especially good if the group is wandering off the subject, however, because when the organization, the agenda, of the discussion is being tracked in white and black, it is easier to spot the digressions.

3. Drop one of your prepared questions, situations, or com-

ments into a lull in a wandering discussion, to redirect thinking onto the subject.

4. Ask a participant who insists on discussing something off the subject, "Will you show a little more clearly how what you are saying ties in with our topic?"

5. Summarize from time to time. There is nothing like a summary to show that what you are summarizing is not what you are supposed to be talking about. A return to the subject is usually readily agreeable to the group.

KEEP DOWN ARGUMENT OVER UNIMPORTANT DETAILS

Keep down argument over or discussion of hairsplitting details. It is amazing how time can fly when people start arguing tiny pet points. In such cases you might ask, "How much real difference to our solution does it make?" Where the answer is "Little!" either drop the subject or arbitrarily specify a compromise solution.

RELATE NEW ASPECTS TO PREVIOUSLY DISCUSSED MATERIAL

Tie in new aspects of the topic with previous ideas; keep a plain thread or pattern of organization running through the discussion. Take a minute—or ask the person bringing up a new idea to do so—to show how it relates to the themes previously developed. Even when there has not been a digression, this is a good idea—as is using the blackboard to record your path.

RESIST REOPENING TOPICS ALREADY FINISHED

Do not permit drifting back to talk over a second time a topic that has already been completed. Discussions sometimes go around in circles like a dog chasing its tail because someone drops back from the current topic to some phase of a previous one, and the group starts over the same ground again. Blackboard outlining of discussion is good for preventing this. If you do not use a blackboard, resolutely say, "I believe we have already talked about that. Let's cover some of the other material we have to con-

sider and wait until the end for a reopening of that area."
Usually it is never reopened.

ENCOURAGE EVERYONE TO PARTICIPATE

To separate your trainees into suitable discussion groups, you
had to know something of the background or experience of each
one. Here is where you can get additional value from the things
you learned about your trainees to group them, to lecture to them
most effectively, to demonstrate something to them—or from your
casual conversation with them. When the discussion touches an
area in which a reticent member has some knowledge or experience, you can bring him into the discussion in a complimentary
manner by singling him out with questions on the area. A discussion is not successful as a training device if it is carried on only
by the *reaction* of a small proportion of the participants.

DO NOT LET ANY ONE PERSON (YOURSELF INCLUDED)
DOMINATE THE DISCUSSION

If a participant is too thick-skinned to take a hint such as, "Let's
see if some of those who haven't been talking much can give some
ideas," he is thick-skinned enough to be told frankly in private
to let others talk more.

CLINCH EACH TOPIC

Clinch a topic being discussed by succinctly summarizing the
consensus on it before moving to a new topic. Let the trail of
your discussion be marked by a series of incisive agreements or
conclusions, not wander vaguely through a mist of not-quite-
resolved issues. It is doing the latter—letting a discussion drift
aimlessly through subjects without ever clinching anything—that
has caused some people to mistrust the discussion method of instruction as a mere bull session. The learning outcomes of your
lesson plan show you what to look for and what to emphasize as
the final trainee conclusions on each topic. This incisive summarizing promotes comprehension of the significance of what has

been said because the instructor emphasizes the significant aspects of the discussion when he summarizes.

PUSH THE DISCUSSION ALONG

Generally speaking, it is better to pass from one topic to another before quite everything has been said than to let it go on until everyone is tired of it and wants to move on to something else.

DIRECT ATTENTION TO ANY ASPECT ABOUT TO BE NEGLECTED

Use one of your questions or comments to direct attention to any aspect of the subject which the discussants seem about to overlook or pass by without proper attention. These questions can also be used to call attention to errors the group may have fallen into which are leading them toward faulty conclusions. It is the duty of the instructor to see that the thinking of trainees in discussions and conferences leads them to the desired knowledges and understandings, just as it is his duty to see that his lectures give them correct information.

Concluding the Discussion

For greatest effectiveness a discussion has to be closed—not run down. If the discussion has proceeded smoothly through a clear agenda, with a clear recognition of each important point discussed and what was decided about it, and if a blackboard record of the proceedings was kept, this is easy. It involves no more than summarizing for the group the proceedings recorded on the blackboard and emphasizing the learning outcomes achieved. If discussants are required to take notes of this summary, the discussion period ends with all having in mind a clear outline, which is available for review as desired, of important points on the subject discussed.

The degree to which the discussion fell short of the criteria just enumerated increases by just that much the difficulty of (and need for) a forceful and effective conclusion to the discussion to insure comprehension of the subject discussed. If important points were not clearly identified and clinched as they were made, it is doubly necessary that the instructor do so in his terminal summary of the discussion. If a blackboard record was not kept, or if it does not reveal a systematic exploration of the topic under discussion, it is doubly desirable for the instructor to make his summary not merely a recapitulation of what the group *did* discuss, but a short presentation of what they *should have* discussed, as well. He should draw on his lesson plan as well as his notes on the discussion. A good way of rounding out a discussion which did not accomplish all that was expected of it is to write up an outline of the learning outcomes *planned* for the discussion, worded and arranged to come as close as possible to representing the discussion as it actually took place, and give it to the discussion participants as soon after the meeting as possible.

It is desirable to make this outline of the discussion reflect the planned learning outcomes as completely as possible without departing from the true picture of the discussion so far as to make the discussants feel they are not really receiving a record of their work. The degree to which the true outline of the discussion and the lesson plan actually coincide is one measure of the degree to which the discussion achieved its goals.

Sometimes a discussion will be conducted not for the purpose of instructing trainees but to gain group agreement on some point. In some cases agreement will not have been reached at the end of the discussion. In such cases, conclude the discussion with a summary such as "The group failed to reach an agreement on . . . because of unresolved differences on . . . , and. . . ." Make your discussion end on a definite, unequivocal note, even if that note can be achieved only by identifying and specifically stating why more was not accomplished. This statement leaves discussants with the feeling that the discussion accomplished *something;* it at least revealed the basic problems that have to be resolved in order to reach an agreement. This leaves the group in a much better spirit to accomplish something at the next meeting than if they break up in an attitude of vague, pointless bickering. End by dismissing the group. Do not permit it to run down and expire.

Special Types of Discussions

Chief differences in the form of group discussions, as far as the instructor is concerned, lie in the degree of responsibility he has to see that they achieve intended results. In the *directed discussion*, the form most commonly employed in training programs, the job of the instructor is to guide trainees' thoughts and discussion to definite, known answers. In *conferences*, more likely to be encountered in in-service training of experienced personnel, the topics discussed are less likely to have pat answers. Here more emphasis is on the constructive imagination of the participants and the pooling of their experiences to come up with better ideas, understandings, and appreciations through the stimulation of discussion than each would have done alone.

Finally, there is the *seminar*. Here, discussion is on a topic regarding which the leader is seeking an answer, a solution, or policy and hoping the discussants can discover one. Here the function of the leader (as he is usually called, rather than "instructor") ranges from being merely the traffic cop who regulates the flow of words among the discussants to one who, having perhaps studied the problem more than the other participants, has some suggestions as to agenda, assumptions, and pertinent data which give him more authority than other members.

Following are examples of each of these three types of discussion, with suggestions as to appropriate procedures for the instructor-leader in each type.

THE DIRECTED DISCUSSION

Suppose you are a training director in a retail store. The sales manager calls you one day to talk about the failure of recently employed sales personnel to make sufficient effort to find adequate substitutes when the particular object requested by a customer is not in stock. There have been several instances where dissatisfied customers have sought the help of more experienced clerks, who were able to produce satisfactory substitutes for the article desired. Training lectures have been given new clerks on this subject, directives have been issued, and informational brochures on identifying substitute merchandise of various types have been published. Nothing seems to have done any good. The sales manager asks if you will try to devise a training program which will alleviate the situation.

This is an ideal situation in which to use the directed discussion, starting with a case and leading discussants to perceive and understand the principles the store wishes followed when customers call for items not in stock. A customer asks for a type of drapery fabric which the store does not stock. What should the salesperson do? A directed discussion will have several advantages over other methods which may already have been used in attempts to get sales personnel to try to find acceptable substitutes for merchandise not in stock. First, the answers arrived at in the discussion will be *their* answers (stimulating their thought or reaction to the subject), their own brain-children, in which they will have a personal interest and which they *have* to make work to prove to themselves that they are right.

Second, it is obviously impossible to anticipate all the articles a customer might request and the store not have, much less calculate adequate substitutes or other ways of handling all situations satisfactorily. So sales personnel may have been taught an incomplete list or inadequate enumeration of ways to handle such situations, ways whose futility they probably recognized. Now, on the other hand, they are getting the actual sort of situation they will face on the sales floor and are acquiring practice in thinking through the answers to those situations. They are comprehending principles, not merely memorizing facts. Doing the same sort of thinking to help the customer will be easier as a result of the experience in the discussion group.

Third, the salespersons know there are no pat answers to cases of this kind, because so much depends on the attitude of the customer. The comments of other members of the discussion group regarding proposal of certain substitutes may closely approximate actual customer reactions they have encountered and show up the sound and unsound ideas that come forth. So your discussion of the problem will have the advantage of involving the salesclerks personally in making their ideas work and of giving them practice in doing the exact thing they are supposed to do as a result of the training. The instructor's job is to keep the thoughts of the group directed toward the solution, ideas, and principles the store management wishes salespersons to adopt.

Here is a suggested representative plan of preliminary preparation for such a directed discussion:

1. Determine the objectives of the program, i.e., what skills and abilities trainees are expected to have as a result of it (the "objective" element of *motivation*).

2. Analyze these course objectives to determine what trainees need to know and what patterns of thinking and reasoning they need to develop to achieve the objectives (the need element of *motivation*).

3. Develop a logical, integrated outline of the material, ideas, and situations they must be led through in the discussion to achieve these knowledges and thinking and reasoning patterns (*organization*).

4. Construct a lesson plan showing the integration of instructor activity, trainee activity, discussion material, learning outcomes, and objectives.

5. Develop an ample reserve of thought-provoking questions, situations, and new ideas to keep thought and discussion flowing freely, and to shift attention to each separate topic on which discussion is desired (*reaction, concentration*).

6. Study the subject thoroughly enough that you will not be caught unprepared by an unexpected turn in the discussion.

7. Prepare summaries based on anticipated trainee comments

to cover concisely and forcefully the ideas you want trainees to carry away with them (*repetition* of important ideas brought out in the discussion, and promoting *comprehension* of crucial ideas).

8. Write up, in the form of a problem, a situation, a case, a series of questions, or an idea or proposition, the topic to be discussed. Give this, along with any available study references, to the trainees a day or so in advance with some encouragement to study the subject before coming to the meeting.

Conducting the directed discussion does not differ appreciably from conducting a discussion of any other type, as far as general rules go. However, in the directed discussion the instructor will participate more, exercise more guidance on the direction discussion takes, and hold more closely to his planned agenda and lesson plan than in the other types.

THE CONFERENCE

The illustration involving the crew and the discussion on emergency first aid procedures is a good example of the conference. There are certain definite things, in the form of facts and ideas about injuries and the proposed emergency procedures, which the company wants the conferees to learn. There are also several areas in which the company wants the conferees to come up with their own ideas, such as how to get thorough acceptance of the plan by crewmen and how the presently proposed plan might be improved. The chances are, too, that those calling this conference hope that through talking about the subject, the conferees will convince themselves of its importance and acquire a new attitude on the matter of safety.

There will be several specific points which you, as the instructor or leader, will want to cover, such as provisions of the present plan, why certain provisions are as they are, or exceptions to the standard procedures. Your objectives, learning outcomes, and body of material will not be so tightly controlled as in the directed discussion, because one of your purposes is to allow leeway for the conferees to give each other and the company good ideas based on their own knowledge, experience, judgment, and ingenuity.

You will find your conference will move along more easily, participants will feel it was more worth while, and you will enjoy a higher feeling of success if you have gone through each of the steps discussed under "Preparing a Discussion Period." But in preparing the agenda you can afford to allow more latitude for deviation in your schedule of going from this point to this at a certain time during the period than you can allow in the directed discussion because you are not obliged to arrive at such specific, predetermined conclusions in the conference as in the directed discussion.

You pay for this partial relaxation of schedule, however, in your personal preparation and the pains you must take to insure that none of the psychological causes of learning are neglected. Presiding over a group of conferees with some know-how on the subject means that, to keep your position as intellectual leader of the conference, you must be thoroughly informed on all aspects of the subject. Otherwise, you will find the group leading you, instead of you it, and while this *may* indicate fine accomplishment on the part of the group, it is not a pleasant experience for a leader. Follow the general rules given for conducting a discussion. Be tactful and considerate in easing conferees in a certain direction, and with experienced people such as those you will have in most conference situations, be careful to avoid reflecting on their knowledge or experience in fields where they are expected to know something. Keep a firm grip on the steering wheel nevertheless. If the conference is going to accomplish anything constructive instead of drifting by chance, it has to have firm, competent guidance. You, the leader, are the one who should be providing it. Do so.

This is why the instructor-leader must go through all the steps of preparing for a more tightly led discussion even when he is actually going to lead a conference. It is often considerably harder to manage and control a loosely directed conference of people who know something about their subject than a tightly directed discussion by people who are just learning.

THE SEMINAR

The seminar presupposes an issue, problem, situation, or proposition on which there is no single correct answer—at least as far as anyone knows. The seminar group is a deliberative body. It is looking for evidence in the reading, experience, and minds of its participants, and as such evidence accumulates, an effort will be made to develop a better policy or solution than has existed heretofore.

Just how far the steps in preparing for a discussion will apply in preparing for a seminar depends largely on how complex the seminar problem is, how expert the leader is in the problem area, and how skillful he is in guiding a group through the process of learning. In cases where he knows enough about the subject, or can find out enough through reading and interviews, to be able to define objectives, outcomes, and agenda and to be able to state the problem definitively, he will find it greatly to his and the group's advantage to do so. This simply gets the seminar group into the subject, and through it, with a minimum of skidding around trying to get their feet set on a constructive path. If he is not pretty expert in the area himself, or if the area is so big and complex that an attempt to reduce it to a lesson plan is clearly beyond the leader's ability, another basic preparatory approach is indicated.

That is the problem-solution approach. A seminar is for the purpose of solving or attempting to solve a problem. A well-thought-out approach to systematic problem solution constitutes a generalized agenda which can be used to order and systematize a seminar discussion of a complex problem. If you will hold your discussion to this general pattern, maintaining this approximate order of discussion but not attempting to eliminate all overlapping of steps, you will find it a helpful approach to directing a seminar discussion.

Steps in Group Problem Solving

IDENTIFY THE PROBLEM

Identifying a problem involves more than merely naming it or stating it. It involves digging down to determine the real inner nature, the crux, of the problem. It also involves all participants' getting the same idea of what the problem is, all "speaking the same language" as far as the problem is concerned. Spending as much as 10 per cent of the total discussion time developing a thorough mutual understanding of the problem is likely to save several times that amount of time which would be lost later in waste motion if everyone were not on the same, and the right, track. Sometimes, indeed, the nature of the problem is such that when it is fully identified, the solution becomes almost routine, and this step becomes practically the total problem-solving process.

GATHER DATA

Gathering data takes two forms—each seminar member contributing his personal knowledge and experience to accumulate a sizable body of know-how from the group itself and systematic data gathering by the members or their staffs from the field, libraries, or other sources. In the first instance, gathering the data will consist in talking over various aspects of the problem, preferably maintaining a blackboard record of facts, ideas, and approaches developed, and converting the store of knowledge of each member into a warehouse stock on which the whole group can draw. In the second instance, it involves recessing the seminar and permitting members to gather such data as they can, reconvening, and assembling the data into a usable form.

ANALYZE THE DATA

Look over the warehouse stock of knowledge the group has accumulated. What does it mean? Are there any significant things about it that stand out, that give some leads in some direction?

Try it in different combinations; sometimes the order in which you look at a group of facts and ideas holds the whole key to solving a problem. Ask, "What would these data mean if we assume that . . . ? How would the significance change if we find that . . . ?" Look for implications, hints, trends, clues. A moment's reflection will tell you that it takes more skill and know-how to make an accurate diagnosis and interpretation of facts than it does simply to collect facts. Spend time on this step.

FORMULATE HYPOTHESES

When you formulate a hypothesis, you are taking direct steps toward a solution. List every possible solution, answer, or explanation you can think of. Do not evaluate them critically at this time. Just encourage everyone to offer as many possible solutions as he can. The members have been spending considerable time thinking about the seminar subject by now. Their minds are pretty well steeped in it. The group will discard at least nine out of ten of the hypotheses mentioned after the most perfunctory examination, but with good minds thoroughly steeped in a subject, all working to get as many potential solutions as possible, sometimes some of the wildest-looking ones turn out to have some sound, usable attributes. So for the time being, work for sheer quantity, not quality.

TEST THE HYPOTHESES

The time for critical evaluation comes when you test the hypotheses. Put each of the hypotheses formulated in the previous step under the microscope of known fact and predictable probability. See which ones stand up best. Your seminar members will find this more natural than the free-wheeling crystal-balling of the previous step, but that step of formulating hypotheses gives them the variety of approaches they must have to explore all the possibilities in this one. Some hypotheses will offer a partial solution to the problem and can be combined with others to produce improved solutions. Some aspects of some of the hypotheses will be found unsuitable and can be discarded. As portions of the list of possible hypotheses stand the test of critical evaluation, your seminar is ready to move into the last stage of the discussion.

FORMULATE A CONCLUSION OR SOLUTION

After all the hypotheses are evaluated, take the soundest ones and build the best possible answer to the subject the seminar was convened to explore.

At any point in this process, a new slant on the real meaning of the problem or new evidence or interpretations may emerge which causes the group to drop back into an earlier stage again, and sometimes a brilliant idea will pop up before its appropriate stage of problem solving is reached. But following this general step-by-step sequence has proved a sound basis for running many seminars. It will probably help you run a better one than you could without some such guide to systematize the discussion of your group.

SUMMARY

TO PLAN FOR A DISCUSSION

1. Read up on the subject and assign for study any topics requiring research.

2. Divide trainees into groups comparable in knowledge and experience with respect to the subject to be discussed.

3. Determine or define specific objectives to be achieved; decide exactly what you want to accomplish.

4. Identify the desired learning outcomes.

5. Clearly establish the problem, and describe it so others can see clearly what it is, too.

6. Prepare and issue preliminary study materials to trainees.

7. Develop an agenda to include all points required for treatment of the problem.

8. Prepare a lesson plan.

9. Arrange a discussion room with blackboard, where all participants can sit facing each other.

TO START A DISCUSSION ALONG PROFITABLE LINES

1. Briefly outline the situation to be discussed; see that everyone understands what is to be accomplished in the discussion.

2. State an opinion or ask a thought-provoking question.

3. Keep injecting questions on vital points that bear on the problem.

4. Use a demonstration, an illustration, or a lifelike case.

TO KEEP A DISCUSSION MOVING SUCCESSFULLY

1. Select and use a recorder; outlining the discussion on the blackboard is a good idea.

2. Make your questions and points require comment; if no comments come, rephrase to hit from another angle.

3. Find some justification for each view expressed; make contributors feel they are helping.

4. Tie in new topics with old ones.

5. Avoid premature introduction of new topics—wait until one is sewed up before starting another.

6. Keep members from wandering away from the subject; tactfully lead them back to the particular point under discussion.

7. Do not allow anyone to dominate the discussion to an obvious degree.

8. Encourage contributions from all.

9. Use blackboard, pads, or handouts to keep the group together.

10. Summarize frequently the contributions that bear directly on or aid the discussion.

11. Clinch each topic with some definite conclusion.

12. Keep outlining the discussion on the blackboard if it has a tendency to become vague.

13. Be ready to come up with a comment or question to redirect discussion if it is led to a "dead end."

TO CONCLUDE A DISCUSSION

1. Summarize discussion—use blackboard outline if kept.

2. Reach some definite conclusion, even if a compromise—do not just fade out, leaving the discussion hanging in mid-air.

3. State your conclusions specifically and definitely.

4. Record conclusions in writing.

5. Dismiss the group—don't let them just drift off by ones and twos.

SUGGESTED READINGS

Baird, A. C.: *Discussion: Principles and Types*, McGraw-Hill Book Company, Inc., New York, 1943.

Ewbank, H. L., and J. J. Aver: *Discussion and Debate*, Appleton-Century-Crofts, Inc., New York, 1951.

Haiman, F. S.: *Group Leadership and Democratic Action*, Houghton Mifflin Company, Boston, 1951.

Hammock, R. C., and R. S. Owings: *Supervising Instruction in Secondary Schools*, McGraw-Hill Book Company, Inc., New York, 1955.

McBurney, J. H., and K. G. Hance: *Discussion in Human Affairs*, Harper & Brothers, New York, 1950.

Muehl, W.: *The Road to Persuasion*, Oxford University Press, New York, 1956.

Sandford, W. P., and W. H. Yeager: *Practical Business Speaking*, McGraw-Hill Book Company, Inc., New York, 1952.

Zelko, Harold P.: *Successful Conference and Discussion Techniques*, McGraw-Hill Book Company, Inc., New York, 1957.

8

The Role-playing Method

This chapter describes the method of instruction known as role-playing. Role-playing is a uniquely effective method of simulating real-life situations in which persons are trying to persuade each other or reach an agreement. It allows supervisors, salespersons, instructors, executives, and others who must work extensively with people to experiment with ways of handling people in different situations without the loss and expense which would result from practice in real-life situations.

SOME JOBS REQUIRE no particular skills in human relations for their successful accomplishment. Machinists, bookkeepers, and many other workers can perform their work about as well, whether they are skilled in dealing with people or not. On the other hand, many jobs require two sorts of knowledge and skills, analogous to the two wheels of a bicycle: technical knowledge and skill to propel their work forward and human-relations skill to keep it moving in the right direction. Salesmen, supervisors, training directors, and executives fall into this latter category. Their jobs require skill and knowledge of a specialized sort pertaining to their work, but they also require knowledge of the human factor in business and skill in dealing with people.

Knowledge of principles and techniques of human relations

can be developed in employees through lectures and reading assignments. A certain feel for dealing with people can be cultivated through discussions. But in the final analysis, feel and skill, the ability to *apply* the principles and techniques, come only from actual practice in handling human-relations situations. This practice can be obtained by putting the person on the job and letting him work out his own application of what he learned in lectures and group discussions and through reading, but the learning-on-the-job procedure has its drawbacks. Salesmen may lose sales that they would have made had they brought to the sales floor more skill in handling customers. Workers, or worker productivity, may be sacrificed while the supervisor is learning his human-relations techniques on the job. Training programs can bog down badly and entire organizations can become demoralized if training directors and executives have to learn the fine points of human relations through trial and error.

To teach human-relations skills through actual practice in a laboratory situation, a procedure known as "role-playing" has been evolved. Role-playing is just what the name implies: a situation is described, the characters in it are identified, and people are assigned the character roles and told to compose their own lines and act the part of these characters. In doing so, they get actual practice in conducting themselves in situations like the one in which they are acting. Their learning is reinforced by analysis and discussion of the little drama—why the actors said and did what they did, how they felt, how else they might have reacted, and so on. Here is a sample role-playing episode:

SITUATION:

Scene is the After Dark Shop of a large department store. (The term "scene" is used in the sense of "situation." Props and scenery are seldom used in role-playing episodes.) A woman and her teen-age daughter are looking for an evening dress for the girl. The girl likes a black strapless, while her mother favors a fluffy, frilly, pastel blue, slightly lower in price.

CHARACTERS:

MOTHER, early forties, well dressed, outspoken in her opinions

DAUGHTER, barely sixteen, attractive, inclined to be plump; angry, and determined

SALESLADY, has a teen-age daughter of her own, agrees with the mother but hates to lose sale, and fears girl will not accept the blue (NOTE: The person playing the part of the saleslady might be self-conscious and embarrassed and the attitude of the whole group toward the training program might be injured if she were told merely to act *herself* and then an analysis were made of how well she did. By specifying her role, especially if it is specified so that it clearly does not apply to her, the element of personal criticism is eliminated. It was the mythical saleslady doing so and so, not really Miss Blank here.)

DIALOGUE:

(Of course, the characters compose their own lines as they go along. Here is a transcription of one play-through of this situation, with trainees taking all roles, as will naturally be the case in a training program.)

DAUGHTER: I wouldn't wear that thing! It looks like an elementary school graduation dress!

MOTHER: Honey, it matches your eyes just perfectly. And this lovely full skirt . . .

DAUGHTER: It's like a tent! I want something that makes me . . . that people will say . . . something that looks *cool*. Like this! (*Holds up black strapless dress.*)

SALESLADY: You want something a little different from the ones you have, don't you? Look at this red tulle . . . these flowers caught . . .

DAUGHTER: It's still a tent, just another color. Can't you *see?* For Pete's sake . . .

MOTHER: Jeannie, honestly, that black strapless is simply out of the question for you. It makes you look like you are trying to imitate somebody.

SALESLADY: Where will you be wearing the dress, honey?

MOTHER: She'll have to wear it *everywhere* for the next year, unless she wears one of the ones she already has!

DAUGHTER: I might as well wear what I have now as that thing! What do *you* care? *I'm* the one who will be wearing it! *I'm* the one knows where I'll be wearing it!

CUT:

At this point the play was interrupted for a discussion. The director asked several questions such as: What is the daughter thinking? How does she feel? What is *really* in the mother's mind? How do you think the saleslady feels? What is she thinking? (Only the participant involved was told the attitude she was to play in this particular instance, although the audience may be told, if desired.) What position should the saleslady take? How should she handle the situation?

After the group had discussed the feelings and thinking of each character and suggested several ways of handling the situation, new persons were assigned the roles. Each was told to adopt one of the ideas brought out by the group about the character she had been assigned and act in keeping with that idea. The saleslady, for instance, should decide to follow one particular line of behavior which the group suggested. No character identified the plan she was actually following, except by her dialogue and actions.

After the scene has been played to a close, or until the instructor-director feels it has served its purpose, there is more analysis. Actors may be asked how they really felt about the people they portrayed. (You will find that people sometimes become quite wrapped up in their roles when a long episode is played. They acquire the emotion and determination of the characters they portray and gain real insight into the inner feelings of some of the persons they previously had viewed only from the outside in their day-by-day work. This can be a valuable help in developing better understanding of workers by foremen, customers by salespersons, and so on.) The way the saleslady—always "the saleslady," never Miss Blank, who played the role—handled the situation is discussed, and ways of improving on it are developed, if possible. The group may be broken into casts of three, and everyone play a role, following one of the group's ideas. In conclusion, the group or the director may discuss what generalizations or principles can be deduced from the episode.

That, in brief, is the substance of the training method known as role-playing. It is an extremely powerful and effective technique. It possesses to a strong degree the psychological causes of learning. *Motivation* in a role-playing session is seldom a problem. Everyone is interested because people readily perceive the application of the episode to themselves. *Concentration* is likewise easy to maintain. As a rule, everyone in the audience quickly identifies with one or another of the characters and follows the flow of emotions, thoughts, and interplay of personalities with real intensity. Of course, this is *reaction* in the fullest sense of the word. The *organization* and *comprehension* factors have to be worked for. How well they are achieved depends largely on the skill and thoroughness with which the analysis of episodes is carried out and how well the generalizations and principles are deduced and incorporated into the thinking of the group. *Repetition* can be carried out to whatever extent is desired through replays of a scene, with a different cast or approach, or through analysis of an episode.

Producing a Role-playing Episode

Role-playing as a training method has occasionally acquired a bad reputation through being misused. Untrained people have mistakenly thought that all you had to do was get your group, foremen, for instance, together and say, "All right, today we are going to work on effective use of the reprimand. Let's have a volunteer who will be the foreman and somebody who will be a worker who has been goofing off. The foreman is mad and wants the worker to do better. The worker thinks he is doing all right. Let's go." Use the role-playing technique this way and you will get results of the exact quality you would get from a lecture if, as you walked to the classroom, you began your thinking on your lecture, "Let's see now, I've got to talk about something this period. . . . Quality control. There's something they need to know more about! Today I'll tell 'em about quality control."

You would not expect highly efficient learning from a lecture prepared in that manner. To realize its maximum potential a role-playing episode has to be planned quite as carefully as a lecture, perhaps even more carefully, because in the lecture the instructor controls what develops and does not have to guard against odd-ball developments which might throw him off track. In the role-playing situation the actors compose their own lines and determine the direction the episode will take, and the instructor has to be prepared to take what happens and model a worthwhile learning experience out of it. To give himself a reasonable chance of success requires careful planning of the episode. Here is a suggested step-by-step procedure for building a role-playing episode which will produce maximum learning for all concerned.

DETERMINE THE OBJECTIVE OF THE EPISODE

Decide exactly what you want trainees to learn from the episode. In the supervisor and delinquent worker situation sketched above, for instance, is the purpose to teach supervisors how to get better work from delinquent workers? Is it to learn how to criticize, reprimand, or make suggestions in a manner which will improve production? Is it to develop a specific technique for supervisors to use? Or is it to produce an understanding of some general principles and concepts of handling people? It makes a difference in the way you plan your scenario. If the purpose is to develop a specific technique, you will want to describe the situation and delineate the characters carefully, so that the episode will develop along the lines you wish and you can spend the training time polishing the technique rather than playing through episode after episode trying to find one that accidentally brings out the technique you wish to study.

"Blunderbuss" objectives which merely indicate a broad general area of human relations in which increased knowledge and skill are desired are unsatisfactory. They lead to role-playing episodes in which participants gradually come to concentrate on thinking up clever lines, displaying their theatrical ability, or making the audience laugh, instead of trying to resolve the human relations situation in the most satisfactory manner. "Rifle" objectives, identifying exactly what you are aiming for in each episode, keep trainees' attention focused where it ought to be—on handling the situation in the best manner possible, not on showing off their cleverness.

To sum it up, "Incidental learning is *still* accidental learning." (Look back over Chapter 1.) Blunderbuss objectives may easily result in a half-dozen role-playing episodes all covering the same point, leaving uncovered five equally important learning outcomes. Only by planning your whole coverage, dividing it into specific points, and then structuring your episodes to insure their application to those points can you be sure of including all learning outcomes you *intend* to accomplish. Only by this systematic planning can you achieve best results from your use of the role-playing techniques.

In preparing the lesson plan, the situation and characters should be described in the paragraph, "Plan for Conducting the Period." The "Learning Outcomes" column is unusually important because the instructor has to use it to build the period on the run more than in any other method of instruction. He should do as much advance planning of his activities as possible and list questions, explanations, and ideas for variations in roles and in the basic situation beside the learning outcomes they might promote. The "Trainee Activity" column should list any special directions or ideas the instructor wishes to give actors and observers. Special thought should be given to ways of involving everyone in the group as an actor or an analyst of each episode, and these ways recorded in the "Trainee Activity" column. How the instructor can do all these things is discussed in the remainder of this chapter.

STRUCTURE A SITUATION

There are several ways of composing the situation to be played. The instructor, or a group of instructors, may design the situation to fit the objectives and learning outcomes they are most anxious to achieve. This method, of course, offers the best guarantee that the episode will develop along the precise lines desired and will produce the outcome desired. From time to time, however, it may be found profitable to draw on the knowledge, experience, and problems of the trainee group in deciding what type of situation will be played. A committee of trainees may be appointed and asked to design one or several situations on problems which they think would be of greatest value to the group. This method has the advantage of focusing on problems of greatest *conscious* concern to the trainees themselves. Finally, it is sometimes permissible to ask the group for suggestions as to situations which might profitably be played and quickly construct a situation in terms of their suggestions. This is by far the least reliable method and least likely to secure thorough coverage of desired learning outcomes, but it tends to spur group interest and enthusiasm and to produce natural, spontaneous role-playing, and it is useful as a variation from the more carefully planned situations.

You will find that observing a few principles in constructing situations to be played will produce smoother, more profitable episodes.

1. Structure the situation to fit the specific learning outcome you wish trainees to achieve (except, of course, when basing it on spontaneous suggestions from the group).

2. If your objective is to explore the personality and methods of a character (an executive type, a certain type of supervisor, etc.), define the *situation* closely to direct players into the course of action desired, but do not describe the characters minutely; let the actors explore and construct them. On the other hand, if a problem, a situation, is to be explored, concentrate on describing the *characters* so that they will develop the situation along

the general lines desired, and do not tell them too specifically just how they should handle the situation. In short, give your actors freedom to explore and exercise initiative *in the area you want studied*.

3. Make the situation resemble conditions the trainees actually face in their daily work. Keep it *believable*, typical of situations they will face, not a fantasy.

4. Describe a situation in enough detail for everyone to envision the same circumstances surrounding it. You will have confusion if, for instance, one player thinks the situation is laid in a preseason showing and another at an end-of-season sale, or if one thinks a foreman can hire and fire and another that he can only suggest and recommend. Such misunderstandings will be minimized by having conditions coincide with actual conditions in the company employing the trainees, except where otherwise specified.

Here are some sample lead-off descriptions of situations. They are by no means models which should be copied, but represent descriptions well suited to the learning outcomes and objectives they are intended to support.

1. The Vice-president in charge of Production has just completed a study on production costs and ways to lower them. He found that switch-over costs involved in producing small runs of articles increased gross cost per article considerably, so he determined on a new policy of much bigger runs, less frequently repeated. In a few weeks the Vice-president in charge of Distribution was receiving complaints from warehouse personnel that big surpluses of some articles had piled up, straining their storage facilities, while they were short on other lines and were delayed in filling the orders sent them by Sales. Upon talking with the Vice-president in charge of Production, the Vice-president in charge of Distribution was told the reason for the imbalance, was shown that the new method would materially raise company profits, and was asked to work out some plan which would support the new production scheme. He did not see how this could be done without increasing warehouse facilities, and

about this time the Vice-president in charge of Sales approached him with the complaint that salesmen were getting cancellations on orders because of delayed shipments. They went to see the Vice-president in charge of Production, who again explained the new system and appealed for cooperation during a period of readjustment to the new plan. Before the discussion was over, considerable acerbity had developed, and by common consent they decided to discuss the situation with the President. They are now seated in his office, and he asks them what their problem is.

This is obviously a human relations problem at the executive level, which might be appropriate to a program of executive development. Highly specific objectives and learning outcomes are less practical at this level than at levels where more specific skills and less broad grasp of things are required of people. It is suitable to a general objective such as developing skill in resolving a conflict situation, "reconciling irreconcilables," as one person put it. It could also be used as a vehicle for teaching administrative practices, lateral coordination, or executive decision making. The objective would determine the point of view from which the situation would be approached. Any desired slant can be given the episode by specifying the points of view of the characters in casting them, for the situation itself is flexible, permitting much exploration and experimentation in the way the parts will be played.

Suppose your objective is to cultivate in instructors skill in remotivating trainees who have become apathetic or uninterested in the program. An appropriate situation could be as follows:

2. It is the third week of a six-week training program in insurance underwriting. Mr. Joles failed the weekly test and is depressed, resentful, and considering withdrawing from the program. You are one of a half-dozen instructors conducting the course, and Mr. Joles is your advisee. You think Joles has possibilities as an insurance man, and since the company by now has several hundred dollars invested in him,

you would like him to continue the course. The interview begins.

Left like this, the person playing the role of the instructor-adviser would be free to turn the interview into one of persuasion, encouragement, appeal to pride, or simply inducing the trainee to consider logic as well as his feelings in making his own decision. The situation could easily be elaborated to specify one or the other of these courses by stating that it is the policy of the company to place maximum responsibility for decisions on trainees and to refrain from high-pressuring them in any way, or the contrary.

A phase of a supervisors' training course may be concerned with handling problems of tardiness and absenteeism. A role-playing situation with the objective of emphasizing the necessity for supervisors to exercise sympathetic discretion in handling such problems might be composed as follows:

3. Joe has been from five to thirty minutes late six times during the past month. His desk is a clearing point for papers to be worked on by others. The first part of the day is the busiest period, as far as his work is concerned. The supervisor knows Joe's wife has been ill and that Joe has two small children, but the work of the remainder of the office staff is being seriously impeded by his tardiness in getting the papers out the first thing in the morning.

The supervisor's responsibility for structuring the interview can be decreased by specifying the time and circumstances in which the interview is to be conducted—or that may be left to the discretion of the person playing the role. Explicit company policies which he must observe can be written into the situation; he can be told to conduct the interview in line with actual company policy as it exists; or he can be told that in Joe's particular case the general manager wants him to proceed on his own judgment, without feeling bound by customary regulations.

Perhaps you would like supervisors to handle better the employee whose disposition suddenly goes sour.

4. Mai is one of the best receptionists the company has ever had, but recently she has been touchy, rude, and irritating to visitors and staff alike. Her eyes are frequently red in the morning. There are vague rumors . . .

By the way in which various parts in the drama are described, this situation can be developed into the supervisor's handling of an employee with a domestic-relations problem, an attempt to divorce the office situation from the employee's private life, handling a drinking problem, or almost any desired special case. It is a basic situation easily adaptable to different objectives through further elaboration.

ESTABLISH ROLES AND SELECT PARTICIPANTS

As was said earlier, if a character study of an employee or superior is desired, specify the *situation* in detail and let the actors develop the characters naturally in relation to the situation. If the emphasis is to be on handling the situation, sketch out clearly the types of *people* involved, and let the participants develop a bare skeleton of a situation as their characters dictate. In the first instance, the character of Mr. Joles might be described as follows:

Mr. Joles, would like to get into the insurance underwriting business, but fears injury to his prospects with the company if he finishes the course with a low grade.

In the second instance, the description might be:

Mr. Joles, has recently left the navy, where he held the rank of commander. He has limited formal education and is sensitive about it, but has succeeded quite well in practical business life. He resents the long-hair approach to selling insurance and is sure that he can do well if just given a territory and turned loose.

In the case of Mai, the receptionist-gone-sour, the emphasis could be placed on getting all pertinent information about the case by describing the supervisor as follows:

SUPERVISOR, kind, but firm, with a statistical sort of mind. He believes that in the long run everyone will get along best by following a policy of complete honesty. He is tactful in handling people, but feels that it is necessary to know all about a situation before you come to a conclusion about it. His life is closely bound up with the company, and he feels that the company's interests are more important than personal reticence or self-consciousness.

It could be placed on achieving impersonal office efficiency by describing him in this way:

SUPERVISOR, a reserved, impersonal man. He is careful not to let personal feelings influence his decisions in office matters, and feels that others should do the same. No one has ever questioned his complete fairness, and he is generous with time and money when any appeal is made for an employee who has suffered some disaster. In return, he expects employees to give their best to their jobs, regardless of any outside problems they may have.

It is seldom wise to have a player act himself. He will usually be more concerned with covering up than with expressing his real feelings; he expects to be exposed to possible criticism and painful analysis, and the training possibilities of the episode suffer accordingly. Much can be gained by having him literally act a part. In the executive-problem situation mentioned earlier, it can prove highly educative to have, for instance, the real-life Vice-president in charge of Production play the part of the Vice-president in charge of Sales, and so on. If it is made clear that they are expected to play their roles with sincerity and genuine sympathy for the parts they portray, participants can, by playing those roles, develop good, sympathetic insights into the problems and procedures other executives face.

To avoid having people thought of as doing and saying things *themselves*, where it should be clearly recognized that they are merely acting parts, *always* give players names different from their own, as well as characters and descriptions easily recognized as not genuinely fitting them. By doing this you can minimize self-consciousness in your players, make the audience feel freer to analyze and criticize the action, and get heartier cooperation from everyone.

It is generally better, in a training situation, for the instructor to assign people to the different roles rather than ask for volunteers. The ones who volunteer might indeed identify better with the roles, but they are also more likely to volunteer for a role-playing situation which they can use as a sounding board for display of histrionics or personal prejudices. Furthermore, they are likely to be the ones least in need of the particular experience which playing the role would give. Of course when a group is composed strictly of volunteers, participating in a program just because they want to (as in a training program for employees volunteering to participate in a welfare fund-raising campaign), it is wise to cater to their preferences in the playing of roles. But when role-playing is an integral part of a regular training program, formal or informal, the instructor can use the casting of players to give specific experiences to the people who most need them.

Is there a person in the group who is overly brusque and unfeeling in handling subordinates? A sincere playing of the role of Joe, who is late because he has a sick wife and two small children at home, may do more to show him the other side of the picture than any amount of lecturing or explaining. Does a salesman make careless errors in writing up sales tickets? Let him play the role of a departmental bookkeeper trying to get better cooperation from departmental personnel in keeping accurate records.

Try to avoid casting two or more persons in roles which will enable them to play up strong conflicts of opinion you know to exist between them. You will turn your training session into a boxing ring, and they will merely emerge more strongly entrenched in their respective positions. The idea is for each player to get a broadened viewpoint, an insight into the position or feelings of someone else, or a new or improved way of handling a situation.

If possible, cast your characters and assign each his part a day or so before the episode is to be played so they can be thinking about their roles, identifying themselves with their parts. Tell them the roles they are to play and the situation to be played. You may want to give them written character sketches of the persons they portray, or a written detailed description of the situation of the episode. Encourage them to do some thinking as to the best way of playing the roles—not, of course, to compose lines beforehand, but to think about their parts and the episode until they get the feel of it.

PREPARE THE AUDIENCE AND PARTICIPANTS FOR THE EPISODE

This is especially necessary when players have not been assigned their parts a day or so in advance, but is extremely helpful even when everyone has known of the situation to be played some time in advance. It is a matter of getting everyone in the mood. The beginning of most motion pictures contains some footage of film which is designed to help the audience get the feel of what is to come. Radio comedians have long striven to have a studio audience laughing heartily as they go on the air, to put the radio or television audience in a mood to join in the mirth. Probably as much loss of potential learning in role-playing instruction is due to starting everyone off cold on a situation instead of warming them up to it as is attributable to any other one defect.

Talking about the objective of the role-playing during the present period, explaining the skills and insights it is hoped will be acquired, is a good starting point to warm up the group for a situation. If you can get trainees to talk about what insights they think they might get, that is fine. Read the situation aloud, even if everyone has had a copy, and invite comments or questions. Describe a roughly similar situation which actually existed in the company some time in the past. Talk a little about the nature of the characters, but do not give away secret instructions you may have given players. Perhaps ask the group for further interpretation of the probable nature of characters, extrapolating from the descriptions given the group.

Then take the players one at a time and engage in a little discussion with each, to get him accustomed to thinking along the lines of the character he is to represent:

INSTRUCTOR: I believe you are Mrs. Ames, interested in buying a refrigerator?

MRS. AMES: Yes.

INSTRUCTOR: How many adults and children in your home, Mrs. Ames?

MRS. AMES: Three adults. My husband's brother boards with us. Four children.

INSTRUCTOR: Why are you shopping for a refrigerator? (Notice that the instructor is not playing the part of a salesman, trying to ingratiate himself with a customer. He is trying to make the actor begin to feel and think like Mrs. Ames.)

MRS. AMES: My old one is too small. I particularly need some more freezing space. Besides, it's getting old and worn-looking.

INSTRUCTOR: I see. Do you have any help in doing your cooking and housekeeping? (He is trying to get the actor to think of Mrs. Ames as a *person,* to be *her,* not merely a character named Mrs. Ames.)

Or the instructor is trying to get a director of personnel to become, for the time of the role-playing episode, president of the company:

INSTRUCTOR: Under what circumstances did you become president, Mr. Hughes?

MR. HUGHES: I was senior vice-president when Mr. Ordan became chairman of the board. I was offered the presidency and accepted.

INSTRUCTOR: Will you give us a little resume of your experience with the company?

MR. HUGHES: I came with Worldwide in 1934 as bookkeeper. I became . . . , etc.

INSTRUCTOR: Thank you for that nice resume, Mr. Hughes. What do you think is Worldwide's greatest need for the next five years? Your No. 1 project?

The audience will have got much into the spirit of things as a result of these conversations with the actors, especially if both the director-instructor and the actor-trainee use imagination and ingenuity in formulating questions and answers. But the group is not there merely to be entertained. Ideally, every person in the group should have an active part to play in each role-playing episode. If the group is large, this may best be achieved by dividing it into smaller groups of three or four and asking each group to pay particular attention to one aspect while watching the action. After the play-through, or any time during it that the instructor thinks appropriate, they may be called upon to go into conference and make a quick analysis of what has developed in the area they are watching, after which the instructor will call on a representative to give a report. The instructor may say:

> I want the people on the right-hand half of the third row to watch for indications of *emotion* in the players. Watch for signs that someone is peeved, triumphant, fearful, or what have you. Try to decide what effect that feeling had on the progress of the situation, how it affected the agreement or lack of agreement they achieved. Some time during or at the end of the episode I'll give you a couple of minutes to discuss and compare notes, then call on you for an interpretation.

Or perhaps:

> Often one point, one statement by someone, is the turning point in a discussion. In the next situation, Juanita, I want you to watch for any such key statements. When you identify one, ask yourself what the person's purpose was in saying it, and what effect it had on the discussion. We'll hear your report after the episode.

If everyone is thus involved, as an individual or member of a small group, in a particular task during the role-playing, it will greatly increase *motivation, reaction, concentration,* and *compre-*

hension throughout the group. It also provides much richer analyses and interpretations than the instructor could make all by himself. (Of course, he will supplement the interpretations made by trainees whenever he thinks it desirable.) By the time these assignments are completed, the group should be warmed up and ready to make the episode a real learning situation.

PLAY THE SITUATION

The preparation in the previous four steps constructs the skeleton of the episode and determines the basic form and shape the flesh, i.e., the play-through, will take. The play-through is the meat, the substance of the role-playing method, but it has to be based on all the parts of the skeleton to insure that the substance will assume the right shape. And after the skeleton has been fleshed out, there is still the step which puts nerves and blood into the body and makes it instruction instead of mere entertainment. That step is discussed later under the heading "Analyze the Episode." It is illustrated intermittently in the dialogue, then discussed at the end of the dialogue.

At this point we shall consider a role-playing episode in its entirety, from determination of the objective through the play-through of the situation. The play-through may be interspersed with analysis and concluded by replays by all trainees to gain practice and skill in the techniques and principles included in the play and the analysis. These replays may be followed by further analysis if the instructor thinks this is wise.

Sample Role-playing Episode

OBJECTIVE:

To cultivate insight into employees' need for belonging and to develop supervisory skill in meeting this need.

SITUATION:

Lou is a clerk-typist in the personnel department of a large organization. She has held this position six months, and while her performance was better than average at first, lately it has dropped off considerably. She has come to the Personnel Director with a request to be transferred back to the stockroom, where she had worked for a year before taking her present job. She says the other girls in the personnel department are not friendly. The Personnel Director does not wish to lose her.

CHARACTERS:

LOU, a plain single girl in her mid-twenties, pleasant and rather quiet, at present is resentful and depressed and determined to do something about it. She feels her situation in the personnel office is intolerable and that nothing can be done to change the social climate.

MR. NIX, the Personnel Director, honestly doesn't see what all the fuss is about. He tries to make things pleasant for his staff and is liberal in granting time off and adjusting routine to suit the convenience of individuals as long as the work is done promptly and well. He is the only man in the department of eight people and mixes little with the group. He feels vaguely that it is a reflection on him that a person would wish to leave personnel and return to a job previously held.

DIALOGUE:

INSTRUCTOR-DIRECTOR: It is human nature to want to be a part of the group you are thrown with. The person left out of the camaraderie of a group is likely to leave himself out of the productive teamwork of the group. This is what is the matter with Lou. At the same time, as long as a person draws a salary, he is obligated to do the work required to earn that salary, whether everything is just as he would like it to be or not. The department head wants to keep everyone in the department as happy as possible; that is the way to get the best possible work from them. At the same time, his primary job is to get the work done, and if he comes to be regarded as a "softie," he may lose control of his organization. The ideal supervisor is skilled at managing things so as to minimize the human relations problems, the interpersonal frictions, within his unit. But he has to know where to draw the line and say, "I'm sorry, but this is the way it is going to be. You will have to decide whether you can adjust to it or not." To accomplish all this, he has to be able to see things from the other person's point of view—to put himself in the other's shoes, so to speak. He has to exercise ingenuity and tact in handling tender feelings and finding ways of working out difficulties. And he has to know how far to go and when to put his foot down. I hope that from our experience in this episode we will get a greater sensitivity to the feelings which actuate people—feelings which may not show up on the surface at first glance. I hope we will get some usable ideas as to specific techniques which can be used to help a lonely person feel more at home on the job, and that we will develop some skill in handling an unhappy employee. After this scene is played through, analyzed, and interpreted, I am going to break the audience into groups of four, and let two play it through and the other two analyze and interpret, then swap places and have another play-through, analysis, and interpretation. First, Butch will play the part of Lou, the clerk-typist, and Andy the part of Mr. Nix, the personnel director. Let's talk about these people a little bit. Where do you live, Lou?

LOU: I share an apartment on Woodland Drive with another girl. She works in the stockroom.

INSTRUCTOR: Do you have a pretty active social life? Any boy friends?

LOU: I guess so. I have three or four men I go with some. No steady.

INSTRUCTOR: How did you happen to take a job with Worldwide?

LOU: I had been working as clerk in a shipping company since getting out of business school. I wanted more money, so when I saw an ad in the paper I applied and got a job here in the stockroom.

INSTRUCTOR: Do most of your friends work at Worldwide?

LOU: No, only Lane, my roommate. Most of them I met through my Sunday school class.

INSTRUCTOR: Well, thanks, Lou. Now I'd like to talk to Mr. Nix, played by Andy. How long have you been director of personnel for Worldwide, Mr. Nix?

NIX: Six years. Before that I had been in Billing and Receiving for four years.

INSTRUCTOR: Does Worldwide have a big personnel turnover?

NIX: No sir! The people we hire stay with us! We select good people, pay well, treat them well, and they stay! We have one of the lowest turnovers in the industry!

INSTRUCTOR: Good deal! How do you get along with the girls in your department?

NIX: Why, uh, all right . . . I mean, I like them all, and I suppose they like me . . . I sort of think I shouldn't mix too . . . I mean, I don't want jealousies . . . and I'm married!

INSTRUCTOR: Sounds logical all the way through. Do you have much trouble with department heads wanting personnel shifts, or things like that?

NIX: Sometimes. Never anything serious. Sometimes someone tries to hijack a good person from another department and I have to step in. Things like that.

INSTRUCTOR: That's good, Mr. Nix. I think you have your part well in mind. Now for the rest of you. Seven, isn't it? Mr. Nix, Lou, please step out of the room a minute while I tell these people what to watch for. I don't want to give you ideas or make you think you've got to put points in just so these people can find them. Lem, I wish you'd see if you can get any hints as to why Lou hasn't been accepted into the group. Dora and Steve, see if Lou and Mr. Nix ever get to seeing eye to eye, and why or why not. Gene, how does Nix's nature, as described in his character description, influence the way he handles this situation? Mary, see if Lou and Nix make any physical movements or gestures which would reveal to an acute observer their feelings. Ed and Sue, you decide what will be the probable long-term effect of whatever happens in this situation, and evaluate the result. All right (raises voice), Lou, Mr. Nix, come in! There is Mr. Nix's desk. Sit down and get started.

NIX: Lou, I've been looking over this application for transfer you submitted. What's the matter, don't you like it here?

LOU: I like the work all right, Mr. Nix. But the folks here don't seem to like me. Somehow I just don't fit in.

NIX: You mean the girls are rude to you?

LOU: No, not that. They just don't seem to notice me at all. They talk and go out for coffee or get together for lunch, and I'm left all by myself. I'm just left out.

NIX: Uh huh . . . I can see how that would be unpleasant. Have you tried to strike up any acquaintances? Tried to make friends?

LOU: Well, I said "Hello," and talked to some of the girls when I first came up here, but nothing happened. I mean, they were polite, but they didn't follow up on my speaking to them. A person can't do all the being friendly . . . it's got to be on both sides. For some reason they just leave me out.

NIX: Lou, I don't think they consciously do that. Maybe if I talked to them . . .

LOU: No sir! How do you think I'd feel, knowing they were being nice to me just because you told them to! Besides, I doubt if they would do any differently even then. They are a tight little group.

NIX: Isn't your work here a little more pleasant than in the stockroom? You *make* some more, I know. I'd hate for you to go back to a poorer job.

LOU: I'd hate it, too. I can use the money as well as anybody. But . . . well, I spend a lot of time on the job, and the extra money isn't worth spending all that time just sitting here like a lump. In the stockroom people were nice, they were free and easy to know.

NIX: I see your point. Lou, do you think there is any particular reason why the girls here haven't been more friendly? Can you think of any reason why they wouldn't?

LOU: I've thought about it a lot. I don't know if they think that working here puts you in a different class from working in the stockroom or what. Maybe they liked the girl who had this job before me and aren't friendly to anyone taking her place. I don't know. I just know things aren't friendly or pleasant here.

NIX: Well, if you don't want me to talk to any of them about it, what do you think we can do?

LOU: All I know to do is move back to the stockroom. That's why I put in for transfer.

NIX: But Lou, it takes a good while to train a person for this job you have here. I hate to have to start over again. And your old job in the stockroom is filled, you know.

LOU: I'll wait awhile for a vacancy. I know you can't just change things all at once. I hate for you to have to train a new girl. But I just don't like it here.

NIX: There are bad things about every job, I guess. Maybe we can plan something, talk it over, see if we can't work out some plan so you will like it better here.

LOU: I like the work. I like you. I guess I'd like the girls if I had a chance. But I don't know how to do anything about it. Do you?

NIX: Not offhand, I don't. How about letting it wait a week and see what we can do?

INSTRUCTOR: Cut! O.K. Let's stop a minute and talk over what has happened. We can carry it on further if we want to, after talking about it awhile. Let's take a few minutes to think over what transpired and then we'll discuss it.

(*Two or three minutes later.*)

INSTRUCTOR: Dora, Steve, how do you think they are coming along? Any chance of reaching an agreement?

DORA: It seems to me that Mr. Nix isn't taking Lou's complaint very seriously. He seems to think it isn't important. Steve has another idea on it, too.

STEVE: If Nix hadn't noticed that Lou was not in the run of things it means he wasn't keeping up with his staff affairs very well. Particularly with a staff that small. I don't believe he has enough feeling about the people in his office.

INSTRUCTOR: You think he sort of lives in an ivory tower?

STEVE: Not exactly. I think he thinks you just *work* in an office, doesn't realize that people want to *live* there, too.

GENE: That ties in with what I saw. The description of him, what he said when you questioned him, the way he handled Lou . . . it looks like he just doesn't realize that people keep on living while they are working.

LEM: I think you're being too hard on Nix. I got the feeling that not being accepted into the group wasn't the real basis of Lou's trouble. Oh, I know that she doesn't like not being accepted, but it seemed to me that she hadn't *tried* to make friends, hadn't tried to get into the group.

DORA: Wait a minute! A newcomer isn't supposed to have to cultivate people. Common courtesy demands that the old hands make her feel at home; it is their place to draw her into the group, not hers to claw her way in! I believe the group has formed a little clique somehow.

INSTRUCTOR: That's just speculation, isn't it? We have little to go on as to how the group feels, how it sees the situation. We have to concentrate on what is happening to Lou, and between Lou and Nix. Did you get any indication of their feelings, Mary?

MARY: Not much. Lou's head jerked up when Nix said he would talk to the girls and she said "No sir!" I think she got a little mad there—I wouldn't be surprised if that made her more determined than ever to leave. Nix picks something up and fumbles with it when he is thinking hard about what to say next.

INSTRUCTOR: Ed and Sue, you haven't said anything yet. How do you think the interview is going? What are the chances of Lou and Nix reaching some sort of an agreement?

ED: I . . . we think he's getting nowhere fast. He is trying to persuade her to stay, and what she is interested in is not staying but in getting where she likes the people she works with. They are at cross purposes.

SUE: He's trying to solve *his* problem of keeping the personnel nicely situated instead of Lou's in getting a more pleasant working situation for herself. As long as that goes on they won't get anywhere.

INSTRUCTOR: Let's see what Mr. Nix himself has to say about it. What *were* you trying to do?

ANDY: I was trying to find some way of getting her to stay on her present job. Preferably by making her happy on it. I didn't seem to get anywhere.

INSTRUCTOR: Let's give Nix some help before starting the play again. What are some approaches, some techniques, he can use?

BUTCH: Can I talk on this, too?

INSTRUCTOR: I don't see why not. Talk as Butch or Lou?

BUTCH: As me. But trying to think like Lou, I got an idea. Maybe she likes being with the men in stockroom. The script says she's single. I said she . . . I . . . *Lou!* had several boy friends. Even if the girls *were* friendly, and we only have Lou's word that they aren't, I'll bet she'd want to go back to the stockroom!

INSTRUCTOR: So you think her admitted reason may not be her *real* reason. In that case, what does Nix do?

ED: First he's got to recognize it!

INSTRUCTOR: Should he ask her if that is a reason? Not necessarily *the* but *a* reason?

MARY: It would be all right if he did it tactfully. And if he did it tactfully, he could find out from some of the other girls what they thought the situation was, too. I'll bet their angle on it would be completely different from Lou's.

INSTRUCTOR: Talk about it to some of the girls? Risky, since Lou didn't like the idea, but a possibility. Maybe one girl? What else?

DORA: Let Nix mix with the girls a little, know what's going on without having to ask. Also he can manage things so Lou is drawn into the conversation, the group, at coffee breaks or before everybody gets to working in the morning.

ANDY: Wait a minute. That's causing me to step out of character. I'm aloof, remember? The leopard can't change his spots . . . at least not in the middle of the play!

INSTRUCTOR: That's something to consider. But anyway, we have to work on the interview. You can remember the possibilities of Nix's doing something with the staff, but what is he going to say to Lou right now?

LEM: Ask her to make another trial at getting with the group, try talking to one a little in the morning, whenever they meet anywhere.

STEVE: Put her on an office entertainment committee or something that will tie her into the group's activities. Ask her to help out on it. Maybe she would.

SUE: Ask her frankly if she honestly feels the girls are cold-shouldering her or if there is a possibility that there has just been no good reason for her to be absorbed into the group.

INSTRUCTOR: There are some possibilities. Now let's go on with the play. I'd like to see the feminine mind at work on the problem. Sue, you are Mr. Nix. Dora, you are Lou. You are continuing the conversation I interrupted a few minutes ago. Stay within the character sketch on the script I gave you, but you don't have to try to follow the personalities developed by Butch and Andy. Work them up in your own interpretation. Maybe some of the ideas people had will help you work toward a mutually acceptable way of meeting the problem.

NIX: Lou, do you feel that the girls are deliberately shutting you out in spite of sincere efforts on your part to become a member of the group?

LOU: I don't know. I know that in the stockroom everyone was friendly and here no one pays any attention to me.

NIX: Have you asked any of the girls to go have coffee, lunch, or anything with you?

LOU: No, I don't guess so. But it isn't my place to. I was new here. Common courtesy would demand that they try to make any newcomer feel welcome.

NIX: That's so. At the same time, people may watch a newcomer and try to take their cue from what that person seems to want —does she seem to want to become involved in the group's affairs or does she want to be left alone? Have you considered that they might think you were cold-shouldering *them?*

LOU: You're determined to make out that it is my fault, aren't you? Not the fault of your little bunch of girls. Well, if you don't like the way I act toward them, just let me go back to the stockroom. That's all I asked for in the first place.

NIX: Come on now, Lou, you know that what I'm trying to do is keep you here, because I think this is a good job for you and that you can do more for the job than anyone else I could get. I certainly wouldn't want to keep you in my department if I thought you were to blame and couldn't get along. It would be the easiest thing in the world, since I'm personnel director, to just reassign you to the stockroom. No trouble at all. But I want you *here,* and I'm willing to go to some trouble to make things pleasant enough for you that you want to stay here.

LOU: That's nice of you, Mr. Nix. You've been very nice all along. I'm sorry I blew up. If the others were as nice as you . . .

NIX: You've given me an opportunity to be nice to you. Do me one favor, Lou. Stay here for another month. Make an honest effort to be friendly to the girls, to make them like you. If at the end of the month you tell me that it's no go, I'll get you transferred back to the stockroom. O.K.?

LOU: Well . . . I guess it's the best I can do, if you don't want to transfer me now.

NIX: Lou, grudging agreement won't do. I'm asking a favor. Will you make an honest effort to work up a companionship with the girls?

LOU: Yes, I will, Mr. Nix. It's nice to have someone interested enough in you to want you to stay somewhere. I hope that I can.

NIX: Good, Lou. I'll be pulling for you . . . and for my department!

INSTRUCTOR: Well, that seems to be a natural ending place. Dora, why did you blow up at Nix?

DORA: Lou felt that she was being pushed around, that everybody was being taken care of except her.

INSTRUCTOR: Sue, why didn't Nix get mad and blow up right back at her?

SUE: It was pretty obvious what was the matter with her. I did feel that I . . . I mean Nix . . . wanted to throw up his hands in disgust, but he knew it would only be cutting off his nose to spite his face. His job was to keep a productive worker on her job.

BUTCH: Was anything settled? I mean will this take care of the situation?

INSTRUCTOR: What does someone think?

ED: Sue and I were supposed to be studying that, and since she took a role, I guess I'm left. I wouldn't say it *settled* anything, but it gave things a chance to get settled. I mean, it looks like Lou will try to be friendly with the other girls. I guess Nix would try to drop a word here and there to some of the girls he knows best. The chances are that the girls have nothing against Lou, but just haven't thought she was interested in going around with them.

INSTRUCTOR: What makes you think that?

ED: Well, she never claimed that they had shut her out, as far as I remember. She just indicated that they hadn't drawn her in, and it seemed pretty obvious that she hadn't given them any encouragement to try to draw her in.

INSTRUCTOR: What do you think of the personal appeal approach Nix took?

BUTCH: I'm not sure it was in character with Nix, as I understood him. But it seemed to work. Would Nix have done that?

SUE: He *did* do it! You know what I mean . . . but if there had been another Nix, he might have handled it another way.

INSTRUCTOR: Let's see how else it could have developed. You who have not taken a role yet, divide up and take parts of Nix and Lou, and you who have had roles listen and see how else the interview might have developed. We'll have each group report to the other on what happened. I'll drift from one to the other. You two who are not acting, in each group, see what you can dig out about why the interviews develop differently from the ones we have just had. See what makes the difference. They'll certainly be different, because different people are playing and interpreting the roles. I want to identify the key to the differences. Go ahead, decide your exact roles among yourselves.

If the instructor desires, each group may be asked to analyze its play for the benefit of the other groups. Everyone will be motivated, and the repetition may aid comprehension. Obviously, as many play-throughs as desired can be conducted, varying approaches, roles, or attitudes, depending on the degree of practice the instructor wants each trainee to receive. A good policy, although it calls for more work on the part of the instructor, is to design several situations to practice on, rather than working on one situation until everyone is burned out on it. This variety approach can be overdone; it benefits a group relatively little to play through a situation, give a perfunctory analysis of it, and dash on to another situation for an equally superficial treatment. Painstaking analysis and a play-through arrangement giving every trainee an opportunity to develop some approach, principle, or observer's skill on every situation are probably desirable. It is not until the fourth or fifth play-through that lack of interest sets in if the program is well handled. Knowing when to terminate an episode, an analysis, and replays is one of the instructor's skills which will determine how successful the role-playing method of instruction will be in a given instance.

ANALYZE THE EPISODE

This is the point where the skill of the instructor really determines whether the role-playing episode will produce valuable understandings and skills in the trainees or whether it will be merely an amusing little caper from which some people might pick up some ideas. If he asks questions and makes comments which direct attention to crucial elements in the episode and which stimulate mental reaction about the implications of those elements, no other method can approach role-playing as a technique for developing human-relations skills and understandings.

Analysis of a role-playing episode is too complex and judgment-involved a process to be reducible to a pat formula. After all possible guidance is given, it still depends on the instructor's insight, professional knowledge, acuity of observation, and skill in drawing people out. However, there are a few requirements which should probably be met in every analysis. These are minimums—maximums are determined and limited only by the resourcefulness of the instructor and his skill in extracting the most learning possible from each individual situation. But at the least, these points should be covered.

What Happened? Did people reach an understanding? Was the problem solved, or was a temporary solution reached? What went on in the episode? What was the status of affairs at the end? It should be borne in mind that the value of a role-playing episode has no relation to whether or not a solution was reached. Indeed, much of the potential value of role-playing will be lost if trainees feel that they must end all episodes with some sort of agreement. In real life, discussions do not always end in agreement, and to expect role-playing episodes to do so is to expect them to be unrealistic.

Why Did It Happen This Way? Whether or not an agreement or solution was reached, the analysis should probe for the reasons for it. What made the agreement possible? Would this agreement factor have occurred in real life? How can a trainee encourage the occurrence of such agreement factors in real-life situations? If a mutually acceptable conclusion was not reached in the episode, why was it not? What got in the way? How could it have been avoided? Circumvented? Overcome? In short, why did it turn out as it did, and what could have been done about the reasons?

What Were the Motives and Feelings Involved? Any human-relations situation is influenced, if not dominated, by the emotional side of people as contrasted to their intellectual side. One of the valuable things about role-playing as a method of teaching is that it clearly brings out the fact that in human-relations situations people's feelings get into the act quite as much as their minds. So in the analysis give this important factor its full due. Have observers watch for indications of feelings helping or hindering cooperation. Analyze the characters and how they played their roles, and try to determine what these feelings were, where they came from, how they affected the progress of the discussion, and how they could have been accentuated or diminished.

Every person in a serious conversation has in the back of his mind many things which he does not bring into the open. The man debating whether to buy an insurance policy is mentally weighing his desire for a new car against the cost of the policy, his wife's attitude about it, whether it will affect his credit rating, his personal feeling about the underwriter who is talking to him, and his desire to terminate the interview and get on with the job he was doing in his shop. He doesn't *say* these things, but they influence whether he buys the policy. The acute salesman comes to sense some of these hidden agenda or unseen rivals and allows for them in his sales plan. Role-playing episodes are excellent devices for making people conscious of the covert, unadmitted motives with which they have to deal. This can best be done by the instructor's cultivating an acute sensitivity to feelings mani- fested by players and by comments and questions leading trainees to an intense consciousness of the feelings and motives suggested by the words and actions of players.

What Variations Would Have Produced Other Results? This element of analysis is basically to stimulate trainees to use their powers of observation and interpretation to find alternate ways of handling a situation. It is imagination applied to human-relations situations. Its keynotes are such questions as, "What other way could Mr. Nix have . . . ?" "What would have happened if Lou had . . . instead of . . . ?" The answers to such questions sug- gest variations in the episode which can be made the basis of replays. It makes trainees conscious that every human-relations situation is a living, changing thing, presenting an infinite number of possible courses of action every instant. It keeps them from getting into a rut, from settling on one pet way of handling situa- tions and sticking to it, regardless of the superior potential of other methods in various situations. It is a fine last step in analysis because it leads naturally to the instructor's saying, "Let's play it over again, with you two handling it this way, you two this way, and then meet again to see what happened when you followed these paths."

EVALUATE, SUMMARIZE, AND DISCUSS THE EPISODE

The final step in any episode should ordinarily be looking at it as a whole and determining what can be concluded or surmised from it. This makes sure trainees comprehend the significance of what they have heard and seen. The instructor can lead off by saying, "What can we conclude from the play-throughs we have just done?" It is the wrap-up, the synthesis, of the lesson.

In the episode of the personnel director and Lou, the evaluation might bring out facts and ideas such as:

> A job that seems better to one person may not seem better to another.
>
> Things other than amount of pay influence a person's willingness to stay on a job.
>
> A supervisor needs to keep in close contact with the unofficial interpersonal relations among the people who work for him.
>
> To get anywhere in persuading a person, you've got to try to see his point of view and appeal to the things which are important to him, rather than the things *you* want.
>
> Showing the employee you are primarily interested in keeping him on the job, not fixing blame on him, can pave the way for solving supervisory problems.
>
> Things not on the surface sometimes are the real determiners of how a person reacts. Maybe we never found what Lou's *real* motive was in wanting to change.
>
> Perhaps we would have got further if Mr. Nix had worked harder to find out more about Lou, what she was like, what she wanted out of life, how she spent her free time. We worked too much on superficialities, just arguing over surface symptoms without hunting real causes.

The instructor can use this evaluation period as a valuable training device for himself. If he cultivates a free, frank attitude of analysis and discussion among the trainees, he can find ways of polishing his techniques in composing, directing, and analyzing role-playing episodes in every evaluation. He can rapidly acquire skill and facility in making the episodes educational devices by adding to his own ideas the ideas and observations of all his trainees after each session.

At first glance, the role-playing technique of instruction appears deceptively simple and to impose minimal demands on the instructor. On closer inspection, it is seen to require an extraordinary amount of skill, finesse, and acuity of observation and analysis. Extensive exploitation of the evaluation step is the instructor's best means of developing these skills and insights on the job.

SUMMARY

Some jobs require a high degree of skill in human relations. Role-playing is an outstandingly effective method of instruction where learning outcomes such as skill in human relations, insights into human behavior, and sensitivity to interpersonal contacts are desired. To realize its maximum effectiveness as an instructional method, a role-playing episode has to be carefully planned and conducted. Basic steps in securing most learning from a role-playing episode are as follows:

1. Determine the objective of the episode.
2. Structure a situation to achieve that objective.
3. Establish roles and select participants.
4. Prepare the audience and participants for the episode.
5. Play the situation.
6. Analyze the episode.
7. Evaluate, summarize, and discuss the episode.

Wise use of the evaluation step can help an instructor increase his skill and proficiency in using role-playing as an instructional method.

SUGGESTED READINGS

Buxton, C. E.: *College Teaching: A Psychologist's View*, Harcourt, Brace and Company, Inc., New York, 1956.

Carter, M. D., and L. Schryver: "Human Relations—Best Public Relations," *Library Journal*, vol. 83, pp. 129–132, January 15, 1958.

Klein, A. F.: *Role-playing in Leadership Training and Group Problem-solving*, Association Press, New York, 1956.

9

A System for Conducting Instruction

This chapter gives a rationale, or philosophy, of instruction. It is based on the premise that the purpose of instruction is to help people learn, and therefore instruction should help trainees achieve the factors influencing learning. To fit the particular requirements of each instructional situation faced, careful blending of the ingredients of other chapters best achieves the effects discussed in this chapter.

IN THE LAST ANALYSIS, most periods of instruction are likely to involve combinations of methods, rather than solely lecture, group discussion, or demonstration. In most instances, then, an instructor is faced with a more complex task than merely performing a demonstration or lecturing for three-quarters of an hour. Even when one method is principally depended on for a period, it must never be forgotten that the purpose of the period is to produce a learning outcome, not to cover a subject or to give a performance. For this reason, teaching is a profession, not a technique. It is too complex in its procedures and objectives, and depends too much on achieving a good balance among diverse considerations and influences to be done effectively by mastering a few narrow skills and following a formula. Nevertheless, a system for conducting instruction *is* a convenient thing to have, especially for one who is attempting a relatively new project.

Master cooks do not depend heavily on recipes—minute differences in the strengths of different batches of seasonings, atmospheric conditions, the nature of the occasion on which the dish is to be consumed—all these things make the great chef prefer to depend on his art and genius rather than a set formula to produce the best food possible. But a novice will find a recipe a mighty handy thing to have while developing the intuitions and subtle skills which go beyond the mechanics of a formula. So it is with teaching. A master teacher will blend methods and techniques to fit a particular classroom situation better than any set scheme for instruction will do, but a beginner may need a teaching formula.

Good instruction is partly an art and partly a science. Partly it depends on the personality, flair, and delicate nuances of understanding of the instructor; partly it depends on systematically carrying out well-defined workmanlike procedures, so that trainees' minds come in contact with the material and effective learning is likely to take place. Fortunately for the effectiveness of training programs, there *is* a well-defined plan for instruction which, if followed, will permit even instructors with a minimum of experience to conduct periods of instruction in a professional, competent manner and be reasonably assured of achieving solid, substantial student learning as a result of their efforts. This method has been used by good instructors in an intuitive form ever since teaching has existed, but has seldom been spelled out in systematic steps for a beginning instructor to follow. You will recall that Chapter 3 dealt with the psychological effects which an instructor must achieve in his trainees in order for his instruction to produce effective learning. This chapter presents a step-by-step procedure, which is adaptable to all instructional methods, for producing the psychological conditions which, in turn, produce learning.

Whether you use group discussion, lectures, demonstrations, or just assign reading material which you want to be sure your trainees will learn, try this system of instructing. It not only will multiply the chances of your trainees' learning effectively but it will also help you to develop swiftly and efficiently the feel of instructing. The steps described are a system for conducting instruction. If you follow this system intelligently, you are virtually guaranteed, if not a superb period or one wildly popular, at the least a period which will impel your trainees to learn and to *know* that they are learning.

Preview

Motion picture houses show previews of coming attractions to awaken audience interest in the pictures. People working jigsaw puzzles begin by looking at the over-all picture formed by the pieces they will be working with, so that they will have a better idea of how they fit together.

Similarly, previewing can contribute to two of the psychological factors involved in learning—motivation and organization. You should exploit this fact to the utmost in your instructing. When you assign your trainees something to read or do as preparation for a period or a job, give them a little preview of what the assignment is about. You may have a chart outlining the steps or principal points of the assignment. You may tell them what to look for and why to look for it. This use of the preview step gives you a head start in instructing by getting your trainees started on the path you want them to follow even before the period begins.

When your class period begins, give a short preview of what you intend to cover, do, and accomplish. Even if there was a previewed assignment in preparation for the period, it is a good idea to preview just what you are going to do during the period because what you want to accomplish during the period will seldom be exactly the same thing you wanted class members to get from their assignment. And your trainees will learn a lot more and learn it better if they know exactly what they are expected to learn. They will be more interested in the material you cover when they know what it is for and what it is all adding up to, and they can learn it better by knowing in advance what pattern it *should be* adding up to. Previewing gives them organization and both the interest and the objective components of motivation.

In conducting your preview of a period, and especially in explaining what the objective of the period is, remember that in the last analysis the objective consists in getting the trainee to do his job better. This improved performance is achieved by developing *skills, knowledges,* or *attitudes.* The attitude aspect must usually be taught indirectly, but it is wise to identify for your trainees exactly the ability to do, the skill or knowledge, that they are expected to gain during the period. Keep their eyes fixed on the exact goal, *improving their ability to do their jobs,* all the time. In the preview step, you can set their sights on it; then watch to see that they keep that goal uppermost in their minds throughout each period.

Yes, previewing will pay off in your instruction, but only if it is done well. You may have heard an instructor at the beginning of his period rattle off something like, "Thisperiodwearegoingtotake upthefourstepsinapproachingacustomergreetingestablishing, etc." And then he goes into his instruction under the impression that he has previewed the period. This is no more a preview than a patent medicine salesman's description of his product is a laboratory-tested analysis of its benefits. It is not a preview, because it does not give the audience a clear picture of what is coming.

To have given a real preview of the period, the instructor just quoted would have said something like this:

This period you are going to develop an understanding of and skill in carrying out the four steps in starting your sales talk to a customer. You have all heard that first impressions are lasting. The customer gets his first impression of you from your approach. The first step in your approach, of course, is greeting him, saying "hello" or however you speak to a person you meet.

But there are some other steps in approaching a customer, too, before getting right down to talking about his buying your product, and we are going to discuss those additional steps, too. The second step we call "establishing rapport." This means getting acquainted, telling him who you are and what you are there for. After he knows *you*, you introduce him to the product you are selling and, when he has a clear idea of what it is, you "establish a need," that is, you show him how your product can be valuable to him.

These four steps flow one into the other as naturally as any kind of conversation. You greet a person, introduce yourself, tell him your business, and explain how you can fill a need he has. For the sake of convenience we will discuss them separately first, and toward the end of the period talk about how to move from one stage to the other. Now, starting with the first step, the greeting . . .

That is a real preview. A group of trainees introduced to a subject in this manner—whether a reading assignment, lecture, demonstration, or discussion is to follow—will be better motivated and better able to arrange the ideas in their minds in orderly fashion. A real preview takes time and trouble to prepare, and time to present to the class, but it is well worth that time and work.

In addition to previewing assignments and periods of instruction for your trainees, you will be materially contributing to their education if you teach them to preview all material they study. The time spent in leafing through the pages of an assignment, glancing at each paragraph just enough to get the drift of the assignment as a whole, can contribute as much to the amount learned as three times that much time spent in reading the assignment. Try it yourself. The next time you start to study a chapter or article, preview it first. You will often find that you get half as much again out of your reading as a result of the two or three minutes spent in previewing the material.

Question

We have already mentioned that looking for the answers to questions can help to increase concentration on material being studied. The instructor can turn this fact to advantage. Trainees who have in mind questions about material and are looking for answers to these questions listen and observe more closely and with greater concentration than they are likely to do otherwise.

So, following the preview portion of your period, ask your trainees, "What are some of the questions you think should be answered in a period (or assignment) such as the one I just outlined?" Try hard to induce them to think—it *does* take thinking to produce intelligent questions about a subject. Repeat a little of what you said in a preview, if necessary, to give them time to think of some sensible, pertinent questions about the subject. You may find it helpful to pose a couple as illustrations of what you have in mind. You may find it impossible to get your trainees to produce good questions the first time or two you try, so have a good assortment tucked away in your mind to offer as substitutes if they do not suggest enough. Tell them that they should watch for the answers to these questions during the period. (In addition, the questions can be worded so as to keep the over-all objective, better job performance, uppermost in their minds.)

The chances are that the questions you get from your trainees will not be questions of narrow fact, such as, "Is it better to say 'Hello' or 'How do you do' when you greet a customer?" They are more likely to be questions like, "Where do you draw the line between being friendly and being too familiar in greeting a customer?" This latter type of question is better for your purposes. When you formulate your questions be sure that they are of such a nature that they are not answered in so many words during the period, but that the answers have to be fitted together from the general ideas brought out. This will insure that trainees do not merely concentrate on watching for a few key words to give them the answers, but have to sort out and mentally digest all the material to get the necessary information to figure out answers.

We have frequently referred to the necessity of trainees' mentally reacting to things they see, hear, or read if they are to learn from them. Well-directed questions virtually guarantee mental activity of the highest sort, first in thinking up logical questions and second in figuring out the answers to them. Following this step faithfully takes a little of the class time, just as does carrying out the preview step, but it is time well spent, since it gives your trainees a challenge to keep them busy in purposeful mental activity throughout the period. If you have to provide the questions the first time or two, start a systematic program to elicit questions from the class members. Before starting your preview, announce that you will call on individuals for pertinent questions after the preview. Put the pressure on for trainees to think, to anticipate what the important ideas are that they might get from the period. Both they and your training program will profit in better attention and better learning.

This question technique can be used to good advantage in making assignments, too. While making the assignment, you can ask trainees to formulate questions whose answers they will watch for as they study. It is certain that if they learn to formulate such questions about their assignments, they will study with greater concentration and perception.

Remember four points in going through the *question* step of this system for teaching. First, try to get your trainees to formulate the questions. Second, if you do not get enough questions from them, have a few of your own to give them as examples, as well as guidance in studying. Third, keep insisting that they produce good questions, even to the point of announcing that individuals will be called on for questions (and calling on them) if necessary. Fourth, by example and guidance steer them into general questions which require thought and reasoning to answer, not questions of fact which may be answered by catching a few key words.

Relate

This is the body of your class period. It is the lecture, the discussion, the demonstration, or the role-playing episode discussed in a previous chapter of this book. It will be more effective, whatever it is, if you have prepared your trainees for it by judicious use of the preview and question steps. Whether you relate your material by demonstration, by lecture, or by getting your trainees to say it themselves, they will get more out of it as a result of the five minutes or so it required you to do the first two steps. Since most of the other chapters of the book are about the different ways of performing this step of relating, or telling, your material to your class, we shall not discuss it further here, but shall go on to the other steps in this plan for teaching.

State

This is really a return to the old study-and-recite method of teaching. There has never been a method that worked better as a device for getting pupils (or trainees) to learn and retain what they read, saw, or heard.

So, plan your instruction to leave time at the end of the period or the end of each topic in the period to ask your trainees questions about what has just been said or done. Call on people by name and ask them to state in their own words the substance of what was said about various topics covered in the period or the assignment. If a trainee knows that he is likely to be asked later in the period to state the substance of what was said, what was done if it was a demonstration, what was covered if it was a discussion, or what happened if it was a role-playing episode, he is apt to work pretty hard at comprehending and organizing the material covered in the period.

In some respects, asking a trainee to state, or summarize, what was said about a topic (teachers sometimes call it asking him to "discuss" the topic) puts him to a more severe test than asking him more specific questions. Both require him to recall what was said or done in the period or assignment, but stating or discussing a topic requires, in addition, that he have the material well enough assimilated to be able to reproduce the essential thought in his own words. It requires that he have mentally organized and comprehended the material as well as remembered it. More specific questions can be used to explore specific points which are not adequately covered in the trainees' discussion. They can also be used to probe an area covered when a trainee appeared to be inattentive.

Thinking through material to the point of being able to state it is the very finest kind of learning activity. It is so good that it would be a fine idea to ask every trainee to state his impression of each topic covered in each period or assignment. This idea is seldom practical, but it can be fairly well approximated when you are teaching a subject especially important for everyone to think through well. Say, "In a minute I am going to ask someone to tell me the substance of what we have discussed in the area of introducing your product to the customer. I want everyone to think it over and be ready, and I'll call on someone in a minute." You can depend on it, *that minute of thinking will be the most learning-producing minute in the entire period.*

It takes some ingenuity to capitalize fully on the state step when manual skills are being taught. Ask a trainee to explain why another did a job in a certain way. The thinking he must do to answer your question will promote his comprehension of the point at issue. Ask another to describe how he would have done it. Remember the technique of asking the question and giving the class a minute's time for thought before calling on someone to answer it. Judicious use of this technique can multiply a dozen times over the value of your question-recitation aspect of teaching.

As an instructor, you are responsible for seeing that your trainees leave each class period with a clear, coherent, and reasonably comprehensive concept of the material studied that day, so arranged in their minds that it will increase their ability to do their jobs. Therefore, note the answers given by students not only to grade them, but also to supplement, correct, or amplify the answers as may be necessary to cover the topic adequately. You may wish to do this by calling on someone else when one trainee's coverage of a subject is incomplete, or you may prefer to do it yourself. (A good rule of thumb is to call on another if the answer was conspicuously unsatisfactory, and do it yourself if the answer was reasonably good and only needed a little polishing up. Just be sure the question is well answered before you move on, to insure that trainees were not left with faulty or incomplete concepts in place of an accurate picture of the subject reviewed.)

Test

Material covered one day and never referred to again will be forgotten or neglected much more than it would if reviews had carried the members of the class over it a couple of times at intervals after it was originally studied. The reviewing that trainees will customarily do in preparation for an announced test is a cogent reason for having tests and for announcing them in advance. However, an instructor can achieve the review benefits of a written test without the actual written test. Divide your class period into two parts—today's lesson and a review (remember the repetition factor in learning?) of the lesson of exactly a week ago. Allow ten minutes or so for this review. Conduct it just as you do the *state* step of instruction: that is, ask a question on the lesson of a week ago, pause to let everyone try to remember it, then call on someone to answer it, and supplement the answer with such explanations as you think necessary to give the class a well-rounded review of the subject. If you do this consistently, you will spend exactly the same amount of time on each assignment, but the time will be divided between an original study period and a review period a week later. This is likely to result in better retention of material than would a single going-over.

It would be unbearably repetitious to divide each chapter of this book which deals with an instructional method into five parts and discuss the lecture method as a device for carrying the class through the *preview, question, relate, state,* and *test* steps, then do the same for the group discussion method, and so on. The *preview, question, relate, state, test* method achieved its wide usage down through the centuries (not under those exact titles, of course, but in so far as the essential substance of the method is

TABLE 2. INSTRUCTOR'S APPLICATION OF PQRST TECHNIQUE FOR TEACHING
TO DIFFERENT INSTRUCTIONAL METHODS

Step	Lecture	Demonstration-performance (manual skills)	Role-playing (human-relations skills)	Group discussion
Preview	Outlines material to be covered in lecture	Explains what the demonstration-performance is to include and what is to be learned from it	Explains what roles the participants are to play and expected learning outcomes	Outlines agenda and objective of discussion
Question ...	Poses important questions to be answered in lecture	Identifies key things to watch for in demonstration	Suggests elements which are crucial in situations such as one to be demonstrated	Identifies questions to be answered
Relate	Gives lecture	Performs demonstration or has it conducted	Has participants present the demonstration	Conducts discussion
State	Has trainees give gist of what was said on various topics	Has trainees summarize what was done, identifying crucial elements and performing the operation	Has trainees analyze what happened, interpreting the significance	Has trainee summarize result of discussion
Test	Reviews lecture later by abridged run-through of state step	Has trainee later explain or demonstrate operation	Has trainees later recall and interpret important elements of demonstration	Conducts follow-up discussion or gives hand-out

167

concerned) because it is both an effective method and an easy, natural one to use. You can adapt it to your instructional method and situation easily *if you consciously try to do so,* but do not depend on chance to cover all the five elements of the method. You will omit one or more if you do, and the period when an element is omitted will not produce the maximum learning possible in your class.

Examination of the Sample Lesson Plan in Chapter 4 will reveal the presence of all five of these steps: The instructor begins the period with an explanation of what the period will cover; he raises questions in trainees' minds, giving them something to watch for; he explains each element of people's psychological needs; he asks trainees to interpret and apply these needs to actual situations they have encountered on their jobs; finally, he leaves time at the end to review the lesson of a week ago. In the process of covering these five steps he insures thorough coverage of all six of the psychological factors affecting learning, and keeps his instruction sharply pointed toward the over-all objective of skills, knowledges, and attitudes which will result in better performance of jobs.

Table 2 outlines the four principal instructional methods, following the PQRST technique for teaching. Each lesson plan you prepare should include provision for each of these factors; this is as good insurance of an effective learning period as you can devise for yourself.

SUMMARY

Regardless of the specific instructional technique you may use in a period, you can follow this system to insure that you are carrying your trainees through the steps that lead to most effective learning.

This plan provides for:

Preview of the period, so that trainees can know what the general plan of the lesson will be

Questions to give the group specific points to watch for, helping them stay alert

Relating (or having related or demonstrated) the topic to be covered

Stating or summarizing the material covered, in trainees' own words, with the mental reaction required for each of them to compose his best answer to each question

Testing trainees' memory of the lesson of a week ago, to provide review and refreshing of memory

Following this plan will carry trainees through the psychological factors producing learning and help you keep the period focused on knowledges, skills, and attitudes which will enable them to do their jobs better.

10

Instructional Aids

*Properly used, instructional aids can increase the amount
of trainee learning from a period of instruction and speed
up the whole training process. Improperly used, they can
give a wrong slant to a subject and seriously interfere with
trainees' getting the learning outcomes desired from a lesson. This chapter explains how instructional aids can be
used to best advantage, common types of instructional
aids and the special merits and limitations of each, and
principles for using instructional aids.*

TRY DESCRIBING THE FLOOR PLAN of a house to someone, then asking him to draw the plan from your verbal description. Try following a route through a strange city from oral directions and the
same route from a road map. Try putting a disassembled piece of
machinery together from written instructions, without looking at
the illustrations included in the directions.

These three exercises illustrate how much easier it is to understand, learn, or do certain things when visual aids supplement
words of direction. Instructional aids which will make the descriptions and instructions clearer may involve only the simplest sort
of visual supplement to verbal directions—a diagram, the penciled
tracing of a route, or a few simple pictures or sketches. Remember
how frequently you reach for a pencil and piece of paper when
trying to explain something to someone in ordinary conversation.
With a few strokes, even though you are not an artist or drafts-
man, you halve the time of explanations and double the under-

standing they produce. Sometimes you do not even use a pencil. Suppose you are going to describe, to a person who has never seen the instrument, a man playing an accordion. Almost without thinking, you begin to use your hands, showing the motions he goes through, with an auditory accompaniment of words telling what the gestures mean. And you have an audio-visual aid which carries a message simultaneously to the eyes and ears of the person you address.

The common term "instructional aids" can apply to written materials as well as to films, records, pictures, and the like, but for purposes of this chapter we shall limit it to basically nonverbal aids. This omits written materials and concentrates on aids which clarify, illustrate, or interpret words, rather than on those which present words in different forms.

Visual aids are commonly classified on either of two bases: the way the aid is *presented* (slide, transparency, film, flip-stand, opaque projection, etc.) or the way it is *represented* (picture, drawing, chart, diagram, etc.). In this chapter, we shall first discuss the different ways of *presenting* aids and then consider the ways of *representing* them in connection with the discussion of principles of using instructional aids.

Presenting Instructional Aids

BLACKBOARD

If only one method of presenting instructional aids could be selected, most experienced instructors probably would choose the blackboard. Any time a wiring diagram needs clarifying, any time a chain of associations between what a supervisor does for his subordinates and superiors is to be compared, any time the general formation of a machine or a specific piece of it is to be learned, the instructor can seize a piece of chalk and produce his visual aid to the accompaniment of clarifying explanations. His products may not be pretty, but produced on the spot, with explanations as he draws the lines, they have a teaching value hard to duplicate in ready-made aids. Their very crudity often is an advantage, because it emphasizes the exact points the instructor wants attention called to, and does not distract from the main idea by containing unneeded details or elements other than the point being studied.

So do not hesitate to use the blackboard just because you cannot draw. And do not waste time and effort trying for artistic accuracy. For purposes of illustrating a lecture on calisthenics, a stick figure is a better picture of a squatting man than something from the Louvre. The escapement of an alarm clock, if you explain it as you draw it, is perfectly understandable in the form shown.

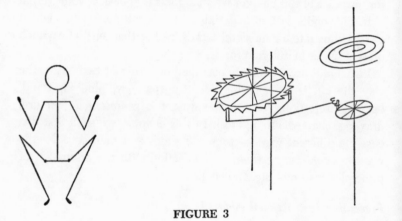

FIGURE 3

It is not artistic, but it graphically illustrates that this is not the sort of mechanism on which to use a screwdriver. Anyone can make such drawings and, made before trainees' eyes, they have a special punch. So use the blackboard any time you can think of a way a drawing could help your class to see what you are trying to put across. It will hold interest as well as clarify your explanations and make your instruction more effective.

SLIDES

A photographic negative reduced to a size of about 2¼ by 3 inches and mounted between two glass plates about 3¼ by 4, the plates being bound together at the edges by masking tape, makes a slide suitable for projecting a photograph onto a screen. Such slides have the advantage of being adaptable: they can be used with an audience, a room, or a screen of any size, and they do not require extreme darkness. They do require fairly expensive equipment to project and considerable time to prepare. They are worth the trouble if you are going to use them a number of times, under conditions that vary from time to time, and where you would like to leave enough light in the room for people to take notes. These slides will show up well on any screen or, in a pinch, on an ordinary wall.

Slides also come in the convenient 35mm size. These are much lighter, easier to carry, and project from cheaper and lighter-weight equipment than the larger slides. They are not quite as well adapted to large rooms and audiences, and the reproduction on the screen is not likely to be so clear unless you sacrifice cheapness and lightness in your projector and get a really fine machine. They are very fine if you are going to have to carry your projection equipment around yourself.

FLIP-STANDS

Where it is advisable to have full light in the room and for the instructor to be in full control of his instructional aids, the use of pictures, charts, or diagrams is often best. Where only a single aid is to be used during a period, it can be mounted on a wall. Where several are to be used, it is convenient to fasten them together at the top and mount them on a stand so that they can be turned back as used and new ones revealed.

MODELS

Scale reproductions of machines or devices being studied are the ultimate in bringing reality into the classroom. Small articles can be enlarged so as to be easily visible by more people. Parts can be made in different colors to reflect their functions or relationships. Details not pertinent to the matter being studied can be omitted, although this treatment can result in oversimplification which may confuse trainees when they face the greater complexity of the real object.

FILMS AND FILMSTRIPS

A filmstrip is a film which does not portray motion. It is a series of still pictures which are shifted from frame to frame as the instructor desires. Like films, some filmstrips are accompanied by recorded sound. Usually a training film must be produced by a professional, at considerable expense. Therefore, except in the case of large organizations, training films are rented from companies specializing in their production or distribution.

Filmstrips can often be produced by amateurs, using relatively inexpensive equipment. Such strips possess the advantage of being tailored to the exact situation and needs of the company rather than trying to illustrate a subject in a manner which will more or less fit a great many situations. Films and filmstrips commonly come in 16mm and 35mm sizes. The larger size is, of course, more expensive. However, for use in training programs the greater versatility and durability of the larger size may justify the greater cost.

Films and filmstrips are the instructional aids most useful in teaching most human-relations skills, such as salesmanship, supervision, and conference procedure. They are also, in the long run, often the least expensive way of teaching manual skills and processes. They are least useful when material to be taught is of an abstract or idea type, such as bookkeeping procedures, basic science and electricity, or logic and reasoning.

TRANSPARENCIES IN OVERHEAD PROJECTORS

One of the most convenient and practical instructional aids combines many of the advantages of the blackboard and the slide. On clear sheets of plastic the instructor (or an artist, if desired) sketches the pictures or diagrams to be used as aids. A light shining from below throws these lines on a screen, giving the vividness of a slide and the convenience of preparation of a blackboard illustration. Transparencies are usually about 5 by 5 inches and are drawn with wax pencil or special inks. The sheets can be cleaned and used again. Next to the blackboard, they permit greatest flexibility to the instructor in their preparation and use. Their chief disadvantage is that they require greater darkness for clear projection than do slides. Also, whereas the instructor can be reasonably sure of finding a slide projector if he goes to another plant or city to give a period of instruction, he is not so likely to find a transparency projector.

OPAQUE PROJECTOR

Did you ever wish you could project a picture from a book or magazine directly on the screen, without having it redrawn, a picture made of it, or a slide prepared? You can with the opaque projector. Just put the page in the machine, and it is reproduced on the screen. To make the image clear, the room has to be considerably darker than with other types of training aids, and you will probably have to cut the page out and mount it on cardboard or heavy paper for a really fine image. But the opaque projector is about the ultimate in convenience as far as preparation of materials is concerned. Its peculiar limitations make it advisable to test it thoroughly under the conditions in which you would be using it before you buy, but if it meets your needs, it can be very useful. As an example, if you are teaching a course in which trainees are required to complete a work sheet on bookkeeping, fill in a sales slip, produce a wiring diagram, or do similar paper work, you can put trainees' papers in the machine, flash them on the screen and use the actual work of trainees as material to illustrate your points.

FLASH CARDS

If your class is small and if you dislike sketching words or pictures on the blackboard in front of everyone, flash cards may be good visual aids for you. As the name implies, they are merely cards of whatever size you want to use, with the words, diagrams, or pictures you want drawn or printed on them. You can have a number of such cards on your lectern, picking each up and flashing it before the class as you need it. If you will cover the face of the card with a sheet of transparent plastic, you can supplement the basic sketch on it by marking on it with a grease pencil as you talk or demonstrate, just as you would on a blackboard. Later you can remove the plastic or wash it off, leaving your basic sketch uninjured.

FLANNEL BOARDS, MAGNETIC BOARDS, AND CORK BOARDS

These devices are really display stands for flash cards, charts, etc., rather than aids themselves. By mounting a piece of rough-nap flannel on the wall or on a board and fastening a strip of coarse sandpaper to the back of a light card or paper, you can fasten your card up in front of the class merely by pressing it against the flannel. A magnetic board consists of a sheet of metal on a stand or attached to the wall. To use it, put your card against the board and place a small magnet against the card, which is held in place by the attraction between the magnet and the sheet of metal. A cork board is a piece of beaverboard, insulating board, or other soft substance to which display materials are fastened with thumbtacks. If you procure tacks with "handles" or finger holds on top, a cork board is as convenient and versatile a display stand as can be had.

TELEVISION

Television is basically an adaptation of film, as far as its use in training programs is concerned. It permits the use of live demonstrations, whereas films are necessarily "canned" records. Thus, it permits more flexibility in use than films do. However, adequate projection and reception equipment for using television in training programs is expensive and usually requires a considerable technical staff to support. It is too complex to be discussed in any detail in this book, especially in view of the relatively small percentage of training programs where the expense and staff required would be justified.

Guides in Using Training Aids

Basically, instructional aids are supplemental devices to assist instructors in producing the psychological causes of learning in their trainees. This is always the principal criterion of whether or not an instructional aid should be used: Will it promote desirable *motivation, concentration, reaction, organization, comprehension,* or *repetition?*

Here are some specific techniques and principles to follow in designing and using instructional aids. (One or more causes of learning which the principle or technique may promote are listed at the end of each rule.) An aid should do as many of the following things as possible:

PROMOTE UNDERSTANDING OF THE SUBJECT

Use an instructional aid whenever you are teaching something which can be understood better by being heard about *and* seen than by being heard about only (promoting *comprehension*).

Words are not objects. They are not qualities. They are not relationships. They are not processes. They are simply *symbols* of things, qualities, relationships, and processes. They are abstractions. They require the user or hearer to visualize the things which they represent. Words are not, in short, realities. They are symbols which may stimulate their users to conjure up in their minds the realities which the words *suggest.*

In studying the electrical system of a complicated piece of machinery, words alone may give an imperfect or erroneous picture. They may prove unequal to the task of suggesting reality accurately and completely to the student. A properly designed instructional aid would do the job. This aid might be a diagram of the machine in which the electrical system would be traced in colors. It might take the form of the actual machine, and the trainee would learn by physically touching and feeling the units of the electrical system, as well as by seeing them and hearing words about them. Not only that, but he may also push buttons and make the system work, watch it work, and control its working by manipulating portions of the system. In such a situation, the learner is dealing with reality.

POINT TOWARD EXACT OBJECTIVE

Tailor your instructional aids to achieve *exactly* the objectives of your instruction (*Motivation:* objective).

If instruction is to stand a good chance of being successful, it must be aimed at the student's achievement of definite objectives, and both trainees and instructor must be aware of these objectives and constantly aiming for them. Instructional methods, and therefore instructional aids, must be determined to a great extent by these objectives.

If the object of the instruction on the electrical system of an office machine is to enable a trainee to use that machine, methods would be largely concerned with explaining what each button caused to happen, what each dial indicates, and what to look for and how to interpret it in reading the dials. Instructional aids in this situation might take the form of an actual instrument panel of a machine, plus diagrams showing the portion of the machine operated by each button or represented by each dial, plus *words* explaining the various relationships and their significance.

If the object of the instruction is to prepare a mechanic to service the electrical system of the machine, use of the actual instrument board might not be profitable at the start of the study, and much more elaborate wiring diagrams of the machine might be required.

If the object is to give background information to a group of electrical engineers who are to work on the problem of eliminating electrical "bugs" from a redesigned machine, the present system of dials and buttons on the instrument panel hardly need be mentioned, and the details of the wiring can be subordinated to charts showing the main trunk lines of power, rheostats, and safety devices.

Aids must always be aimed at the specific objectives of instruction and designed in a form which will best achieve the objectives.

STIMULATE INTEREST IN THE MAIN SUBJECT

Remember that instructional aids are tools, and while it is desirable for the tool to be attractive and amusing, it should primarily stimulate interest in the main subject rather than in itself (*Motivation:* objective; *concentration; reaction*).

Instructional methods or aids are not good or bad in themselves, but only in so far as they contribute to the achievement of the specified objectives of instruction or fail to do so. This fact has important implications for the instructor beginning to plan his attack upon a subject. Traditionally, in such a situation the instructor proceeded to break down the subject into what seemed to be a logical group of subpoints, break down each of the subpoints as necessary, accumulate required material on each subpoint, and then cover the subject by presenting a lecture on each of the subpoints. Instructional aids, if any, were incidentally included.

With a wider recognition of the instructional value of audiovisual aids and increasing emphasis on their use, many instructors have fallen into the error of either of two extremes:

1. After having organized their instruction, they look back and think, "Now where can I stick in some instructional aids?" This is better than ignoring instructional aids altogether but leaves much to be desired.

2. Or they get an idea for some instructional aid—a film they want to use, a clever cartoon series they would like to see developed, a system of graphs or charts that is the apple of their eye —and build the instructional program around that idea. This is putting the cart before the horse.

A third course is possible—and recommended. The instructor may determine the over-all objective of his instruction and then analyze it to determine the specific objectives which must be achieved in order to accomplish the general end result desired. Then he may ask himself, "How can I best handle the instruction to achieve each of these specific objectives?" Some objectives may be most readily attainable through lectures, some through group discussions, some through lectures or discussions supplemented and clarified by instructional aids. Occasionally an instructional aid (especially a film) will by itself achieve an objective.

The crucial point is that the aids are neither superimposed extras nor the backbones around which a subject is organized, but are an integrated portion of the treatment of the subject, making their unique contribution to the achievement of the common objective. They may clarify and dramatically portray otherwise abstract ideas. They may reproduce or approach reality, replacing the imperfect symbolism of words. They may simply awaken and amuse or stimulate the interest of an apathetic class. Humorous cartoons, aids stressing sex appeal, and highly imaginative or vividly colored aids are likely to fall into this category. Such use of aids is perfectly permissible, but they must be so closely related to the subject under consideration that their entertainment value does not actually detract from the main subject but rather enhances it.

MAKE AIDS AN INTRINSIC PORTION OF THE INSTRUCTION

Design your training aids to be a natural, intrinsic portion of the sequence of instruction. A good rule of thumb is: "Would achievement of the objective be hampered if I had to do without this aid?" If the answer is "No," the aid requires revision to justify its inclusion (*organization, comprehension*).

Instructors occasionally get the idea that to be good, instruction must have instructional aids. As a result, they decide to work in a few pictures, charts, or graphs somewhere in their instruction. This addition may be good, especially if they have not previously given proper attention to a real possibility of service from training aids while developing the plan of instruction. However, it may also result in the use of aids which have little relation to the real objective of instruction and sometimes even require (so plainly that the class can see it) that the instructor take time out from his subject to work in his aid. This interruption breaks the continuity of the subject, to say the least.

A philosophy governing the use of instructional aids cannot be developed in isolation from the broader concepts of educational philosophy and methodology any more than a set of instructional aids can be developed in isolation from the objectives of instruction. Therefore, effective use of instructional aids requires an understanding of basic principles of learning and instruction such as are found in other chapters of this book. Successful use of this chapter on training aids requires previous assimilation of the ideas and principles of instruction presented in the other chapters.

PROMOTE DESIRABLE LEARNINGS IN TRAINEES

Make your final determination of the nature or use of an aid on the basis of the effect it will have on the trainees, especially the nature and direction of the activity it will stimulate in them (*reaction, comprehension*).

Remember, students do not learn directly as a result of what instructors do, books say, or instructional aids show. They learn only as a result of what the instructors, books, or aids *get them to do*.

You cannot pass this off lightly by saying, "It amounts to the same thing in the end." It may not. The lecture, reading assignment, or instructional aid which seems to the instructor to be most valuable as far as the *subject* is concerned may not be the most valuable as far as stimulating the trainee to *activity* on the subject. Student activity is the keynote of successful teaching and learning. In picking material, methods, or aids, the instructor should not ask himself, "What will bear most closely on the objectives of *my instruction?*" but rather, "What will stimulate most and best direct *student activity* in regard to *their objective?*" Instruction is for P-E-O-P-L-E! (See Chapter 5.)

CLARIFY OBJECTIVE FOR TRAINEES

Use instructional aids to motivate the trainee by clarifying the objective which is being sought or by showing him how achievement of that objective will enhance his effectiveness on the job (*Reaction; concentration; motivation:* need to know; *comprehension*).

Showing a picture of a worker doing what a trainee is being taught to do, showing him taking a procedures manual from a shelf and hunting up the point you are teaching, then showing him returning to his job and doing what he just read how to do can impress trainees with the importance of learning your point. It can be much more convincing than merely telling them they will need this knowledge later to do their jobs. A snapshot of an executive studying a production record held in one hand and a manning chart held in the other can impress a group of foremen with the importance of accurate production records more than any amount of talking about it. A diagram showing the informal flow of information through an organization can point up the importance of a discussion on how to facilitate official communication up and down.

SIMPLIFY COMPLEX INTERRELATIONSHIPS

Use instructional aids to show interrelationships too complex and extensive to be presented verbally, or to show them more clearly than they can be presented verbally (*organization*).

Except in a very small and simple organization, an explanation of the organization will probably be clearer if shown by an organization chart as well as expressed in words. The relation between the thermostat of an automatic choke and the action within the carburetor can be pictured more clearly than it can be described. The shifting relationships of the stockroom, sales department, and accounting office to an electric stove received and later sold by a retail store (illustrating merchandise flow to a group of junior executives, for example) can be kept straighter in everyone's mind if the store is pictured on a chart and tags representing the different departments and their different functions are put on and taken off to the accompaniment of verbal explanations.

REINFORCE POINTS ALREADY MADE

Use instructional aids to drive home points previously made in other ways (*repetition*).

Few things are learned on one exposure so thoroughly that they are not forgotten. Generally, some repetition of a fact, a principle, or an idea is necessary to insure its being remembered. If this repetition can present the same idea in a different form or context, it affords a richer set of associations built around the idea and increases the chances of its being remembered. Also, this type of variation promotes comprehension and application of ideas better than simply presenting the idea over and over in the same form and way. Instructional aids afford an opportunity to repeat an idea to the group with a minimum of monotony and with a maximum of variety in showing the application of the idea.

Some instructors like to list important concepts of their course on cards and display them permanently in the classroom. This has a disadvantage—distraction from other instruction—but certainly provides repetition. A cartoon shown a class after an explanation has been given, representing the point of the explanation in a humorous fashion, provides repetition of the idea described.

Many books have been written giving information about the nature and construction of instructional aids, examples, types, and ways of using them, but no instructional aid is any better than its fit into the objective and method of instruction. This chapter has provided several rules of thumb for guiding the instructor in the use of instructional aids and some suggestions as to the psychological processes of learning which may be helped along by instructional aids. In a very brief form, it has presented a few highlights of instructional principles and practices. This chapter, however, cannot discuss adequately the whole psychology of learning and instruction which the instructor must have if he is to realize the potentialities of aids in improving his instruction.

Therefore, it should be repeated here, the instructor should make no attempt to use instructional aids on the basis of this chapter alone. Accompany study of this chapter by careful study of the earlier portion of the book. Get a clear picture of the real nature of instruction and learning and how learning takes place. Then, in the light of this knowledge, continue to use this chapter as a ready reference to suggest *techniques* which will *supplement* the *professional knowledge* without which the techniques alone would be impotent.

SUMMARY

A multitude of books have been written on how to produce training aids of various sorts, as well as directions for the mechanics of using them. Unfortunately, much less has been written on principles and procedures for their effective use, such as the guides discussed in this chapter.

The following is suggested as a step-by-step procedure for developing training aids which will contribute most to the achievement of the objectives of your instruction and most effectively activate the psychological factors of learning:

1. Prepare your period of instruction as usual.
2. Examine your lesson plan to see whether any learning outcome could be achieved better through supplementing words with audio-visual aids.
3. Upon identifying such an objective, sketch out several aids which would help to achieve it. Settle on the best one you can produce (meaning "best" in terms of helping students master the learning outcome).
4. Ascertain the manner of presentation—chart, slide, transparency, etc.—best adapted to your needs and resources.
5. Produce the aid, or have it produced.
6. Rehearse your presentation and see if the aid really contributes to the clarity, interest, or completeness of your period of instruction. If not, alter it so that it does, or eliminate it.

SUGGESTED READINGS

DALE, E.: *Audio-visual Methods in Teaching,* The Dryden Press, Inc., New York, 1954.

HAAS, K. B., and H. Q. PACKER: *Preparation and Use of Audio-visual Aids,* Prentice-Hall, Inc., Englewood Cliffs, N.J., 1955.

McKOWN, H. C., and A. B. ROBERTS: *Audiovisual Aids to Instruction,* McGraw-Hill Book Company, Inc., New York, 1949.

SANDS, L. B.: *Audio-visual Procedures in Teaching,* The Ronald Press Company, New York, 1956.

WITTICH, W. A., and C. F. SCHULLER: *Audio-visual Materials; Their Nature and Use,* Harper & Brothers, New York, 1957.

11

Preparing a Classroom

This chapter sets forth the conditions and equipment for best instruction in a training program.

IT IS POSSIBLE for effective learning and effective instruction to take place in almost any physical surroundings, but effective learning is most likely to take place in surroundings well selected and well equipped for instructional purposes. This is partly because good instructional facilities make it easier to get the job done, just as good facilities and equipment always help get any job done.

Perhaps even more important is the fact that trainees tend to judge the importance of the training program partly in terms of the prestige of the quarters it occupies. It is hard to get people to take a program seriously if it is obviously stuck away in a corner that no one else would want or have, or conducted here, there, and yonder, wherever some space is available. It is easier to get them to take the program seriously if management attaches enough importance to it to take pains to provide the best possible physical plant. Of course, training programs involving the use of heavy or complex equipment must be conducted where that equipment is, but where the nature of the equipment does not dictate the location of the training program, it is good economy to make the classroom as impressive, convenient, and comfortable as possible. Other things being equal, such a classroom will simply produce more learning in trainees.

Desirable Characteristics of a Classroom

ATTRACTIVENESS

Numerous psychological studies have demonstrated the effect on spirits, enthusiasm, and efficiency of attractiveness of the physical surroundings in which work is to be done. Management consultants have said that the best single, quick check of the efficiency of a plant is the cleanliness of its working space. For best educational results, a classroom needs to be attractively constructed and finished, with furnishings that emphasize the importance attached to the instructional program. Dirty, unpainted, or chipped walls, crude seats, castoff office furniture, an unfinished floor, and sheeted stacks of supplies pushed to the side of the room all mutely testify that the higher-ups are not attaching much real significance to the training program. Board rooms do not look like that! On the other hand, a room appropriately decorated, furnished with careful attention to the physical and mental requirements of education, makes trainees feel that the program is a high-priority portion of their career with the company. (It also subconsciously affects *management's* thinking about the program.)

ILLUMINATION

Plenty of light to do the work without eyestrain, preferably coming from in back and the left of the students, is the traditional ideal of classroom lighting. However, more and more schools are being built with primary dependence on artificial lighting, and the availability of natural light should not be an influential factor in selecting a classroom. Fluorescent lights are generally recommended for classroom use, with well-diffused incandescent bulbs as second choice. Altogether, the general rules for lighting an office where considerable paper work is done amply cover the lighting requirements of a classroom.

Unlike an office, however, a classroom must sometimes be darkened for showing slides, films, and the like, and therefore all outside windows should be provided with heavy, opaque curtains to shut out light when needed. These curtains or draperies should be permanently installed rather than put up and taken down each time they will be needed, because, human nature being what it is, instructional aids requiring a darkened room will be used more nearly whenever they are needed if they can be used with a minimum of work and bother.

QUIET

A classroom should be as free from outside noise as possible. Assuming, of course, that there is no noise so loud as to drown out conversation in the classroom, probably the worst sort of outside noise, as far as instructing and learning are concerned, is the sound of people talking, particularly if words can be distinguished. Such audible conversation distracts both instructor and trainees and makes concentration unnecessarily difficult. Another particularly annoying noise is intermittent noise, which comes and goes, rises and falls, changes in nature, so that it is impossible to become accustomed to it and one must readjust to its changing nature every few minutes. The least objectionable outside noise likely to be present is the steady, unchanging drone of machinery or traffic. Such a noise can be adapted to fairly readily and poses minimum threat to instruction or learning, other than the necessity for speaking a bit more loudly. This can be tolerated, although the quieter the environment of the classroom, generally speaking, the better.

COMFORTABLE TEMPERATURE

A classroom needs to be slightly warmer than working space where people are moving around, if the training course demands much sitting. Temperatures from 68 to 74° are generally considered optimum, although if the higher temperatures are used a low relative humidity, probably in the neighborhood of 15 per cent, is needed. Normal ventilation such as is required in any heavily populated room is adequate, but care should be taken to avoid drafts, for people sitting in relative immobility are vastly more subject to discomfort from slight drafts than are people moving around, turning, or changing position frequently.

Furnishings

TABLES AND CHAIRS

For training programs, tables and chairs will generally be found preferable to desks, benches, or chairs with writing arms, for they give a maximum of flexibility in classroom arrangement. They can be aligned in rows for formal lectures, can hold demonstration equipment, or can be formed into units of any size for discussion groups of half a dozen or seminars of half a hundred. Their expanse permits comfortable spreading of instructional and note-taking materials, and they are easy for an instructor to walk among when supervising individual trainee work. There is no optimum size for classroom tables; five to six feet long and thirty to thirty-six inches wide are common dimensions, providing ample working space for from four to six people and yet being light and handy to move around.

Chairs should be as comfortable as possible, for no chairs suitable for use at tables will be comfortable enough to encourage falling asleep, and physical discomfort is a powerful distractor of minds. Cushions in the chairs will probably pay for themselves many times over in better attention if trainees must spend long periods of time sitting.

EQUIPMENT FOR THE INSTRUCTOR

Presumably the instructor will have the use of a table, unoccupied by trainees, whenever he needs it. He may or may not need a desk in the classroom. If there is to be much lecturing in the program, a lectern should be provided. An instructor can maintain better eye contact with his audience with a lectern than by having his notes flat on the table, and can lecture with less fatigue by using one. It can be either a small one which sits on top of the table or a heavier one tall enough to be used on the floor.

Some lecterns are built with a fluorescent light across the top, giving localized illumination to notes lying on the lectern. In an adequately lighted classroom such lights are seldom of value, however, unless an instructor speaks from notes extensively while showing slides or filmstrips.

GENERAL CLASSROOM EQUIPMENT

Blackboard. This is one of the most important single items of equipment for the average training program. A permanently installed board is a fine investment if a room will be used more or less permanently as a classroom. If different rooms will be used temporarily by the training program, a portable blackboard of the type which flips over, making two usable sides, is convenient. Get one with a surface rough enough to take chalk well. A sheet of plywood painted with black enamel is unsatisfactory; one painted with flat black paint is usable, but hard to erase. There are several satisfactory board surfaces. Try each one at your dealer's and get one that takes chalk well, erases well, and has minimum glare reflection from light. If soft strips of wood are secured around the frame, charts can be pinned to a permanently installed or a portable blackboard, making it serve a double purpose. Do not put tacks into the writing surface of any board, however, and be cautious about using adhesive tape of any kind to fasten anything to the blackboard surface; the adhesive may gum up the surface and be troublesome to remove without marring the board.

Projection Equipment. Projection screens may be permanently attached to the wall and unrolled like a window shade when needed. They are also available mounted on a variety of stands so they can be moved about. There are two general types of surface of screens: plain glass and beaded glass. The beaded glass gives a brighter, sharper picture, but the plain (which is cheaper) can be seen more easily from extreme side angles. A test of different finishes in the classroom where projection equipment is expected to be used most, under the lighting conditions which will prevail, is advisable before a final selection of a screen is made. If there is difficulty in darkening the classroom appreciably, you might consider a special daylight screen which is constructed to provide clear images even in a light room.

Projectors, slide and film, are too complex a subject to attempt to cover in the limited space of this book. A small, home projector is usually adequate if training groups are small, but inadequate if large groups must view the picture. A photographic supply dealer can give needed help in the selection of equipment, and a list of helpful books dealing with the subject will be found at the end of Chapter 10.

Storage. If at all possible, it is desirable to have somewhere in the classroom facilities in which to store material not in use. Lockers, a closet, or simple shelves may suffice, depending on the degree of security the materials require. If shelves are used, they should either be at the back of the room or be provided with curtains, screens, or some other covering so their contents can be hidden from view. It is a general rule of good instruction that the classroom be as uncluttered as possible and that equipment used in a specific period be kept out of sight during the portions of that period when it is not in use. The ideal is to have all instruction interesting, but also to have the classroom so bland that there is nothing in it to compete with instruction for trainee interest and attention. Any sort of mechanical equipment, or even a row of books, can be distracting if the instruction is particularly uninteresting to the trainees. Piles of papers and manila folders are hardly distractions but may look untidy, and should be concealed to add to the general attractiveness of the room. Have your storage facilities conveniently placed and easy to use.

Bulletin Boards, Chart Boards, Etc. These are useful adjuncts to instruction and good to have in any classroom. However, put them at the back of the room to avoid their possible distracting influence during instruction.

SUMMARY

It has been said that "Mark Hopkins on one end of a log and a student on the other is a university." This is a fairly accurate representation of the relative importance of physical facilities and instructor competence in producing a good training program. However, even Mark Hopkins could teach a student better if he had better equipment than the log. And there are very few Mark Hopkinses. In general, if it is worth a company's money to place personnel in a training program, it is worth the relatively small additional expenditure required to provide the program with the classroom and equipment which will impress trainees with the importance attached to the program, and provide them the best opportunity of realizing the full learning opportunities their instructors present them.

SUGGESTED READINGS

ALEXANDER, W. M., and P. M. HALVERSON: *Effective Teaching in Secondary Schools,* Rinehart & Company, Inc., New York, 1957.

MACCONNELL, J. D.: *Planning Tomorrow's Secondary Schools,* Stanford University Press, Stanford, Calif., 1954.

————: *Trends in School Planning,* Stanford University Press, Stanford, Calif., 1955.

TAYLOR, J. L.: *Planning and Designing the Multipurpose Room in Elementary Schools,* U.S. Department of Health, Education and Welfare, U.S. Office of Education Bulletin 83.

12

Measuring Achievement and Performance

This chapter shows how to construct instruments with which you can measure the results your training program is achieving. It points out principles of evaluation which you can follow to gain the best and most accurate picture of the achievement of individual trainees and of your course as a whole. It concludes with suggestions as to how the results of an evaluation program can be used to best advantage.

IN A TRAINING PROGRAM as much as in an advertising campaign, results are what count. In an advertising campaign results are measured in terms of new customers and increased business. In a training program results are measured in terms of trainee learning and, ultimately, worker performance. The evaluation procedures designed to measure the results of a training program can usually be extended beyond the limits of the formal training program and produce worthwhile information on worker performance generally. Properly used, the evaluation program can be a valuable quality-control instrument of management. It can yield evidence on how to improve training and supervision, and be of assistance in counseling trainees on how to improve their work. It can provide sound bases for worker promotions or discharges.

There are two principal types of evaluation—testing and performance rating. Testing is useful in determining how much knowledge a trainee (or worker—throughout this chapter the statements regarding evaluating trainees can be applied with equal pertinence to other workers) has about a subject. Performance rating indicates the degree of skill the trainee has acquired in applying his knowledge or in performing his work. The former is usually accomplished by subjective or objective tests, the latter by observation, using a rating scale.

Constructing and Using Evaluation Devices

To give accurate results, any evaluation device—essay test, rating scale, or objective test—must be *reliable* and it must be *valid*. For an evaluation device to be reliable, it must give approximately the same results each time it is applied to one particular thing. If five observers, each using a particular rating scale designed to measure how well a worker did a job, watched a worker doing the job and, guided by the rating scale, each one independently gave the worker the same grade, you could regard the rating scale as reliable. In short, as applied to evaluation, "reliability" is practically synonymous with "consistency." A reliable evaluation instrument is one which gives the same results every time it is applied to the same situation or object.

To be valid, an evaluation instrument must actually measure what it is intended to measure. If the rating scale which gave the same results in the hands of five different observers did not give results which actually showed the competence of the worker, it would be reliable, all right, but it would not be valid. This sometimes happens. In preparing all sorts of rating scales and tests, people sometimes get off the track and produce an evaluation instrument which measures something entirely different from what they want to measure. A rating scale sometimes proves to be measuring conscientiousness instead of competence. A test sometimes turns out really to be testing, for instance, knowledge of the history and development of time-motion study instead of knowledge of how to conduct time-motion studies. Essay tests are invalid when they actually test how well a trainee can write instead of how much he knows about the subject he has been studying.

SUBJECTIVE TESTS

Subjective tests are so called because the grade a trainee receives on this type of test depends on the subjective (i.e., personal) judgment of the one grading the test. Subjective tests usually consist of a number of questions the trainee is expected to answer or topics he is asked to discuss or explain. Their chief advantages are that they are easy to construct (if you are not particular about how accurately they can be scored) and can easily be designed to require trainees to demonstrate their ability to organize and express their thoughts and to reason about a subject. Their principal disadvantages are that they are difficult, if not impossible, to grade accurately and, since writing out answers to questions is time-consuming, one test can usually cover an extremely limited number of topics.

Subjective tests are often called "essay tests" because of the essaylike form of the answers, discussions, and explanations. The very wordiness of the answers makes grading difficult. A clever trainee who does not know the answer to a question will almost certainly try to conceal the fact by choosing words for his answer which can be interpreted in either of several ways, while a conscientious student, who not only knows the expected answer but also some exceptions to it, may answer the question in almost the same way.

For instance, an instructor thought he was asking a question whose answer he could accurately grade as "right" or "wrong" when he asked his class of prospective stock clerks, "How do you go about locating an article in the warehouse to fill an order?" The expected answer was, "By consulting the master locator index." However, one trainee replied, "One of the first things a stock clerk should do is familiarize himself with the location of types of stock so that he will know instantly where to locate the 'family,' and thus can locate the specific item in a few seconds." That answer sounds like a good idea. But is it a disguising of the fact that the trainee was daydreaming when the master locator index was being explained? Some instructors would say "Yes" and score the trainee zero on that question. Others would say it showed initiative and an understanding of the true use of the master locator index, and give the answer full credit.

When the same answer is given different grades by different instructors, it is obvious that the grades must represent something other than the quality of the answer. If the primary purpose of a test is to motivate study and attention, to encourage review, or to require trainees to organize and express their knowledge, this is unimportant, and the essay test is an easy, convenient, and satisfactory evaluation device. If, on the other hand, the primary purpose of the test is to measure accurately trainees' knowledge, it is desirable to make essay tests, which are naturally subjective, as objective as possible. Here are some rules which may assist you in preparing essay-type tests which can be graded with some degree of accuracy, and which capitalize on the essay test's advantage of requiring reasoning and clear expression.

Guidelines in Constructing Subjective Tests

1. Make questions precise. Say, "Explain (a) the difference between alternating and direct currents, (b) the advantages of each, and (c) the principal uses of each," rather than "Discuss alternating and direct currents."

2. Ask questions which require reasoning or application of knowledge to answer, rather than questions which merely measure factual recall. (The latter can be measured more easily and accurately by objective tests.) Ask, "What was the practical effect of the decision to make this a mutual rather than a stock company?" not, "Name three characteristics of a mutual as contrasted with a stock company."

3. Identify how fully you want each question answered. In an actual test it would help both the trainees and the one grading the test papers to put after each question a notation such as "(50 words or less)," "(25 words)," etc.

4. Check questions carefully to be sure they are worded clearly

and accurately. Do not say, "How could you determine whether a motor's failure to start is due to faulty ignition?" if you really mean, "What is the recommended way to determine . . . , etc.?" The two are not necessarily the same!

5. Break questions which would require long answers into several, each of which can be answered more briefly. This will minimize your being lost in a wilderness of words when trying to grade the papers. Carried to its extreme, this rule produces the "completion" question which can be answered in one to a half-dozen words. This can be more accurately graded than the other subjective test questions, but it sacrifices the advantages of forcing trainees to show their reasoning processes and facility in organizing and applying their knowledge. How far you want to go in following this rule will be determined by what you are more interested in—accurate grades or trainee exercise and demonstration of reasoning and organizing.

6. Before starting to grade the papers, write out what you consider accurate answers, expressed in terms of the criteria which an answer must meet to earn maximum credit. To earn full credit, the answer to the question about mutual and stock companies, stated above, might have to mention lower rates, greater flexibility in policy, faster reaction to changing situations, and simpler corporate structure. By checking answers against these criteria instead of depending on over-all impressions, you can grade more accurately.

7. Grade one question for all papers, then grade the next question for all papers, and so on, rather than grading one entire paper, then another. Also, after grading all the papers on one question, look again at the first three or four you graded. You will frequently want to change these grades after comparing them with others.

As was pointed out in the beginning of this chapter, test results can be used for several purposes besides passing and failing trainees, and for most of these other purposes the relative inaccuracy of grades given individual papers on an essay test is not a serious disadvantage. It is no disadvantage at all for purposes such as stimulating trainee study and learning. Use subjective tests for the purposes they are suited to, but keep in mind that actual experience has shown not only that different instructors give widely differing grades to the same essay test answer, but also that when *the same* instructor grades his own essay test papers a second time (if he did not mark on them the first time), it is a rare accident when he gives a paper the same percentage grade the second time that he gave it the first. So be wary of using essay tests as bases for making important decisions about individual trainees.

RATING SCALES

Another major form of subjective evaluation is evaluation by observing, or rating. This is by far the most common of all forms of evaluation. It is the evaluation a foreman, supervisor, or department head makes through his observation of the people working under him. Often the observer is not conscious that he is rating a worker, but when the time comes for a personnel change, when someone is to be promoted, discharged, reprimanded, or complimented, the person in authority is guided in his decision by the day-to-day observations and conscious or unconscious ratings he has over a period of time given the various people under him.

In training programs, evaluation by rating is likely to be more formalized and systematic and therefore more accurate. Of course, it is highly desirable for ratings of workers *not* in training programs to be accurate, too, and the principles and procedures which will increase the accuracy of ratings of trainees can be applied profitably to all personnel within an organization.

Evaluation by observation has the important advantage of appraising how well a person is actually doing the job he is hired for, not merely how much he knows of the theory of how to do the job. It has the disadvantages of being time-consuming, expensive, and, unless care is taken, extremely inaccurate. Attempts to devise ways of making ratings more accurate have invariably resulted in adoption of some form of rating scale to guide observers in what to watch for and how to measure what they see.

Obviously, unreliable or invalid evaluation instruments may be worse than no instruments at all because they give results which instructors or supervisors act on in good faith, only to find that they were acting on erroneous information.

To give observers the guidance they need to obtain reliable and valid ratings of trainee performance, rating scales are an absolute necessity. These rating scales must usually include two factors: (1) a list of the skills or qualities most important to the job being done, which will serve as a guide to the observer as to what to watch for, and (2) descriptions or explanations placed at various points along each scale to show the observer how high work of a given quality would be rated. Table 3 presents an example of a rating scale designed to assist a department head in rating sales clerks in a ladies' shoe store.

Basic Steps in Constructing a Rating Scale

1. Analyze the job whose incumbents are to be rated. Identify the skills or characteristics most important to the successful performance of the job. (Try to hold the total number to six or eight.)

2. For each of the skills or characteristics identified, write a brief description of what would be required to justify a rating at the top of the scale.

3. Write another brief statement describing what would constitute unsatisfactory or absolutely minimal acceptable performance.

4. Describe in a few words what constitutes typical satisfactory performance of a worker in that skill or characteristic.

5. Condense the descriptions of the different levels of performance to a brevity which will permit them to fit into the space beside their respective scales without extending the whole scale beyond a page or being too complex for convenience in using.

6. Combine the skills and characteristics, and the description of

TABLE 3. SAMPLE RATING SCALE FOR SALESMEN

Trait			
Appearance	Always immaculate — 5	Usually neat — 3	Untidy — 1
Knowledge of merchandise	Wastes time and loses sales because of lack of knowledge of stock — 1	Has average knowledge of stock — 3	Knows stock and its characteristics thoroughly — 5
Attitude toward work ..	Requires pushing to keep working — 1	Works conscientiously and willingly — 3	Eager, cooperative, and industrious — 5
Relations with customers	Liked by all; frequently called for by name — 5	Well liked; seldom any conflict — 3	Frequently criticized by customers; friction — 1
Skill in fitting	Untactful or poor — 1	Satisfactory — 3	Unusually skillful — 5

200

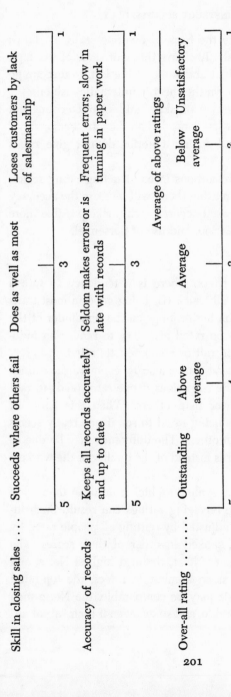

| Skill in closing sales .... | Loses customers by lack of salesmanship | Does as well as most | Succeeds where others fail |
| | 1 | 3 | 5 |

| Accuracy of records ... | Frequent errors; slow in turning in paper work | Seldom makes errors or is late with records | Keeps all records accurately and up to date |
| | 1 | 3 | 5 |

Average of above ratings

| Over-all rating .... | Unsatisfactory | Below average | Average | Above average | Outstanding |
| | 1 | 2 | 3 | 4 | 5 |

Make check marks representing your estimate of the ratee's position on each of the qualities listed. Total the scores you gave the ratee, and divide the total by 7 to get his average score. Your over-all rating of the ratee does not have to be this average of scores, but your over-all rating should be influenced heavily by the qualities on the scale. Therefore, any marked divergence between the over-all rating you give the ratee and the average of ratings you gave him on qualities listed on this scale should be explained on the back of the rating scale form.

201

levels of performance, into the form of a rating scale, as shown by the Sample Rating Scale. In doing this, put some of the high ends of the scale at the right and some at the left, to discourage raters' checking straight down the sheet in automatic fashion.

7. Avoid general categories of skills and characteristics not specifically descriptive of what is needed on the job. "Personality," "health," "knowledge," and such categories do not give raters sufficient guidance.

Observing the above precautions in constructing rating scales, and the following guides in using them, will increase the accuracy of your ratings. This increased accuracy will make possible more effective counseling, instruction, and use of personnel.

Guides in Using Rating Scales

1. Guard against halo effect. There is a tendency to rate a person about the same on all traits. His being good in most traits predisposes you to give him high ratings on the remainder of the skills or characteristics to be rated also. Try to render an independent judgment on each trait or characteristic rated.

2. When more than one rater uses a scale, compare the ratings given by different raters. Be suspicious if one rater tends to rate consistently higher or lower than others. When this happens, check the different groups being rated to see if one really seems to be better or poorer than others. The difference may be due to differences in rater standards instead of the quality of the workers in the different groups.

3. If some raters insist on evaluating higher or lower than other raters, injustices to people receiving ratings can result. Such injustices can sometimes be adjusted by putting all people rated by one rater in a single list, ranked in order of their scores. The highest-rated person becomes No. 1, the next highest No. 2, and so on. If raters have the same number of ratees, the top-rated people on the different lists may be comparable, the No. 2 men on each list may be comparable, and so on, even if their "absolute"

ratings differ. If inspection reveals no other evidence of difference between groups than the absolute ratings given by different raters, it is probable that the difference is in the standards of the raters, not in the groups themselves.

4. In deciding what over-all rating to give a ratee, be guided heavily by the average of his ratings on the different factors listed on the rating scale. If the analysis of factors which determine the ratee's job effectiveness was accurate, his over-all rating should usually closely approximate the average of his ratings on separate factors. However, no rating scale can provide for all the unusual circumstances which might influence the effectiveness of a person as an employee. A gambling habit which caused undesirable companions to visit him at the store might lower the over-all value of an employee without being reflected on any of the specific factors rated. A person of only moderate ability on all of the factors rated might be so versatile in his ability to fill in in different capacities when other employees are out that he is valuable beyond what the average rating indicates.

So consider *all* factors influencing the competence of the ratee as an employee, in making out his over-all rating. But marked divergence between average rating and over-all rating should be relatively rare unless the rating scale is incomplete or erroneous. And since the purpose of the rating scale is to make ratings as specific and objective as possible, any marked difference between the level of competence indicated by the average of ratings and the over-all rating given a ratee should be explained fully. This procedure capitalizes on the objectivity of the rating scale and still retains provision for reflecting exceptional circumstances which materially affect an employee's competence but do not show up on the specific factors on the scale.

OBJECTIVE TESTS

There are two widely used forms of test which can be scored without the exercise of personal opinion or judgment on the part of the scorer, which is to say they can be scored objectively. These are the multiple-choice form and the true-false form. Besides their freedom from influence of personal bias and individual differences in judgment of scorers, objective tests possess the important advantage of being able to cover course objectives and materials with great thoroughness. Because trainees can answer objective items in a fraction of the time it takes them to write out the answer to an essay question, a great many points of material can be covered instead of the half-dozen or so which an essay test might sample.

Objective tests take much longer to prepare than do essay tests, and usually they must be mimeographed or otherwise reproduced so each trainee may have a copy. This requires fairly early preparation of test items, and more arrangement of details than is involved in giving an essay test. Generally, the advantages of objective tests outweigh their inconvenience, and the practice of using objective tests is steadily growing and spreading.

Although the scoring of objective tests is reliable, i.e., it is exact and free from fluctuations due to the nature of the scorer, this does not necessarily guarantee valid results from objective tests. No matter how accurate a score is, it cannot possibly be indicative of the knowledge of a trainee about a specific subject if the test items from which the score is derived do not measure knowledge about that subject. Unfortunately, objective tests are highly susceptible to errors of construction which render their results invalid. The remainder of this section will be devoted to explanation and illustration of how to construct objective test items which truly measure trainees' achievement of course objectives, avoiding the errors which produce tests that really measure one thing while intended to measure something quite different.

Multiple-choice Tests. Virtually every test in wide use educationally or industrially today is of the multiple-choice type. Multiple-choice items are more time-consuming to construct and require more mental effort on the part of the constructor, but their superiority is such that wherever accurate, objective evaluation of learning is desired, they are almost universally used.

A multiple-choice test item is composed of a question or incomplete statement and several (usually four or five) alternatives, from which the trainee is directed to select the one which best answers the question or completes the statement. Here is an outline of procedures which can be used as a guide to the construction of multiple-choice tests which will accurately evaluate trainees' mastery of the learning outcomes of a course. (An elementary course in welding will be used to illustrate the development of multiple-choice items.)

1. Identify the learning outcomes you want to test students on. Do not waste time on detail which was casually mentioned in the course but which the trainee does not need to know to do his work intelligently and well. Test on the knowledges which really make a difference in trainees' effectiveness as workers.

A Poor Item

Fairly adequate welding equipment can be purchased for as little as

   a. $25.
   b. $75.
   c. $150.
   d. $200.

A Better Item

The best heating device for applying solder to sheet metal is

   a. an alcohol blowtorch.
   b. a gasoline blowtorch.
   c. an oxacetylene torch.
   d. an electric arc welder.

This item would be even better if alternative "d" could be worded to include the word "torch," thus making it more comparable to the other three in wording. However, so long as the wording does not suggest the answer or disqualify the alternative for obvious reasons (such as being altogether unrelated to the question, as would be a well-known device—say, a riveting gun—which does not heat at all) such an alternative may be acceptable.

2. Put as much of the item in the "stem" as possible, rather than repeating it in each alternative. This lets trainees concentrate on the real essence of the question by minimizing the number of words they have to think through in each alternative.

A Poor Item

The proper blend and pressure of acetylene and oxygen

  a. burns with a soft, breathy sound.
  b. burns with a crackling sound.
  c. burns with a sharp, hissing sound.
  d. burns with a harsh, blowing sound.

A Better Item

The proper blend and pressure of acetylene and oxygen burns with a sound that is

  a. soft and breathy.
  b. crackling.
  c. sharp and hissing.
  d. harsh and blowing.

3. Do not use words in the stem which will give away the correct alternative. The following illustration contains two such tip-offs.

A Poor Item

Light-gauge metals can best be welded by rotating the torch flame in a

  a. oscillating motion.
  b. eccentric pattern.
  c. up-and-down motion.
  d. circular motion.

Alternatives "a," "b" and "c" above are eliminated because they do not fit with the article "a" at the end of the stem. Obviously "*d*" is the only alternative whose motion fits the term "rotating" in the stem.

4. Keep all alternatives approximately the same length, or at least make sure that your correct alternatives are not conspicuously longer or shorter than the incorrect alternatives. There is a strong tendency for instructors to state their correct alternative with elaborate precision, and the erroneous ones with careless brevity.

A Poor Item

Fusion is best defined as

    a. two things stuck tightly to each other.
    b. fastening things together.
    c. the flowing together of two materials in a molten state in such a manner that they form one piece when they harden.
    d. fastening two pieces together by means of a third.

5. Design your items so that they call for the kind of knowledge a trainee will require to do his work. Avoid testing theoretical or artificial concepts the knowledge of which would have little or no effect on the trainee's ability to do his job.

A Poor Item

Flux

    a. prevents the formation of oxide in a weld.
    b. reduces and removes the oxide which forms in a weld.
    c. floats off impurities such as scale, dust, and sand.
    d. all of the above.

This illustration brings up another point. It is occasionally permissible to use the expression "all (or "none") of the above" as an alternative. Care must be taken, however, to use "all" or "none" as an *incorrect* answer at least as often as a correct answer, or trainees will quickly deduce that it is a wise choice whenever they are not sure of the answer.

A Better Item

For best results, flux should be applied to materials to be welded

    a. at least an hour before welding.
    b. a few minutes before welding.

c. just before lighting the torch.

d. as closely as possible to when they are welded.

e. any time it is convenient, since time of application is not important.

6. When you use "not," "all except," or other negative expressions in an item, emphasize them so they will not be overlooked.

A Poor Item

Which of the following will an arc welder not do as well as a torch?

a. Apply body solder.

b. Weld heavy material.

c. Weld light material.

d. Cut metal.

A Better Item

Which of the following will an arc welder *not* do as well as a torch?

a. Apply body solder.

b. Weld heavy material.

c. Weld light material.

d. Cut metal.

7. Watch for clues in one item which will give away the answer to another item. Trainees will catch them, and you will be testing ingenuity and "test wisdom" rather than subject knowledge. Alternative "*a*" in Illustration 6 eliminates alternative "*d*" in the better item in Illustration 1. One of the items should be altered to avoid this overlapping if both are to be used.

8. Use a picture or diagram in place of words to simulate reality more closely, wherever this is appropriate.

A Poor Item

The best angle at which to hold a torch to weld a joint is usually

a. 10°.

b. 30°.

c. 60°.

d. 90°.

A Better Item

The best angle at which to hold a torch to weld a joint is usually

FIGURE 4

9. Avoid use of involved wording which makes an item, in reality, a test of reading comprehension rather than a test of subject knowledge.

A Poor Item

All welding done on the outside of a body should be done on the inside rather than the outside if possible because

   a. the joint made is stronger.
   b. it is desirable to protect the weld from exposure to weather.
   c. mistakes are not so visible.
   d. it will take less work to put a finish on the joint.

A Better Item

When a body section which is to be welded will be seen on one side and not seen on the other, the welding should be done on the unseen side if possible because

   a. the joint made is stronger.
   b. it is desirable to protect the weld from exposure to weather.
   c. mistakes are not so visible.
   d. it will take less work to put a finish on the joint.

10. Make all alternatives seem reasonable to trainees who have normal intelligence and good general information but do not have the specific information being tested.

A *Poor Item*

To use a lower amperage in a weld, you should use

    a. a coated rod.
    b. a smaller rod.
    c. a larger rod.
    d. more flux.

The relation between amperage and size of wire is probably too well known to make this a valid question. The following item may not fully eliminate the general-knowledge aspect of the question, but it helps.

A *Better Item*

The most reliable way to minimize the chance of burning a hole in sheet metal is to use

    a. a coated rod.
    b. a smaller rod.
    c. a larger rod.
    d. more flux.

In preparing any test, first identify points that are important enough to be worth testing, and then try to devise tests on these points. Do not start by looking for ideas that can be tested easily. The value of a test lies largely in how well it measures trainees' knowledge of *the things they need to know to do their jobs well,* the vital skills, knowledges, and attitudes which determine their ability to do. Therefore, testing on unimportant details or irrelevant facts, or asking trick questions where noticing some minute twist of language is the key to the correct answer, defeats the basic purpose of the test. Before using any test item, let two or three knowledgeable persons look it over and see if they agree that it covers a worthwhile bit of knowledge, that it is easy to read and understand (although not necessarily easy to answer), and that the indicated correct answer is really correct. This little precaution can prevent not only unreliable test results but a lot of trainee dissatisfaction over items which are picayune, misleading, or erroneous.

True-False Tests. While seldom as valid and reliable as well constructed multiple-choice tests, true-false tests are so easy to construct and permit coverage of so many points in a relatively short period of testing that they are widely used. But they require care in their construction. Too often instructors look through their notes or textual material for statements which may be either quoted directly as true items or transformed by changing a word from true statements in the text to false statements. These items tend to measure sheer memory rather than real knowledge and understanding.

By taking time and care and by observing some principles in the construction of true-false items, instructors can construct true-false tests which are adequate for the purposes of most training programs. A well-constructed true-false test is probably better than a hurriedly constructed multiple-choice one. A hurriedly constructed multiple-choice test is likely to have many items which have only two plausible alternatives, thus making them in reality two-choice, or true-false, items instead of four-choice, and it is never a good idea to have a testing device which pretends to be one thing when it is really another.

Careful observance of three simple steps in procedure should enable you to produce good true-false items. First, make a list of important facts or ideas trainees should have learned from the training program. Second, change the wording in these statements until about half are true and half are false. Then go over the list of revised statements and cross out the ones which are so simple and obvious that they will not distinguish between trainees who have some special knowledge of the subject and those who just have common sense. (Common sense is fine, but if that is what you want to test, use an intelligence test and save yourself the trouble of making up your own test.)

Here are some guides to help you prepare true-false items which will stand the test of your close inspection.

1. Cover only one fact or idea in an item. (If you have more than one and a trainee misses the question, you have no way of knowing which part he did not know.)

A Poor Item

T F Oxygen is inflammable and may become explosive if contaminated with oil or grease.

Oxygen is *not* inflammable, although it will enthusiastically support combustion. It *may* become explosive if contaminated with oil or grease. Even if the trainee knows these things, how should he answer? Still worse, if he marks it "false," how can you tell whether he knows that oil or grease in a cylinder to be filled with liquid oxygen may result in the shop's being blown up?

A Better Way of Covering These Points

T F Oxygen brought into contact with anything burning will increase the flame.

T F The interior of cylinders used to hold liquid oxygen should be rinsed with oil occasionally to prevent oxidation.

It is often necessary to change a statement rather radically, as in the latter of the two examples above, to make it plausible as a false statement. Whether or not they knew anything about the explosive qualities of a mixture of oxygen and grease under pressure, trainees would be highly unlikely, just on general principles, to mark "true" a statement such as, "Oxygen and oil under pressure cannot be explosive." But the trainee who knows oxygen and oil can be explosive would recognize that oxygen cylinders must have no oil in them, while to the one who does not know this, the false statement is plausible. That makes for a good item.

2. Avoid the use of complicated items requiring a trainee to mark them true or false because of a reversal in the statement. These measure intelligence or reading ability as much as knowledge, which is not the purpose of your test.

A Poor Item

T F When welding, it is better not to move the flame of the torch toward and away from one's self instead of from left to right.

(Or is it, perhaps, false?)

A Better Item

T F Left-to-right-to-left motion is better than to-and-from-you motion in welding.

or

T F In welding, side-to-side motion usually gives better visibility of the work than does toward-and-from motion.

3. Be as exact as possible in your language; be precise in your wording. Avoid expressions that mean different things to different people.

A Poor Item

T F Acetylene in cylinders is compressed until it exerts high pressure.

The typical pressure of 250 to 275 pounds per square inch in a fresh acetylene cylinder is high when compared with the pressure in an automobile tire. It is low compared with the pressure under which liquid oxygen is kept.

A Better Item

T F Acetylene in cylinders is compressed to a pressure of 250 to 275 pounds per square inch.

This item could reasonably be made false by stating the pressure as 50 to 75 pounds or 500 to 600 pounds. It might well be important for a trainee to know that the pressure is not really as high or low as these limits. Making it false by changing the pressure only 25 to 50 pounds, however, would probably create a problem whose answer is quite unimportant, and besides, different companies might actually use these slightly different pressures. *Test for things it is important for the trainee to know.*

Scoring and Using Results

Some commercially produced tests carry instructions that scores on them be determined by counting the number of items answered correctly and subtracting from that number a stated proportion of the items missed. Little accuracy is gained by this procedure if trainees are allowed time to finish tests and instructed to guess at any items they do not know. Probably the time required for the mathematics of computing scores adjusted for chance would give more valid test results if devoted instead to constructing better items. For instructor-made tests, just count the number right and give that as the score.

When you were in school you were probably graded on the basis that 70 per cent correct answers was "passing," 80 per cent "good," and so on. This is called "absolute" grading, meaning that the instructor sets a standard that getting so many questions right earns a certain mark and then grades to that standard. This works moderately well with an instructor who over a period of years teaches and tests the same material with hundreds of students. But what about the one who does not have those years of experience? How is he to know just how hard to make his questions so that getting 70 per cent of them (or any other specified percentage) right should be a pass? If he makes them easy enough, even the class dullard could get 90 per cent of them correct, and it is probable that he *could* make the test technical enough for few, if any, to get as many as 70 per cent correct. Since what is desired is to measure trainees' knowledge, not instructors' standards, what is the best thing to do?

The answer is simple when we consider just what the objective of testing in a training program is. Fundamentally, it is to identify the people who learn most and those who learn least. If this is true, the important thing is not to determine the exact percentage of training material a trainee has mastered, but to determine the relative order of excellence of the trainees. Of course, it may at times be desirable to require that trainees master a specified proportion of the training material to which they are exposed. Usually though, the sheer amount of material learned is not as important as that certain specific material be learned. As an example, it is *good* for a trainee to know the angle at which to hold a welding torch; it is *essential* that he know that grease must not be allowed to come into contact with oxygen under pressure.

Three conclusions can be drawn from the above considerations regarding the use of test results:

1. For practical purposes, such as determining whom to promote, train further, or discharge, the actual score of a trainee in an evaluation is usually less important than his relative standing among other trainees. This is especially true when tests are used which have not been tried out and improved on a large number of trainees because the test's ease or difficulty may throw the group of trainees high or low, thus making a passing mark vary from test to test. On the other hand, whether the whole group tests high or low, presumably the company would like to keep the best and have least interest in keeping the poorest. Therefore, rank would be more meaningful than score.

2. Sheer percentage of knowledge of training material may be important, but must not be allowed to obscure the fact that some of the knowledge is merely helpful, while other knowledge is essential to successful performance of the job. Therefore, examination of trainees' answers to individual questions, not merely total scores, is necessary to get maximum value from the results of an evaluation program.

3. If a large proportion of trainees miss an item, or a group of items, on one subject, it may be that the instruction on this subject was poor. Thus, examination of evaluation results may afford ideas for the improvement of the training program as a whole.

SUMMARY

Every training program needs an evaluation program to show how well it is succeeding. To be of real value, the evaluation program must reflect *accurately* both how well individual trainees do in their work and how well the program as a whole is succeeding in producing better workers. Therefore, any evaluation devices used should be *valid*, i.e., they should actually measure what they profess to measure; and they should be *reliable*, i.e., they should consistently give one grade for one specific quality of work.

Subjective, or essay, tests are easy to construct but extremely difficult to grade accurately. They afford a good opportunity for the trainee to demonstrate his ability to organize and express his ideas, but grades on them are likely to reflect peculiarities of graders as much as knowledge of trainees. To get best results from essay tests:

1. Make questions precise.

2. Ask questions which require reasoning rather than mere factual recall.

3. Tell trainees how fully you want questions answered.

4. Word questions carefully, to make them clearer and to avoid ambiguity.

5. Break down questions requiring long answers into several requiring shorter answers.

6. Write out an ideal answer in terms of criteria a perfect answer should meet.

7. Grade all papers on one question, then all on another, and so on.

In many instances it is desirable to grade an employee in his actual performance of a job, and written tests are impractical. Such grading is called "rating" and requires highly accurate observation of the ratee and standardized expression of his performance. This necessary accuracy can be most nearly achieved through use of a rating scale, listing the factors on which the worker is to be rated and providing descriptions of different levels of quality on each factor. But the best scale can give no more valid and reliable results than the validity and reliability of the person applying it. To achieve maximum accuracy in the use of rating scales, follow these three principles:

1. Rate a worker on each factor independently; avoid halo effect.

2. Compare ratings of different raters. Be suspicious if one consistently rates higher or lower than others. Check to see if his group is really unusual.

3. Where raters tend to give high or low ratings because of their individual standards rather than as a result of real differences between groups of ratees, converting each rater's grades into rank order instead of handling them as absolute scales may minimize injustices and inaccuracies.

Objective test results are little affected by the idiosyncrasies of the grader, but the tests may be slow and difficult to construct and to reproduce and may require considerable skill for good construction. Multiple-choice tests are frequently the best type of objective test for a particular situation. Following the ten guides discussed and illustrated in the chapter will help the nonprofessional test constructor turn out a satisfactory multiple-choice test.

True-false tests permit fast coverage of many points—fast both in the time required to construct the items and the time required for trainees to take the test. True-false items are easier to construct than multiple-choice items and, if composed in careful accord with the guides given in the chapter, can produce a test which will give a good picture of trainee achievement and program achievement.

In using the results of an evaluation program, remember:

1. Determining the relative standing of a trainee among other trainees is more frequently the practical purpose of evaluation in a training program than is determining his absolute level of knowledge or skill. It is also easier to do.

2. Certain items of knowledge, attitude, or skill may be so vital that deficiency in them is not compensated for by generally high grades. Check trainees' answers to individual questions or trainees' individual factor ratings which deal with such crucial areas.

3. Study the results of evaluation of entire trainee groups. Low grades *can* indicate poor instruction. They can indicate areas where more instruction is necessary and thus aid in improvement and revision of the training program.

SUGGESTED READINGS

ADAMS, G. S., and T. L. TORGERSON: *Measurement and Evaluation for the Secondary School Teacher,* The Dryden Press, Inc., New York, 1956.

GREENE, H. A., A. N. JORGENSEN, and J. R. GEBERICH: *Measurement and Evaluation in the Secondary School,* Longmans, Green & Co., Inc., New York, 1954.

MICHEELS, W. J., and M. R. KARNES: *Measuring Educational Achievement,* McGraw-Hill Book Company, Inc., New York, 1950.

REMMERS, H. H., and N. L. GAGE: *Educational Measurement and Evaluation,* Harper & Brothers, New York, 1955.

SCOTT, W. D., R. C. CLOTHIER, and W. R. SPRIEGEL: *Personnel Management,* 5th ed., McGraw-Hill Book Company, Inc., New York, 1954.

TRAVERS, R. M. W.: *Educational Measurement*, The Macmillan Company, New York, 1955.

WEITZMAN, ELLIS, and WALTER J. McNAMARA: *Constructing Classroom Examinations: A Guide for Teachers*, Science Research Associates, Inc., Chicago, 1949.

WHITEHILL, A. M.: *Personnel Relations: The Human Aspects of Administration*, McGraw-Hill Book Company, Inc., New York, 1955.

WRIGHTSTONE, J. W., J. JUSTMAN, and I. ROBBINS: *Evaluation in Modern Education*, American Book Company, New York, 1956.

13

Principles of Employee Counseling

This chapter explains the benefits a counseling program can afford to a training program, the things a counselor tries to accomplish, and some principles for conducting a counseling interview.

MOST EMPLOYEE COUNSELING is conducted for just one reason: to get better performance from the counselee. In getting better performance from the counselee, counseling benefits both the individual, by assisting him to work at a level of excellence that increases his earnings and his chances of promotion, and the company, by the superior quality of work the individual does in this process of self-advancement.

Counseling is a part of all aspects of improving the job performance of employees. It is a part of the original training by which instructors prepare a new trainee for his job, and it is equally a part of the in-service training of employees which is constantly conducted by foremen, supervisors, and department heads. Therefore, to fulfill a part of their in-service training responsibilities, foremen, department managers, supervisors, instructors, all from time to time need to function as counselors and should be able to recognize where counseling is needed and know how to do it.

Sometimes skillful counseling can salvage a worker who would otherwise leave the company or be discharged. A worker of any degree of experience represents a sizable investment on the part of the company which paid him while he acquired that experience. A trainee represents a considerable investment by the time he is far enough along in his training program to be a prospect for elimination. Therefore, salvaging human resources through counseling becomes, in sheer dollars and cents, as important to a company as salvaging imperfect but restorable material in its physical stock.

The need for employee counseling arises from the occasional failure of an individual to fit perfectly the company's training program or work situation. This failing to fit may take one or more of at least six forms:

1. Doing so well as to be worth some special attention

2. Failing to measure up to expected standards of work or progress

3. Not working up to his level of ability (even though he may be doing as well as others)

4. Not getting along congenially with boss or fellow workers

5. Showing unacceptable behavior or irresponsibility

6. Poor health, appearance of anxiety or depression, or general need of encouragement or help of some kind

The instructor needs to be alert for trainees who show any of these symptoms. All except the first one (doing especially well) cost the company money as long as they go uncorrected, and the first one can be turned to company profit through capitalizing on a good human asset.

It is inevitable that there will be some individuals who do not fit the company's needs without special assistance, because a training program or a work situation is like a ready-made suit of clothes. It is, let us say, a size-42 suit. This does not mean that it will fit every size-42 man who comes along. Some size-42s have longer arms, some a different set to their shoulders, and so on. The basic size-42 suit is altered to fit these individual differences in size-42 men. The fact that alterations are needed does not necessarily mean that there is something wrong with either the suit or the man. It simply means that they were not made for each other, but by skillful adjustment they can be made to fit each other well and comfortably.

Like ready-made suits, training programs and work situations are designed to fit persons of a certain type—the machinist, the salesman, and so on. Some individuals, however, require a little mutual alteration and adjustment between them and the program or the job to get the best fit between the two. It is not anyone's fault; it is simply that a program or situation which fits the average person may need some special fitting to bring out the best in someone who is out-of-the-average in some way.

That we may be using the same language about what counseling in training programs is, let us consider that it is *advising on special problems*. This eliminates the routine guidance and suggestions a foreman or supervisor gives everyone under him in the natural course of daily work. That is standard on-the-job training everyone gets. Counseling is *special* advising that the foreman, superintendent, instructor, or someone else in a "boss" position gives an individual when the routine on-the-job guidance is not having the effect the boss desires. It bridges the gap between what the employee is and what the job demands and helps bring the two together if such a thing is possible.

If bringing the two together agreeably is not possible, a good counseling program helps reveal that fact. This knowledge accomplishes two things: It helps the company rid itself of an undesirable or unadaptable employee, and it helps the employee leave the company with the feeling that he has been given sympathetic consideration, thus minimizing any feeling of hostility toward the company that he might otherwise take away with him.

At this point let us distinguish between two types of counseling which employees may receive—job counseling and personal counseling. Job counseling is the consultations between an employee and his foreman or supervisor or other superior in the company to help him overcome some deficiency in his work or to capitalize on some ability he has, to help him get ahead faster. (*It is important to remember that counseling is for the able, to help them excel, as well as for the deficient, to help them measure up.*)

Personal counseling is counseling involving more deep-seated factors such as emotional instability, marital troubles that are injuring the employee's work, poor adjustment to his job or fellow workers based on fundamental personality disorders or social maladjustments, poor health, or physical disorders. This type of counseling should be left strictly to physicians in the case of health and physical disorders and to psychologists or psychiatrists in the case of personality, social, marital, emotional, and adjustment troubles.

It is now generally recognized that psychological maladjustments are as much beyond the power of the individual to cure by his own "will power" or "straightening himself out" as are physical ailments. What is *not* always recognized is that it is as dangerous for the counselor not trained in psychology to tinker with such ailments as it is for him to prescribe for physical ailments. Refer the personal counseling problems to a physician or psychologist, and lean over backward to make sure that you do not do the company and the employee harm by edging into areas of advisement that are the exclusive and rightful province of the trained clinician.

Guidelines of Job Counseling

The remainder of this chapter will be devoted to concepts, guides, principles, and techniques of job counseling, because this is the type of counseling that training personnel can well do.

Whenever a foreman, supervisor, training officer, or other person gives an employee job counseling he should aim at doing one or more of three things: (1) helping the employee improve some area of his job performance; (2) adjusting the employee's job to his particular abilities and limitations; or (3) creating better adjustment of the worker to the work situation.

These are the things that job counseling can do. Here are some guides in counseling for each of these objectives.

HELPING THE EMPLOYEE TO IMPROVE SOME AREA OF HIS JOB PERFORMANCE

This applies both to trainees and on-the-job personnel. Perhaps the area is his whole standard of performance. To get rid once and for all of the notion that counseling is only to provide incompetents and weaklings with wheel chairs, let us consider how a worker of *superior* ability and performance might profit from job counseling.

A salesclerk in the children's clothing department of a retail store had a pleasing personality, worked hard, took an interest in her work, showed high intelligence, and generally looked like a career girl who could go places. Her departmental manager recognized the importance of helping those in her department get ahead, so in addition to the routine guidance and instruction that she gave all the women in the department, from time to time she called this outstanding girl aside and talked with her about ways she could improve her performance. They had counseling sessions on things the average salesgirl never bothered with. How did the buyer know in the fall what fashions and colors to order for the spring trade? What were the fine points of tailoring that made a discriminating customer willing to pay fifty dollars instead of fifteen dollars for a child's coat? She also passed the word to the store's personnel manager, who made a point of talking with the girl about ways in which she might develop herself so as to qualify for promotion in different lines of work within the store.

This counseling-to-get-ahead with an above-the-average employee is fully as profitable to the company as a conference with a good employee who is having too large a percentage of his machinings rejected at the inspection step. Both can pay big dividends. The company will profit quite as much as the outstanding salesgirl if she stays with it and moves up the ladder of success because she was able to apply the counseling she received.

The company may also profit handsomely if the machinist's foreman has a well-planned counseling session with him. The machinist in question is a valuable, skilled employee. He is too good to let go lightly, but the large proportion of rejected pieces he is turning out is costing the company money. What is causing them? The machinist says his lathe has a "bug" in it, but the man who uses it on the other shift does not have any trouble. In a counseling session with the machinist, his foreman would try to go over just how he does his job, see if there is any regular pattern of when the rejected work is done, get the counselee to take an "I'm going to find out what's the matter" attitude instead of doggedly blaming the lathe, which works satisfactorily for someone else.

With the superior employee, the counselor does not have to watch his *p*'s and *q*'s closely or exercise special tact. Counseling an employee on his below-standard work is a touchier matter. It is a basic fact of human nature that a scared employee, who is afraid he may be fired, may either work harder to improve or do still poorer work through spending time and effort thinking how he will get another job. In most cases one who is left angry after a counseling session, not afraid for his job (because of seniority, scarce skill, or what have you), but feeling that he has been roughly treated, will for days to come have little interest in improving or even in doing his job passably.

Since the true purpose of job counseling is to benefit the company *through* helping the employee, these facts have important implications for the counselor. They mean that, to be successful, job-performance counseling must (1) convince the counselee it is being conducted to help *him* and (2) end on a hopeful note so that he feels he has a better chance of getting along well in his job as a result of it.

Even disciplinary counseling, where the objective of the counseling is to reprimand or punish the counselee, has to be conducted in such a manner that the counselee feels he is getting fair treatment, or the end result will be to make him a malcontent, a focus of employee friction. A good counselor, be he foreman or training director, is one who can find what is the matter and help the counselee overcome it, *and do it in such a manner that the counselee feels the company has been trying to help him out.* There's where good counseling makes for good employee-company relations!

ADJUSTING THE EMPLOYEE'S JOB TO HIS PARTICULAR ABILITIES AND LIMITATIONS

A company which was producing tent poles to meet an army contract was barely breaking even because of the large number of rejects it was suffering. All efforts to make a sizable reduction in the proportion of rejects failed. But they started work on another tack; if they could not cut down the number of poles that failed to meet army specifications, could they adjust the rejects into another form that could be used profitably for something else? They could and they did, and they racked up a satisfactory profit by the conclusion of their army contract.

The same principle may apply in human engineering. If an employee cannot perform satisfactorily on a given job, and counseling has been ineffective in bringing about the improvement needed, can the job or the work situation be altered so he can perform satisfactorily? Will it be good business for the company to preserve its investment in the employee by changing some policy, practice, or procedure so it will fit him, if he cannot be changed to fit the situation as it now exists?

Counseling is a logical first step in finding out. Counseling for the purpose of fitting a job to an employee is likely to require more time and effort, and an infinitely wider knowledge on the counselor's part of what can and cannot be done with the work situation than does counseling to fit the trainee to his present job or a better job. Furthermore, it is likely to require the counselor to explore the employee's abilities and shortcomings much more fully than is necessary merely to identify a deficiency which can be overcome.

The employee's foreman, instructor, or other appropriate person may have a counseling interview with him. What is the shortcoming that causes the trouble? What is the *cause* of the shortcoming, and if nothing can be done about the cause, how might the area in which the shortcoming exists be avoided? If the man is too slow and holds up the assembly line, but is a meticulous, perfection-seeking worker, can he be used on a job where careful workmanship is at a bigger premium and speed not as all-important as it is in his present job? If he gets bored and careless toward the end of his shift, is he a "no-good," or does he have an active, ingenious mind that the company could use to better advantage than by keeping him on the routine job he now does?

As a starting point in helping the counselee to get a job fitted to his particular abilities, identify as accurately as possible his *disabilities*. Then identify, among the jobs which he *might* be able to fill, the places where those disabilities would injure his performance. Then see if there is any way the work could be juggled so the areas in which he is weak could be eliminated from his duties on a particular job. If not, see if by going out of his *primary* skill and into *related* skills you can construct a job that will capitalize on his skills, avoid his weaknesses, and arouse his interest.

Of course, how far it is profitable for a counselor to go in trying to fit a job to a counselee depends on the particular employee's attitude, his skill, the scarcity of those abilities he does possess, his breadth of knowledge of the company's work, the responsibility the company feels for him as an employee, and a host of other factors. But it does not pay to be too cynical and write off too fast a good man because of a deficiency he cannot help. The gratitude of such an employee for the pains taken for him often results in such loyalty, industry, and drive to succeed that it pays the company big dividends. Other workers, too, may have a much kinder feeling toward the company if they see the effort the allegedly "soulless corporation" will take to help one deserving employee.

CREATING A BETTER ADJUSTMENT OF THE WORKER
TO THE WORK SITUATION

Under this head falls counseling the attitude cases, the malingerer, the social misfit, the employee who chronically wants advances on his pay or has his wages garnisheed, or the person who cannot get along with his fellow workers. These are not pleasant cases to deal with, but they, even more than most cases needing counseling, can be fearfully expensive to the company if not handled properly. These cases are the rotten apples, the focal points of friction and discontent, and natural leaders in demoralizing the whole working force. These are not so hard to identify as others who may need counseling. They stand out like sore thumbs! Further, it is seldom much trouble to identify what seems to be the matter. It shrieks to high heaven!

Sometimes the most effective counseling for these cases *is* the plain, old-fashioned raking over the coals, *but ending in a few minutes of sympathetic encouragement, letting the counselee leave the counseling interview with the feeling that he will get a square deal if he will make an honest effort, and that it is worth while for him to make the effort.* If the counselor cannot, with all his tact and persuasion (and with the help of *his* superior before he gives it up as a hopeless case), get this responsiveness and attitude of cooperation from the counselee, immediate steps probably should be taken to get rid of the employee. Counseling is not a device for babying or coddling employees. It is a device for getting the best effort and cooperation from them. Sometimes the mailed fist is required, but unless the employee is to be discharged, it will always be more effective if the velvet glove is slipped over it before the counseling session is ended, so that the employee goes out hopeful, not angry and resentful.

Before jumping to the conclusion that what a particular counselee needs is a thorough reaming out, however, there are a number of possibilities that should be explored. Take, for example, the bookkeeper whose vile temper and nasty disposition made him thoroughly despised by everyone else in the office. On investigation it was found that he was working at a second job from six until midnight to meet medical bills for an invalid father and had contracted stomach ulcers in the process! On the surface it appeared that the counseling he needed was to be treated just as he had been treating those around him, winding up with a firm "or else!" *But a good counselor never goes by surface appearances.* The principle of tact, sympathetic attitude, and considerate questioning applies to attitude cases as much as to the aging craftsman who can no longer read his micrometer accurately with the necessary speed.

A malingerer may be a good-for-nothing, lazy dead-beat. He may also be a man with marital trouble that makes it impossible for him to concentrate on his work. After all, a good husband works to provide for his family. If the prime reason for a man's working is fading from his life, to what extent is a human mind capable of ignoring that fact and concentrating on keeping full bobbins on the spindles? The social misfit may have a defect, trivial in the eyes of others but overwhelmingly embarrassing to him, that he will conceal even at the cost of forfeiting the natural good will and friendship of his fellow workers.

The good counselor will, in all instances, automatically assume that there is some reason, logical at least to the counselee, that accounts for the symptom the counselee displays. He will carefully avoid urging on the counselee a superficial solution based on the symptoms he displays, before looking into the case thoroughly enough to be pretty certain what the underlying cause is. Telling the irascible bookkeeper (who snarled that he never said anything unpleasant to anyone who didn't speak unpleasantly to him) to greet everyone with a happy smile and a cheery word and see how warmly they responded would not have been very effective, would it?

Serious problems of social and emotional maladjustment are frequently camouflaged by symptoms such as headaches, backaches, indigestion, lack of self-control, and inability to get along with fellow workers. As a rule of thumb, if another difficulty or complaint pops up in an employee as fast as one is cleared up, there is good reason to suspect a deep-seated psychological problem. If this is the case, the counselor is merely treating misleading symptoms as he tries to help the counselee get his physical and adjustment problems resolved. Professional psychological or psychiatric help is needed.

By this time it should be fairly evident that most attitude cases should be referred for psychological consultation and a report before any drastic action is taken. Obviously, this does not apply to straight, out-and-out disciplinary cases which occur every day, if there is substantial certainty that none of the hidden factors which the culprit cannot help and which are responsible for his offenses are lurking somewhere in the background.

General Rules in Counseling Employees

There are a few general rules which can assist instructors, supervisors, and others who may counsel employees to get the best results from their counseling interviews. Following them will vastly improve the results the counselor obtains.

PREPARE FOR EACH COUNSELING SESSION BY LEARNING DETAILS ABOUT THE INDIVIDUAL TO BE COUNSELED

Of course, the supervisor, the instructor, or other person who is to be the counselor knows the particular reason he wants to counsel with an employee. It may be an attitude of indifference that needs correcting. Perhaps the trainee is failing the training program or not making desired progress from the on-the-job instruction he is receiving. Maybe he is doing unusually well and is to be sounded out on his interest in an accelerated program with the company. Or he may be just an average person whom the boss cannot quite figure out and of whom he wants a better picture.

A clear idea of the reason for counseling is the first bit of knowledge needed about the counselee, but is by no means all of the needed information. The counselor should look over the coun-selee's application form or personal data sheet in the personnel office. He needs to have some idea of what kind of person this counselee is—a floater, an ambitious up-and-comer, a plodder? Much can be found about the general nature and ability of a per-son from what he did before coming to your company. If he is not a brand-new employee, check his file for any comments or ratings by previous supervisors or foremen. Find out all you can about him from the personnel file. This can prevent your making em-barrassing blunders such as mistaking a glib tongue for brightness, previous experience for unusual aptitude, or a reticent disposition for antisociability.

Before a counseling interview, it is a good idea for the counselor to look up any other people who may have supervised the coun-selee and talk with them. They may be able to supplement the counselor's observations with other information which will help in the diagnosis and counseling.

It is *not* wise to try to gather additional information about the counselee by "tactfully" talking about him with his fellow trainees or coworkers, however. An absolute necessity for effective coun-seling is the counselee's confidence that his dealings with the counselor are personal and private (except as other necessary company officials must be involved), and it is impossible for this confidence to be maintained if the counselor talks about the counselee with other workers. Even though such a conversation might have taken place before the initial counseling session, when the employee learns that the counselor has been discussing him with the people he works with (and learn it he will), his feeling that the interview was confidential will be destroyed, and any good the counseling might have done will be largely offset.

APPEAR TO HAVE UNLIMITED TIME FOR THE COUNSELING SESSION

Nothing can kill the possible effectiveness of a counseling ses-sion more completely than letting the counselee feel that he is being allotted a scheduled portion of the counselor's parceled-out time and no more. It has already been said that a counseling session which does not leave the counselee feeling it has been conducted for *his* benefit is unlikely to be effective, and he certainly cannot be expected to feel that he is the vital element in the interview if he sees that the counselor is conducting it by the clock instead of by his needs.

Even if the counselor knows in advance that he is going to spend only five minutes with a counselee (although such a short interview would probably be more like routine job supervision than what is generally thought of as a counseling interview), he should maneuver to get where they can sit down in privacy, lean back in their chairs and compose themselves in a manner that says, "We are going to spend as long as either of us thinks is necessary to talk this matter through." It is difficult to overemphasize the importance of this rule. Even if the counselor is in a hurry and is going to terminate the interview in the very near future, he will get most and best results if he talks in a leisurely manner and just leaves out things he cannot get to, rather than trying to squeeze in hurriedly everything he would like to cover.

A final tip on this: If you have to check the time, try to camouflage the movement by picking up your pencil or some such move. Try not to let the counselee see you looking at your watch. Remember, the counselee must feel that *his needs*, not your clock, control the interview. It is up to you to create that feeling.

OBTAIN COUNSELEE READINESS

The counselor will ordinarily want to arrange with the employee to get together at a certain time to talk over so-and-so. (NOTE: This arrangement in advance may not be wise if the employee is an attitude case, for the time lag will only give him more time to get thoroughly worked up instead of allowing him to get the right mind set to talk about his problem.) It is usually best to tell the counselee the purpose of the interview. Not only will his mind be focused on the subject to be discussed, but he will also realize that the counseling interview is not just a bull session.

For a counseling interview to have the best chance of being successful, the counselee must recognize it as an interview in which he is to receive guidance, not merely a man-to-man discussion between two equals.

Knowing how quickly or how slowly to get to the heart of the subject of the interview is one of the marks of an effective counselor. Before the interview can accomplish anything you must establish what the psychologist calls "rapport." This means that the counselor and counselee have to get acquainted with each other in this new relationship. They have to feel at ease with each other. The chances are the person being counseled is nervous. He needs to be made to feel that the counselor is friendly and is going to try to help him. Lighting up, if either smokes, casually commenting on his new shoes or his good performance on some piece of work, or even on your own mashed fingernail, can be good techniques for helping the counselee feel that you are his friend.

Establishing rapport is especially necessary if the subject to be discussed is an emotionally charged one such as an undesirable attitude or, in some instances, substandard performance. Sometimes the counselor finds that by the time he has established rapport, the counselee's attitude has changed so much that the conference has already accomplished its purpose! Counselee hostility, distrust, or fear has to be dispelled before anything constructive can be accomplished in the interview. It is better to recess the interview if time runs short and set a date to continue later, rather than to drive into a tender area before the counselee is prepared to talk it over with an attitude of cooperatively doing something about it. Sometimes he may come to the interview prepared to counterattack rather than to try to work things out with the counselor, but the counselor will probably be defeated if he does not postpone really getting to the bone of the matter until the counselee's attitude has softened so that the two can talk together in friendly fashion.

If it is not possible to get this counselee cooperation, the net result of the interview may be that this trainee will have to leave the company. The counselor's time has not been wasted if he has identified a person who just does not, cannot, and will not fit into the pattern needed in the work situation.

A good rule of thumb is this: Where the counselee seems agreeable and cooperative, move into the heart of the counseling right away. If he seems wary, suspicious, hostile, or otherwise uncooperative, do not waste time and risk ruining everything by plunging into a subject that will confirm his apprehensions. Play it easy, play it easy!

ENCOURAGE THE COUNSELEE TO TALK AND WORK OUT HIS OWN SOLUTION TO HIS PROBLEM WHEREVER POSSIBLE

Some psychologists maintain that most people with problems have within themselves the capacities for solving their problems and therefore the counselor should not venture to give advice, guidance, or instructions. Although all psychologists do not agree with this, all psychologists do agree that whenever a person *is* able to diagnose his own strengths and weaknesses and work out his own plans for the future, it is best for him to do so. Not only does the experience make a more mature thinking and better adjusted person out of him, but he is much more likely to remember the ideas developed and follow through with the plans made.

Therefore, it is good, sound procedure for the counselor to promote discussion about the area in which he would like his counselee to improve, but refrain from giving the obvious procedure (obvious to the counselor, at least) the counselee should follow. Discuss the matter with him and get him to talk. See if *he* can come up with some sound ideas as to how he could improve himself. If he is a good man whom you would like to see working toward a promising career with the company, see if he can be guided into talking about how he would like his career to develop and planning how he could help it develop along those lines. It is absolutely amazing how much better a job of solving his own problems a person is likely to do by talking about the problem to an encouraging but noncommittal listener than through just sitting down by himself and meditating about it!

The counselor should not hesitate to step in and give guidance or instructions where the counselee cannot work out his own difficulties or plans if the problem is one that does not require clinical skills beyond the counselor's scope. A counselor is almost always a person of responsibility in his company—an instructor, foreman, department head, supervisor, or other personnel representative whose knowledge and judgment are worthy of respect. The responsibility of advising an employee on a job problem is no greater than other responsibilities the counselor probably performs as a matter of routine in his work. He should not be timid about telling someone else how to manage his business. It is part of the boss's business when the employee's work is involved.

KEEP A RECORD OF ALL COUNSELING

Anyone taking the time and trouble to have an important advisory interview with an employee should by all means make notes on what the interview was about, what was learned from or about the counselee, the impressions the counselor got, and the recommendations he made. These notes may be written on a piece of scratch paper as the interview is conducted and put in the folder in exactly that form if it would be unduly troublesome to convert them into a neat, formal document. The form is not important. Having available the nature and findings of the interview for reference in future counseling of the employee is. If any follow-up of the counseling is done (and it always *should* be), if special notice is taken of the counselee to see how he reacts after the counseling, whatever impressions the observer gets should be jotted down and put in the file also.

In short, information is to effective counseling what lubrication is to a piece of machinery; it is not the only thing that is necessary to make the machinery run, but it certainly will not run well or long without it! Try not to make the counselee self-conscious by ostentatiously recording everything he says, but do get the facts.

down. There is no excuse for starting the next counseling session with no more information to go on than was available when the first one started.

CLOSE YOUR COUNSELING SESSION AS A RECESS, NOT AS AN END

Counseling is best thought of as a process, not an event. It should continue as needed as long as a training course or on-the-job guidance and supervision continues—and some sort of in-service training should continue as long as the employee is working. It is desirable from the standpoint of both the counselor and the counselee to leave the door open for further pursuit of whatever subject seems important enough in the case of the employee to justify counseling. A feeling of freedom on his part to reopen the counseling if he feels the need can result in earlier awareness of situations in which counseling can help. Too, it saves the counselor's time to begin a subsequent session as a simple continuation of what was already in progress instead of building up a new set of reasons for it.

The purpose of counseling is to promote growth and adjustment of the trainee which will make him more valuable to the company. Growth and adjustment are continuous development, not points, and thinking of the counseling process as paralleling growth and adjustment is sound. Finally, each counseling interview should build on the ones preceding it, which is a clear case of continuation rather than a series of disconnected interviews.

SUMMARY

The purpose of counseling in a training program is to benefit the company through helping an employee make better progress than he would make if not helped. Counseling may be as valuable by helping the above-average employee become outstanding as by lifting up the below-average.

To be effective, the counselor must handle the counseling interview in such a manner that the counselee feels it is intended to help *him*, and does not leave the interview feeling apprehensive or resentful. It takes considerable tact and sympathetic handling to accomplish this result when the counselee is being counseled about poor performance or an attitude deficiency. It is easier when the purpose is to boost an already good employee or find a way a job can be adjusted to the particular individual. Adjusting jobs to take fullest advantage of individual skills and abilities is an important possible benefit of employee counseling.

The counselor should always be alert to avoid making snap judgments and recommendations to a counselee without exploring as deeply as possible into causes and conditions which underlie the surface symptoms the counselee presents. He should also be careful to recognize medical or psychological factors in a counselee's situation and refer cases where these factors occur to a physician or psychologist.

In conducting a counseling interview, the counselor will obtain best results if he (1) obtains as much information as possible about the counselee before the interview; (2) seems to determine the length of the interview by the counselee's needs, not the clock; (3) gets the counselee into a cooperative attitude before plunging into touchy matters; (4) encourages the counselee to solve his own problem in so far as possible; (5) keeps a record of all counseling; and (6) terminates each counseling interview as a recess in a continuing process.

This summary can itself be summarized by saying that, like any other educational experience, a counseling session must be *planned* and *prepared for* to achieve best results. A counselor does not talk at random with a counselee, fishing for what to discuss or say. He starts the counseling session with a knowledge of the counselee and an objective for the session. He works for the counselee to want to improve himself, to react to what is said, and to understand how he may improve, and he recesses the counseling session with provisions for later elaboration or repetition.

14

Employee Counseling as a Training Device

This chapter presents some of the basic counseling techniques for determining what is responsible for trainees' difficulties in learning, ways the counselor can help them learn more efficiently, and techniques of counseling on group discussions.

THE BASIC PRINCIPLES AND RULES of counseling discussed in Chapter 13 apply in all employee counseling situations. Counseling employees who are in formal training courses is merely one phase of the improving-performance counseling which should be conducted by all persons responsible for on-the-job improvement of people working under them. However, many training courses require trainees to learn, remember, and pass tests on subject matter covered by lectures and reading assignments. Counseling trainees in such courses becomes something very closely akin to the educational counseling provided for students in school or college.

There are a number of specialized understandings and skills which a person doing such educational counseling should possess. This chapter is devoted to a presentation of these specialized understandings and skills required for educational counseling and is intended particularly for instructors in training programs. A good instructor will become a *better* instructor if, in addition to being able to teach his subject in a superior manner, he is also able to diagnose the difficulties various trainees may encounter and is skillful in helping them to overcome those difficulties, wherever that is possible. In other words, a good instructor who is also a good counselor is a *better* instructor. This fact has long been recognized as it relates to teachers in schools and colleges. It is just as true regarding the instructor-counselor in a training program.

Counseling on Academic Performance

We shall consider here four factors commonly affecting the degree of academic success a trainee achieves.

GENERAL INTELLIGENCE

One factor about which the counselor can do nothing is the native intelligence of a trainee, but very few people work up to their mental limit any time in their lives. Every teacher can cite a number of instances where students of relatively low mental ability did surprisingly well in competition with brighter persons because they made an unusual effort to use the mental capacity they possessed. It is the old story of the tortoise and the hare. A trainee of limited mental capacity may be turned into a valuable employee, often surpassing in skill and accomplishment much more mentally gifted people who are simply not as industrious. So, although native intelligence probably imposes an upper limit on what a trainee can accomplish, few trainees work up to this limit. A counselor may do much to improve a trainee's performance, regardless of his mental ability, by working on the second factor which determines academic success.

DEGREE OF APPLICATION

Merely urging a trainee to work harder or do more home study usually accomplishes little. Such encouragement can be made to achieve much more if accompanied by a few specific suggestions. See if the trainee can be led to work out for himself a *time schedule* which will set aside a certain hour or two in the evening for extra, concentrated study. Perhaps he has been trying to study while surrounded by his children clamoring for his attention. He cannot apply his mind to his work effectively under such conditions. Maybe a full social calendar keeps a girl from the quality and quantity of work she requires to succeed.

The counselor should help each trainee to recognize that an hour spent in concentrated, single-minded study will accomplish more than two or three hours of erratic, spotty study interrupted by the children or by planning for the evening's activities. Also, the trainee can study more easily and more effectively if he studies in the *same place* each time, rather than in any room to which his mood leads him. In short, helping the trainee plan so he will have an established time and place set aside for concentrated study will help him increase his degree of application and materially improve his academic performance.

PERSONAL PROBLEMS

Personal problems may cause an able trainee to do poor work. The instructor should be alert for symptoms such as preoccupation, irritability, lethargy, and absent-mindedness among the trainees. They may signal poor health, overfatigue, severe worries, or emotional maladjustment. A trainee showing such symptoms should be called in for counseling and a sympathetic effort made to see if the trouble underlying the symptom can be located. If so, see what can be done to alleviate his situation, or refer him to the proper source of professional assistance (as discussed in Chapter 13) if the problem is not suited to the counselor's functions.

STUDY TECHNIQUES

The fourth notable factor affecting academic success is study techniques, including reading, listening, note taking, and test taking. Most trainees could improve their academic achievement through help on these study techniques, regardless of their present accomplishment. It is important, therefore, that the training instructor know how to help along these lines. Chapter 2 explained the psychological causes of learning. Here we are discussing how the counselor-instructor can assist a learner in getting these factors of learning to operate when he is reading or listening.

Reading Habits. Probably the most important single thing the counselor needs to correct to improve reading habits of trainees is the common practice of confining study to mere reading and re-reading of material. Psychological experimentation has shown that people of reasonable literacy will learn more through devoting about half of their time to reading material they want to learn and half of their time to *trying to recall the material they have read.*

People sometimes question the validity of this statement. If you care to, you can doubtless prove to yourself its accuracy. Jot down two lists, each containing twenty disconnected words. Time yourself to see how long it takes you to memorize the twenty words in the first list merely by reading them over and over, time after time. Then take the second list. Read it over, then start trying to *remember* each word, looking at the list only when your memory fails you. Most people will learn the list considerably faster by the second method.

In light of the fact that learning is promoted better by conscious effort to recall what has been read than by simply re-reading, trainees should be encouraged to spend a large portion of their study time in attempting to recall material they have read. Urge them to read an assignment, then go over it, trying to recall it, paragraph by paragraph. By the time they have recalled the contents of each paragraph and checked their recall by scanning the paragraph again, they will usually have learned the assignment. Such recalling and checking recall is harder work than mere re-reading, but it produces the most learning per hour spent in study.

Trainees often complain of inability to concentrate as limiting the effectiveness of their reading. Suggest to them that before reading the material they look at the title and, using their imagination, formulate a number of questions they might reasonably expect to have answered on such a topic. *Then* they should read the material, looking for the answers. Reading with the aim of determining answers to specific questions encourages concentration and makes it much easier for the reader to keep his attention focused on the material he is reading. This is the same principle you as an instructor are following by formulating thought-provoking questions or eliciting them from trainees as you enter upon a new topic. (See Chapter 9.)

Listening. Much of the material a trainee needs to learn, however, comes to him not through reading but through the oral explanations and lectures which compose a large part of most training courses. Effective learning in situations where the instructor is orally presenting or explaining material requires skill in listening, and if a trainee is not getting what he should from a training program, it may be because he does not know how to listen properly.

There is an art to effective, perceptive listening, just as there is to efficient reading, and the same fundamental principles of learning apply to both. There are a few techniques which, if mastered, will help a trainee to listen efficiently, and people who counsel trainees will have more successes and fewer failures to their account if they include coaching on effective listening in their academic counseling of trainees.

As in any other form of learning, the first step in effective listening is motivation, wanting to learn, being motivated to learn. It will greatly profit a trainee to shut out other things from his mind a couple of minutes before a training session and begin to think about how a knowledge of the subject to be covered could be of use to him. Perceiving how the subject is *important to him* will give him a reason to listen. He will derive a bonus benefit from the fact that when the instructor starts talking, his mind will already be tuned in on the subject and he will not miss the introduction while shifting his mental gears away from other things which have been on his mind. He is off to a flying start on the subject and wanting to learn!

A listener's eardrums react automatically, with no effort on their part, to the sounds of an instructor's voice. They do all they are capable of doing without the slightest effort on the part of the listener. The brain does not work this way, however. The eardrums may be vibrating with the instructor's words of wisdom, but unless the listener is making a conscious effort to listen with his mind, his brain does not actually hear a thing. It is merely conscious of a noise. Failure to learn from oral explanations is often due to the trainee's not realizing this fact. Putting a live body in front of an instructor is not necessarily the same as putting an effective listener in front of him. It takes will power and a conscious effort on the part of the listener to make his mind react, to capture and examine the ideas the instructor is putting out. Sitting up straight in a seat and keeping eyes fixed on the instructor are surprisingly effective aids in keeping a student's mental reaction to a lecture going at top efficiency.

Intense concentration is even more important in listening than in reading, because in reading one can go back and look again if he realizes he has missed something. This cannot be done in listening, for instance, to the explanation accompanying a demonstration. The technique (mentioned under *Reading Habits*) of anticipating a few questions to keep in mind and watching for the answers during a lecture is a good device to help people concentrate on what is being said. As in reaction, deliberate, conscious *forcing* of the mind to concentrate on what is being said may be necessary. Trainees should be told clearly that willingness and ability to keep their minds on the subject and at work are as much parts of their job as making their bodies show up for work and keeping busy!

Many listeners simply do not realize that it is a normal, natural thing to have to work hard to keep their minds from straying off the subject at hand. They think there is some magic key to concentration without effort which all other people have but which, for some reason, they do not possess. Therefore, they do not realize that they are delinquent if they do not work hard to force themselves to pay close attention. They *are* delinquent, nevertheless. Few people *enjoy* listening intensely and thinking hard about a lecture, but doing so is necessary to learning.

All the intense taking in of facts by listening (or reading) is of little use, however, if the next two factors in learning—organization and comprehension—are not exploited.

A fact is seldom useful in and of itself. It becomes useful as it is seen in its proper relationship to a whole body of knowledge. It does a trainee little good to learn the different parts of an electric motor, for example, unless he also learns how those parts fit together and the principles governing their proper organization. It does a trainee little good to learn that greeting a customer by name is a good sales idea unless he fits that fact into its larger context of showing personal interest in the customer and her needs. A careless "Good morning, Mrs. Brown" tossed flippantly over a saleslady's departing shoulder may follow one rule of good salesmanship to the letter and yet damage customer relations because it did not genuinely indicate the friendly, personal interest that is the reason for greeting the customer by name.

Point out to the academically deficient trainee that the company is not interested in his memorizing facts for facts' sake, but in his learning the implication of those facts so he can apply them intelligently. Organization in listening means constructing a neat mental pattern of what is heard. Comprehension means thinking through what was heard to the point of grasping the implications, significance, and application of it. The listener may not be able to do all this thinking through as the instructor talks. Indeed, if he keeps his whole mind on trying to organize and comprehend all the implications of the facts he hears, he may wind up missing most of what is said. He should listen with the conscious effort of getting *ideas*, not just facts, and later in going over his notes he should think through the implications of what he noted.

When the material is presented in oral form, the only way to exploit the sixth factor in learning, repetition, is by recourse to notes. In studying notes, two practices will help the trainees:

First, in reviewing notes, make the mind do its best to recall everything that was said about each notation, i.e., take the few written words as a starting point and try to remember the whole explanation as completely as possible. Second, do not stop with just remembering what was said—pursue the organization and comprehension steps to the point of converting the collection of facts represented in the notebook to a systematic, rounded-out understanding of the subject. This means thinking of the significance and implications of each point reviewed. Effective listening requires mentally reacting to and thinking over what is heard, rather than passively accepting it.

Notes. In order to be able to carry out your good advice about reviewing notes, however, the trainee must have a set of notes in the first place. Many trainees have only a vague idea of how to take notes, many have never formed the habit of taking notes anywhere in their school careers, and many are pitifully ineffective when they try to take notes during a training program. No matter how good all his other study techniques may be, the trainee who cannot or does not take effective notes in a training program containing much oral instruction is at a potential disadvantage. A counselor should always ask a trainee who is having academic difficulty to bring his notes with him to the counseling interview. By examining these notes the counselor may be able to identify the source of the trainee's difficulty as simply not having the necessary material there to study.

Here are three common defects that an instructor should look for in students' notes, and suggestions as to what can be done about them.

1. Notes are sketchy and incomplete. Occasionally trainees wait for the instructor to come out with an obvious pearl of wisdom before they put anything down. Although such pearls of wisdom do occur from time to time in training lectures, most of the material trainees need to learn is of the plain "oyster" variety instead of the rare "pearl" type. Most of the things you teach that the trainee should learn are unspectacular facts, concepts,

and ideas. Only occasionally is there something of obviously
world-shaking importance. If the trainee sits with his pencil idle
as all the oysters pass, waiting for a pearl to roll by, he is likely
to wind up with insufficient food for study to prepare him for
tests, questions, or doing his job.

When a trainee is having academic difficulty, it may be well to
advise him to get into the habit of taking notes almost constantly
while instruction is being presented. He will get a lot of shell
along with the oysters and occasional pearls that way, but at least
he will have something besides blank pages in a notebook to look
at when he has need to review what he has heard. After having
got into the habit and developed the skill of taking notes com-
prehensively, he can gradually learn how to discriminate and
take notes selectively.

2. Notes are in the form of topical headings, without real information. A counselor will see sets of notes on a period where
the trainee faithfully put down each major topic and major sub-
heading, but did not put down the information under each one.
This practice results in an outline something like this:

    Principles of Electricity
        Composition
            Relation to matter
            Nature
        Production
            History
            Commercial
            Experimental
        Types
            Direct
            Alternating
        Characteristics
            Direct
            Alternating

This is what is called a "topical outline" and is obviously next
to useless for review purposes. To be of value it would have to be

changed to an "informational outline" through including the im‐
portant data under each heading, as was partially done under the
heading "Types."

3. Notes contain useless detail. This does not contradict what
was said under the first point regarding notes that are too sketchy
or incomplete. Generally speaking, the more detailed notes a per‐
son can get, the better, but some unskilled note takers will get
minute, useless detail on some one point and while they are
writing, completely miss the next six main ideas. See that your
trainees' notes are not so detailed that they are spotty, with big
blank spaces between unnecessary details.

Most trainee deficiencies in note taking can be cured by avoid‐
ing these three errors.

Test Taking. Some trainees learn their material but just cannot
give it out on tests. This sort of case is about as rare as hens'
teeth, but it is probably the most common *excuse* for failing tests
a training instructor encounters. He frequently hears a trainee
say, "I know the stuff but I just can't seem to do well taking the
tests." This is seldom true. It is rare indeed for a person who
actually knows the material covered not to demonstrate that
knowledge on tests, but since out of a hundred students who may
give the excuse there are sometimes a few for whom this is
valid, we shall discuss the things most likely to cause this condi‐
tion, and what the instructor can do about them.

1. Student mentally freezes-up from fear when faced with a
test. Diagnosis is seldom a problem in such cases. The trainee
knows it and tells the counselor. If this seems to be really true,
not just an alibi, the trainee should probably be referred to the
psychologist. It is not normal to be *that* scared!

2. Student answers test questions too fast. He glances at the
question, gets a vague impression of it, and puts down his answer
without actually thinking of the question's meaning. Check by
asking him some of the questions he missed. If he can answer
them correctly when they are read to him, this may be his trouble.

The procedure here is obvious: Tell him to read the question carefully and think it over before writing his answer.

3. Student debates words so suspiciously that he reads a meaning into the question which was not there. This is the hairsplitter, the fellow who feels that the simple, obvious answer cannot possibly be the one and starts looking for some tricky complexity. When you ask him to explain his wrong answers to you, his explanations will show whether this tortuous reasoning is his trouble. Advise him to read a question through once rapidly and give his answer on the basis of a quick impression.

At this point the critical reader may justifiably complain that both rapid and slow reading have been blamed for mistakes, and reading more slowly and more rapidly have both been offered as remedies. This is true. The fact is, some people's minds work in a way that makes one method of test taking best for them, while the minds of other people make the opposite way best for them. Unfortunately, there is no simple rule of thumb to show a counselor the correct diagnosis and remedy. The best thing to do is to get the trainee's actual test paper and ask him to give the answers orally as you read to him the questions he missed. Talk with him about the questions he missed and see if you can find a consistent procedure on his part that is causing his trouble. Discuss where he has erred in his system of taking tests and advise him to lean more toward the other extreme. As a safeguard, give trainees this suggestion: Look at the question quickly and make a rapid estimate of the correct answer, then read the question critically. If critical reading shows beyond a doubt that your first answer was wrong, change it. If it is not pretty obvious the original impression and answer were wrong, do not change it. This system usually gives reasonably good results.

If it appears that a trainee can tell his instructor the answers to test questions but persists in answering questions wrong on tests after trying these suggestions, you might refer him to the psychologist. Remember, however, if a trainee is doing poorly on tests, the chances are about ninety-nine out of a hundred that it is simply because he has not learned the material, not because tests exert a mysterious hoodoo on him.

Counseling on Group Discussions

Many training programs depend heavily on trainees' discussing subjects or problems under the instructor's guidance. When a trainee is reluctant to participate in group discussions, it is the responsibility of the instructor to try to help him. As in the matter of taking tests, the most frequently successful way to get a trainee to participate more in conferences is to get him to improve his knowledge of the subject being discussed. Most adults can and will talk coherently and intelligently—if they have something to say. Therefore, when an instructor tries to help a person increase his participation in group discussion, the simplest and most effective way of doing it is *usually* by helping him learn more about the subject the group is considering. Of course, there are instances when a person knows the subject thoroughly but "the cat gets his tongue" in a group discussion, but these are freak cases.

To help a counselee increase his participation in group discussion, ask him to make a special study of the topic the group is going to discuss tomorrow. Suggest that he make an outline of the points he thinks should be covered and do some reading on these points prior to the group discussion. Tell him to figure out the best way of saying some of the things he thinks should be said in a discussion of the topic and come to the meeting with them on the tip of his tongue, ready to talk at the appropriate time. Few trainees are so lacking in verbal facility that they cannot participate to excellent advantage in a discussion if they have *prepared* themselves for the discussion by studying the subject to be discussed and formulating statements highly significant to the discussion.

In the rare case where a trainee does seem to know the subject but is unable to participate effectively, encourage him to extend his preparation for the conference to the point of finding a few people with whom he can discuss the topic before coming into the meeting. Perhaps talking about it with his wife will get his mind and tongue accustomed to working on the subject. If his wife is not available or cooperative, some written notes taken in the course of his study might give him the confidence he needs to try to talk.

If he is simply inept, that is, he says the wrong thing and antagonizes people, the training instructor should give him all the help he can through explaining to him how he might have handled a specific situation better, how he alienated the group, or how he might have used one of his contributions to better advantage.

Counseling on improving group discussion participation involves a mixture of citing specific instances in which the counselee was involved and drawing generalizations applicable to these instances. It means that the counselor-instructor must have paid careful attention to the counselee's participation in group discussions and must have sufficiently complete notes to be able to recall specific situations to both his own and the counselee's minds. This identification of a specific situation is usually necessary before a generalization on how to improve can be applied effectively by the counselee. Counseling on participation in group discussion is more difficult than most types of academic counseling because so many highly abstract and intangible elements are involved. In addition to the dominant factor of knowing the subject under discussion, personality, language facility, skill in human relations, knowledge of technical conference procedures and parliamentary practices, all influence a person's success as a conferee.

However, for work involving human relations, such as sales, supervision, work coordination, and the like, group discussion, along with role-playing, is one of the most valuable of all training techniques, and if a trainee is worth retaining for use in a position in which human relations are stressed, he is worth your spending considerable time and effort to develop in him facility in group discussion.

SUMMARY

Counseling trainees who experience difficulty in mastering material they are expected to learn in training courses requires specialized techniques. There are several things counselors can do to help trainees who are falling behind in their work. Sometimes simply encouraging them to work at the top level of their ability is all that is needed. Sometimes counselors can give limited assistance to trainees who have personal problems, and refer those with serious problems for appropriate professional help. They can also help many trainees by teaching them better techniques of reading, listening, note taking, and test taking. Trainees will learn more from the time they spend studying if they read an assignment and then try to recall what they have read, instead of spending all their study time in reading and re-reading assignments. Their ability to concentrate can be helped by teaching them to read with the purpose of locating answers to specific questions.

Listening is an unusually important learning skill in most training programs, because much instruction is presented in oral form. For most effective listening and learning, trainees should be taught to begin thinking about the subject of the training session even before it starts, sit erect, watch the instructor, and really *work* at holding their minds tightly on his material, even when minds try to stray away. In reviewing notes, trainees should try to recall everything said and perceive the implications of material outlined in the notes, not merely read over the outline. To be useful, notes should usually be taken fairly continuously throughout a period, and the trainee should take care to get real information and not mere topic headings in his notes. Important ideas, not masses of detail, make notes useful.

Most trainees who say they know the material but cannot show it on tests, in actuality have not learned the material. In a rare case, poor reading habits or emotional freeze-up on tests may cause the trouble.

Where a trainee is reluctant to participate in a group discussion, the trouble is often that he has nothing to say because he is deficient in knowledge of the subject under discussion. His trouble may be remedied by having him devote extra study beforehand to the topic to be discussed. If the instructor notes in the trainee manners of expressing himself that antagonize other group members, he should counsel him regarding them. Effective counseling on group discussion requires close, perceptive observation on the part of the instructor.

SUGGESTED READINGS

Buxton, C. E.: *College Teaching: A Psychologist's View,* Harcourt, Brace and Company, Inc., New York, 1956.

Davis, K.: *Human Relations in Business,* McGraw-Hill Book Company, Inc., New York, 1957.

Erickson, C. E.: *The Counseling Interview,* Prentice-Hall, Inc., Englewood Cliffs, N.J., 1950.

Jucius, M. J.: *Personnel Management,* Richard D. Irwin, Inc., Homewood, Ill., 1955.

Laird, D. A., and E. C. Laird: *Sizing Up People,* McGraw-Hill Book Company, Inc., New York, 1951.

Mort, P. R., and W. S. Vincent: *Modern Educational Practice,* McGraw-Hill Book Company, Inc., New York, 1950.

Staton, Thomas F.: *How to Learn Faster and Better,* Educational Aids, 2208 Woodley Road, Montgomery, Ala., 1958.

Traxler, A. E.: *The Improvement of Study Habits and Skills,* Educational Records Bureau, New York, 1954.

15

Broadening Your Qualifications as an Instructor

Instruction is partly an art and partly a science. It is an art in that best instruction occurs when every instructor is allowed the freedom of method and technique to leave the imprint of his particular personality and talent on his teaching. It is a science in that an instructor must have certain well-defined abilities, usually attainable only by disciplined study and practice, in order to do the best teaching of which he is capable. This chapter identifies areas in which the instructor can study and practice in order to improve his quality as an instructor.

IF YOU HAVE MENTALLY assimilated the principles and concepts of this book, you have introduced yourself to the field of education. More than that, if you apply these principles and concepts in the instruction you conduct, you should be able to do an adequate job of teaching a period, a unit, or a course by any of several methods. You should also be able to counsel trainees with some effectiveness and evaluate the results of your training program.

But teaching, the field of education, is a profession. Like any profession, it vastly exceeds in scope the contents of any one book. This chapter is intended primarily for the instructor who wishes to cultivate a broader and more comprehensive understanding of the field involved in instruction than any one book affords. If you are interested in instructing, if you think of it as a challenging activity to be mastered as a phase of your career development, you should familiarize yourself with the literature of (1) the subject you teach, (2) certain aspects of psychology, and (3) the field of education. By doing so, you will come to understand better the *whys* underlying many of the methods, suggestions, and admonitions contained in this introductory book. You will be able to formulate better methods of teaching specific topics in special situations through better understanding of educational psychology. You will acquire *perspective*, an acquaintance with the whole field in which you instruct, and with the field of teaching, which will enable you to cope with training problems in the light of broad knowledge rather than by rule of thumb. You will get ideas for experiments and research on ways of improving your training program as a whole. Wide professional reading is the bloodstream of professional knowledge. Keep it flowing!

Knowledge of Your Subject

With the exception of suggesting a few methods of obtaining information necessary for a lecture, the important matter of *knowing the material you are to teach* has not been discussed in this text. It has been assumed that when an instructor is being selected for a course or topic, the choice will fall on a person who knows the subject that is to be taught. However, there are times when circumstances render it desirable to instruct a group of employees on some subject about which no one seems to know a great deal. Perhaps that is the reason for the instruction—apparently no one knows much about this important matter, so there is a need to teach people about it! In actual practice such situations arise rather frequently. Then the person selected as instructor for the program is faced first of all with the problem of learning enough about his subject to have something to teach!

Even when one is thoroughly familiar with the subject which he is to teach, the need for research before trying to teach that subject may be acute. It is quite a different matter, for instance, to know from bitter experience how to handle a severe traffic jam and to *be able to explain* to a group of traffic squad trainees what to do, how to do it, and why. Many highly skilled people confess that they never worked and studied as hard in acquiring their skill as they did when first called on to teach it to someone else.

Probably the first rule to observe in studying a subject you are to teach is, take a broad viewpoint. When you find a book containing one chapter on the subject of your instruction, look through the whole book. It is a good idea to read it all, if time permits. At the least, glance through each chapter and read the chapter summaries if there are any. This is to give the perspective mentioned earlier. It helps you to see not merely what your subject covers, but how it fits into the broader field of knowledge of which it is a part. Sometimes you will find an idea about a subject obtained from one chapter would be vastly oversimplified if the contents of other chapters were not also considered. As an example, in this text the chapter on the lecture method of instruction contained little reference to producing a lesson plan. Lesson plans are just as necessary to periods conducted by the lecture method as to all other periods of instruction, but constructing a lesson plan had been discussed in a previous chapter and was not repeated in detail elsewhere. The chapter on lecturing confined itself to aspects of instruction particularly pertinent to the lecture method; repeating considerations which apply to every method in the discussion of each method would exhaust the reader. Other authors follow this same plan, and an entirely erroneous impression or faulty concept of a topic often results from studying one aspect of the subject, artificially separated from the broader area of which it is a part.

After acquiring a general familiarity with the literature of a broad field—fire insurance, let us say—you will usually want to begin to narrow your study to the particular subject on which you are to conduct instruction—perhaps the determination of categories of property for fire insurance purposes. Here your intensive study begins. You will want to study the principles of categorizing properties in the light of the perspective gained through your broad reading and then develop a lesson plan which covers those principles. You can save yourself much time and effort in the long run by gathering all the information you can find on property types, then formulating your instruction by picking the bits which best fit your needs. As was said in Chapter 5, *thinking through* your subject is one essential step in preparing a period of instruction. However, supplementing your own thinking through of the subject by selecting ideas and material from authoritative sources is shorter and surer than depending entirely on your imagination to determine the content of your period.

The ability to locate information about a given subject quickly, with the assurance that no significant aspect or source has been overlooked, is a valuable instructional skill. There are several basic sources which should be covered in doing research for instruction on any subject. If you work for a sizable organization, there are company publications. Almost every large corporation has a research and writing staff whose principal function is to gather information on various subjects of concern to the corporation and put it in readable, informative form. If you have not received manuals or pamphlets on your instructional subject, write your home office, asking if anything is available.

If you are with a smaller company, you may not have this resource, but you probably have another source equally good. This is the industry association. Whether your work is with a department store or a machine shop, there is almost surely a national organization of companies in your line of business. These organizations supply their members with up-to-date information and ideas on all sorts of topics of interest to the particular industry. Often they will even provide a nonmember with information on a specific topic, as an advertising or good-will measure.

The librarian at your local public library can help you locate the names and addresses of organizations which would be sources of information on the subject in which you are particularly interested. While at the library, you might also look for magazines slanted toward your line of work. Even if the library does not subscribe to any, it will have a reference volume from which you can obtain the names and addresses of periodicals along your special line of interest. Such magazines depend on the interest, accuracy, and importance of their articles to attract subscribers and advertisers and are a rich source of new ideas and approaches for the instructor.

Of course, all this takes time, which means that preparation for instructing is not something that is accomplished overnight or in a week. As much "lead time" as possible should be provided for all preparation for instruction.

Readers' Guide to Periodical Literature is an invaluable source of information on what has been published in the popular magazines on various subjects. Some professional and technical journals are covered by this index, too. Often articles listed here will contain human interest stories and illustrations not found in the more specialized publications. Such human interest slants and illustrative examples can make the difference between a dull and depressing instruction period and a bright and inspiring one.

The library's subject-card index conveniently locates in one place cards on all the library's books on a given topic. This is an ideal resource from which to work in doing your original broad reading to gain perspective on your subject. Do not overlook references in the books you read to *other* books and periodicals, too. If your library does not have these references, it can probably get them for you on an interlibrary loan from another library at little or no cost to you.

As may be seen from this discussion, the public library is a veritable warehouse of information on virtually every subject in which mankind is interested. It behooves every instructor to familiarize himself with it and its resources, for it can save him untold hours of work and enable him to do a better job.

Talking with other people knowledgeable in your field will give you leads to sources of information, and give you as well the benefit of their knowledge and thinking on the subject itself.

Knowledge of Psychology

We have said that instructors teach two things, subject matter and people. To be more than a technician in the business of instruction, then, the instructor needs to develop a better-than-average understanding of psychology. Do not make the mistake of thinking that because your present work involves dealing with people, you therefore know all you need to know about psychology. One learns a little smattering of a few specific applications that way, comparable to the training as a lawyer one gets from serving on several juries!

Your public library will also have a good assortment of standard college texts on psychology. (If you took a course in psychology in college, you will be surprised to find how much more meaningful a book on the subject is now, since you have acquired more maturity, than it was when you originally studied it.) Look through several of them. Discard those which seem to limit themselves to physiological discussions of man's make-up or tight little compartments suggested by "perception," "sensation," etc., as chapter titles. These can be excellent for the young scholar intent on studying the subject as a discipline, but for your purposes, find a book emphasizing the applications of psychology to man's life. If the book seems to be concerned with such topics as "ways of adjusting," "understanding our emotions," and the like, it probably has the approach that will be most helpful to you. (The suggested reading lists at the end of Chapters 1, 2, 3, 14, and 15 are good starting points for your reading in psychology.

Read your psychology text with a conscious effort to get a perspective on the nature of man. If you will construct a written outline of detailed notes on the book as you read, you will complete your course with a much better understanding of what your students are and why they react as they do. It will help you in understanding and dealing with other people with whom you have contacts, as well.

Having acquired a grounding in general psychology through reading (and especially through taking outline notes on) one or more texts, you will have the capacity to profit from reading in several areas of particular concern to an instructor. One of these areas is human relations, the art of getting along with people. It is particularly desirable to acquire a solid grounding in the field of psychology before beginning your reading in this specialized area because, unfortunately, much of what has been published on the subject of human relations is of a most shallow, superficial nature. You will hardly find a text in psychology which is not a sound, reliable book. By checking your books on human relations against sound psychology textbooks, you can determine which ones are in agreement with the known facts of psychology and which ones merely list and discuss a few tricks and gimmicks. You will probably find a section in the subject-card index in your library entitled "human relations." Whether you do or not, you will find considerable material in this area under the headings "personality," "character," "supervision," and perhaps "management." Much of it will be too technical to be of use to you, but you will find some of it valuable. You will find the books on supervision and human relations in supervision especially helpful, because the relationship between instructor and trainee closely approximates that between supervisor and supervisee. Many of the references cited at the end of chapters in this book include sections on human relations and personality development.

There is no doubt that any normal, intelligent person can improve his whole personality (meaning the impression he makes on people, and how well he gets along with them) by conscious effort directed along the right lines. Even the most superficial self-help books contain worthwhile ideas on what to do and how to do it to get along better with people, and the better ones provide sound guidance toward making yourself a more likable person. It really is important for an instructor to be likable, because trainees' attitudes toward the instructor inevitably color their attitudes toward the subject he is teaching. If an instructor is tactless, prejudiced, or rude, trainees' reception of the material he presents will be lessened. Motivation to learn will be at a minimum and trainees' attitudes toward the subject he is teaching will be tinged with the bitterness felt toward the instructor. A well-liked instructor is not necessarily a good one, but an instructor who raises the hackles of the people who work or study under him will necessarily lower his effectiveness as an instructor (as well as his chances of getting ahead in life generally).

Every instructor should have a good acquaintance with the psychology of individual differences. Many individual differences are superficial and unimportant—a preference for blue as opposed to yellow, hunting instead of fishing, outdoor or indoor work. Others are of great significance to an instructor—whether an individual is motivated more by money appeal or by social approval, whether he works best with moderate supervision or when left to himself as much as possible. In many texts you will find good chapters on individual differences in intelligence and their significance for the instructor. (See the suggested readings following Chapter 3.)

Other equally or more important individual differences are not so well identified in the average text. Differences among trainees in temperament, emotional reaction, and basic character are of significance to the instructor in making recommendations for future placement of trainees, as well as in adjusting the training program and methods to their individual needs. Psychology, generally and properly, concerns itself more with the common nature of all mankind than with the differences between men. However, chapters in psychology texts on emotions, personality, and individual adjustment contain valuable information on how people differ and why. You will find few suggestions as to how an instructor can capitalize on or minimize the disruptive effect of such differences. However, one of the purposes of the whole self-development program being outlined here is to give you the

broad understandings which will enable you to draw rational conclusions and make appropriate applications of professional data,
and not force you to accept uncritically the interpretations or
suggested applications given by others.

A vital sector of your self-education in psychology is the area
of educational psychology. Texts on this subject emphasize the
aspects of psychology having to do with learning and the instructional process.

You will find in these texts valuable additional data on motivation in learning. Various factors which influence the amount of
subject material a learner will understand and remember are
discussed. Some have special chapters on the psychodynamics of
learning physical skills; these will be of especial significance to
you if your instruction involves teaching trainees to assemble or
operate machinery, or perform other work involving eye-mind-
hand coordination. Frustrations—how people react to being faced
with demands they are unable to meet, or how they are affected
by being unable to achieve the goals they set for themselves—
are discussed in many texts on educational psychology. Some discuss the psychological pros and cons of different methods of
instruction—the lecture, the demonstration, and so on.

In reading the text on educational psychology, as in the case of
general psychology, study it systematically from cover to cover.
Do not pick and choose chapters out of context. Outlining, with
copious notes, at least the first book you read will be well worth
the time and effort it requires. Then you are in a good position
to read selectively, picking from a number of books the chapters
of most significance to you. Perspective, again, is the keynote.
One cannot evaluate or apply a segment of knowledge with sure-
ness and appropriateness unless he knows the big picture of
which the segment is a part. Remember how different a piece of
a jigsaw puzzle may look in your hand and in place? The same is
true of a fact or principle.

Knowledge of the Field of Education

The catalogue of a college of education may list from fifty to a hundred or more separate courses on various subjects more or less related to teaching. Degrees are granted in such diverse fields as elementary education, secondary education, school administration, industrial education, education of the handicapped, and physical education. Then there are entire subject-oriented fields of study such as educational evaluation, philosophy of education, and history of education, as well as educational psychology. Innumerable magazines are published on the subject, and in many libraries the 370–371 section (the location of books on education in one widely used system of library indexing) is among the largest.

Standing before such an accumulation of material, one not familiar with the field of education is likely to be baffled to know how or where to start. Much of it is of little use or concern to the instructor who is not in a typical academic situation—teaching literature, fourth graders, or the like—but it is extremely desirable for any instructor to become conversant with some of it. Specifically, if he is interested in broadening his competence as an instructor, he should do some reading in the fields of adult education, technical (or industrial) education, educational methods, evaluation, and speech and language, to say the least. Here are some suggestions on extending your reading beyond the references cited in this book.

ADULT EDUCATION

Years ago children were thought of as small-edition adults, and provisions for them in courts, schools, and at work were made on that assumption. Now it is known that this idea is erroneous, and much literature on education is written from the point of view of the *child's* education. This is reasonable, because most people attending schools are children or, at any rate, adults who have not yet faced the maturing responsibilities of earning a living or supporting a family. So, much of the material you will read on the subject of education will be equated to a group basically and qualitatively different from the group you will be teaching. You will have to depend on your broad understanding and ability to interpret and adapt the ideas you need and make adult applications of child-oriented writings. When you do find a book, article, or magazine on adult education, read it! Here will be a discussion of educational topics from the standpoint of people at least somewhat comparable to your trainees.

The librarian can help you locate materials on adult education and may be able to obtain for you (or find where you can obtain) special materials on the specific type of training you are conducting. You have a real head start if you begin your training program with a knowledge of other similar programs that worked and know why still others did not succeed, instead of having to learn it all through personal trial and error.

TECHNICAL EDUCATION

In many types of work, from selling to machining, through the years so many training programs have been conducted that a body of literature has been developed about principles and methods of teaching these specialized subjects. You will perhaps find little, if any, material on such a specialized subject in your local public library, but the librarian can help you locate it from other sources. The industrywide associations are probably the most fertile fields to search out in this area, as well as in the area of specialized knowledge of subject matter discussed earlier. You will find plenty in your library on vocational education, and while much material on this subject will be of little value to a training instructor, you will find analyses of skills and qualities required for success in different occupations which might help you in counseling your trainees.

EDUCATIONAL METHODS

This book is about educational methods, on the adult level. By choosing among the many available texts, you can find vastly amplified discussions of virtually every topic discussed herein. The references cited at the end of each chapter of this book are writings particularly appropriate for additional reading on chapter subjects. Some books, more specialized than this one, may devote several chapters to "planning a unit of instruction." Others may give such planning only perfunctory treatment, but deal at great length with the employment of the group discussion or conference method of instruction.

Although you are unlikely to find direct disagreements among them, you will find many differing approaches, points of view, and emphases. Most will probably be slanted toward elementary or high school teaching, but you will be able, as a result of the perspective gained from this book and your broad study of the field of education, to make adaptations to adult teaching situations of the good ideas you encounter. The books you will look for in this area can be identified by titles referring to methods of teaching or guiding learning activities. From time to time there will appear in the various journals of education new and useful ideas you can use to improve the effectiveness of your instruction. Make it a habit to look these journals over occasionally.

EVALUATION

Since about 1930 "evaluation" has grown from a fancy name for testing to a broad field which includes determining the overall effectiveness and success of an educational program, its methods, and the current and future success of its graduates. Statistics plays an important part in evaluation because masses of data can be more meaningfully interpreted by handling them according to certain proved rules and procedures. It is worth while for any instructor to read one or two books on educational tests and measurements and to look for and study in books on educational methods and educational psychology chapters that discuss such ideas as measuring the results of instruction or evaluating the success of a program of instruction. Evaluation is to education what control is to management—it is the system by which strengths and weaknesses are detected and ideas stimulated for over-all improvement. (See the suggested reading list following Chapter 12.)

SPEECH AND LANGUAGE

Words are the tools and the stock in trade of the instructor. A good mechanic learns the fine shadings of difference between wrenches of different shapes, types, and even brands. An interior decorator knows the advantages and limitations of different types of fabrics and how to use each to its best advantage. The more an instructor knows about language, the effects words have on people, and speech, how to use words orally to best advantage, the better instructor he is able to become. Correct grammar is important to an instructor, but impeccably correct grammar is probably less important than a number of other aspects of verbal communication. If you take your instruction seriously, by all means read one or two books on semantics, the study of the effects of words and their meanings on people. Some of these books may seem dull or too complicated. Do not bother with those. There are several books on semantics which are not only sound and enlightening but also interesting, stimulating, and easy to read.

You will probably get more practical help from books on public speaking and speech making than from texts on speech itself, although the latter are helpful if you are going into the subject deeply enough to be concerned with the physiology of speech, remedying speech defects, and fine points of enunciation. Books on planning and presenting a talk give greatly elaborated treatment to the topics discussed in Chapter 5 of this book. They go into much greater detail than could be done here on the use of anecdotes in talks, the divisions of a talk, how to use voice inflections to drive home your points, and many other topics related to oral communication. (See the suggested reading list following Chapter 5.)

SUMMARY

This book covers the basic fundamentals of instruction, but the ambitious instructor will profit by doing considerable reading in the fields of the subject he is teaching, of psychology, and of education. Corporations often have research and writing staffs which can provide instructors with special subject-matter information needed. Industrywide associations are good sources of specialized information on technical subjects, and the public library affords ways of locating, and in some instances obtaining, even those books or materials it does not have on its shelves.

A knowledge of the nature of man gained through studying one or more texts on general psychology is a valuable asset to an instructor, and enables him to make a better critical evaluation and application of the ideas he encounters in books on human relations, personality development, and getting along with people. Special reading in the area of individual differences is desirable, and one or more books on educational psychology should be studied carefully.

The discussion of various skills and procedures involved in instructing which this book contains can profitably be supplemented by the instructor through additional reading in the field of education. Of particular value should be books and periodicals on adult education. Technical education, educational methods, and evaluation are other profitable fields for supplementary reading. Finally, a study of semantics and of a few books on public speaking will assist the instructor in putting his ideas across in a manner which will encourage the trainee to listen, learn, and profit therefrom.

SUGGESTED READINGS

BAYLES, E. E.: *The Theory and Practice of Teaching*, Harper & Brothers, New York, 1950.

BROWN, E. J.: *Managing the Classroom*, The Ronald Press Company, New York, 1952.

BUXTON, C. E.: *College Teaching: A Psychologist's View*, Harcourt, Brace and Company, Inc., New York, 1956.

CALHOON, R. P., and C. A. KIRKPATRICK: *Influencing Employee Behavior*, McGraw-Hill Book Company, Inc., New York, 1956.

ELLIS, W. D., and F. SIEDEL: *How to Win the Conference*, Prentice-Hall, Inc., Englewood Cliffs, N.J., 1955.

FRANDSEN, A. N.: *How Children Learn: An Educational Psychology*, McGraw-Hill Book Company, Inc., New York, 1957.

FURST, E. J.: *Constructing Evaluation Instruments*, Longmans, Green & Co., Inc., New York, 1958.

GLOVER, J. D., and R. M. HOWER: *The Administrator: Cases on Human Relations in Business*, Richard D. Irwin, Inc., Homewood, Ill., 1957.

GORDON, T.: *Group-centered Leadership*, Houghton Mifflin Company, The Riverside Press, Cambridge, Mass., 1955.

GRAY, J. S.: *Psychology Applied to Human Affairs*, McGraw-Hill Book Company, Inc., New York, 1954.

JOHNSON, W.: *Your Most Enchanted Listener*, Harper & Brothers, New York, 1956.

LEE, I. J.: *Language Habits in Human Affairs*, Harper & Brothers, New York, 1941.

PLANTY, E. G., W. S. McCORD, and C. A. EFFERSON: *Training Employers and Managers*, The Ronald Press Company, New York, 1948.

RUCH, F. L.: *Psychology and Life*, Scott, Foresman and Company, Chicago, Ill., 1958.

STATON, THOMAS F.: *How to Learn Faster and Better*, Educational Aids, 2208 Woodley Road, Montgomery, Ala., 1958.

————: *Human Relations for Supervisors*, Educational Aids, 2208 Woodley Road, Montgomery, Ala., 1957.

16

Designing and Administering a Training Program

This chapter discusses types of training programs, how to determine the type suited to the needs of a particular organization, and some guides for designing and administering training programs.

EVERY BUSINESS ESTABLISHMENT that hires new people has a training program of some sort. There are broad differences, however, in the degree to which the programs have been formalized. In small businesses they are likely to be completely informal, sometimes almost accidental, consisting in showing the new employee a few things about his job, then turning him loose. The remainder of the training occurs as he runs into difficulties and asks questions or is given instructions.

Where the number of new employees entering a company at any one time is small and where the duties to be performed by the new employees are simple or routine, this may be the most economical system of training. It becomes uneconomical if large numbers of persons have to be trained or if the duties are such that a few simple directions and subsequent use of common sense by the employee are insufficient. It will work admirably, for instance, as a method of training a local girl to work as a salesclerk in a two-clerk store where her customers have known her and her family all their lives. It is uneconomical in a big department store, where customers must be catered to in a professional manner and where many questions of record keeping and stock-control measures are involved.

What Type of Training Program Will Be Best?

The company whose size demands more than informal direction of its employees may find its needs best met by one (or a combination) of three types of training programs: (1) a formal training course, meeting at certain hours each day or week and having a specified program of study, with lectures, reading, and assignments; (2) an on-the-job training program in which an employee is given some explanation of the actual work he is to do and then put to work under the more or less close supervision of a foreman or supervisor; or (3) apprenticeship training, where the trainee is assigned to an experienced worker to serve as helper or be given constant surveillance and tutelage on the work at which they are both engaged.

Whatever the form of the training program, its purpose is always the same: to teach the trainee something he would not learn on the job by his own unaided efforts, or to teach it to him faster, cheaper, and better. It is aimed at developing the ability to do, developing job-related skills, knowledges and understandings, and attitudes. It is a plan to condense the long, expensive, and sometimes painful process of learning through one's own experience to a shorter and more efficient program of learning, and the type of program which will do this best varies with the circumstances of individual companies. The remaining portion of this section of the chapter will discuss some of the considerations which determine the most economical and effective type of training program for a particular situation, and will conclude with a brief check-chart which can be used to arrive at an estimate of an optimum training program, considering several factors.

1. It is usually economical to have a systematized training pro-

gram for jobs involving complex or unique skills or knowledge. As a rule of thumb, jobs which require only simple abilities possessed by most people require little in the way of formal training. Incidental direction by experienced workers or supervisors may provide more economical training than a formal course, but some systematized on-the-job training might develop a more efficient worker. The simpler or more common the skill, the less formalized instruction will be needed. A holiday-rush clerk in a five-and-ten-cent store must have a knowledge of simple arithmetic to make change. She must know the physical location of few, if any, items. Aside from common courtesy, no especial skill in human relations is needed. She is not expected to know any details about the merchandise she sells, its quality, special uses, characteristics, and the like. A few minutes spent showing her the use of the cash register and telling her whom she should call if she encounters a problem, and she is trained.

By way of contrast, the woman selling household merchandise at premium prices by means of neighborhood party gatherings must have an exhaustive knowledge of her line of merchandise. She must be adept at human relations, especially the specialized field of promoting group action. She must know how to counter, without giving offense, adverse comments which might result not only in the loss of a sale to the critical person, but in lessening the buying spirit of the whole group. A training program combining extensive study of the merchandise she will sell with lectures and readings on applied psychology, role-playing, and written tests, together with an opportunity to observe the work of an experienced representative, would probably be profitable both to her and the company she will represent.

Skills of top complexity and difficulty can best be acquired, usually, upon a preliminary foundation of explanation and theory. Skills of lower complexity may sometimes be acquired economically by close cooperative work with an experienced fellow worker—a type of apprenticeship. This is particularly true when two or more workers work in close cooperation on a job where each needs to know and be able to do all aspects of the job. If guidance can be given by a fellow worker without constantly interrupting the trend of his thought and work, the apprentice system of training may prove adequate.

In summary, if the abilities needed on a job are complex, difficult, not possessed by people generally, and cannot be learned by watching and being guided by a fellow worker without considerable complication, some form of systematic training program is worth while. If the abilities are easily acquired, or teamwork is such that personal tutoring is not disruptive to work, a less formal employee training arrangement will suffice.

2. Where a number of employees are to be trained simultaneously, a systematic training program is economical. If a company has forty clerk trainees, each requiring an average of an hour spent by a fellow worker showing her the fundamentals of using the filing system and routing correspondence, a substantial saving may result from having all the new people taught as a group by a well-qualified supervisor. In addition to saving the time of the clerks who would have done the individual tutoring, using one person selected by reason of his special knowledge and skill as an instructor to teach the group is likely to result in better trained, more competent clerks than the forty unqualified instructors would produce.

Where the skills to be learned are more complex, smaller numbers of trainees will justify a formal training course. As few as three, certainly five, stenographers who will be expected to follow an organization's policies or special format can be turned into fully productive workers more quickly and economically by designing for them a short training course, drilling them in the fundamentals their jobs require, than by any form of on-the-job training without the course. Sometimes it may prove advantageous to accumulate as many trainees as a program will readily accommodate and put them through one course, instead of using the personal tutoring system.

3. Jobs regularly performed under relatively loose supervision

call for a more intensive training program than do jobs more closely supervised. If an employee is very closely supervised, he can perhaps be trained in the natural course of that supervision with little extra expenditure of the supervisor's time. If the supervisor must divide his attention over a large number of workers, diverting a disproportionate amount of time and effort to one person who must be trained as well as supervised can result in a serious lowering of the working efficiency of the entire unit through inadequate supervision. Training performed by supervisors not especially trained as instructors almost inevitably becomes training which follows the path of resolving difficulties as they arise. Much working time may be lost by untrained employees' time-wasting procedures before they come to the attention of the supervisor for correction. Incorrect or time-consuming procedures may become habits hard to break before being noticed by the supervisor, and the training process will require more time than would have been necessary to train the employee correctly in the first place.

Teaching, instructing, and training are an art. A person may be quite competent to detect unsatisfactory work, keep employee cooperation good, do the work being supervised, and satisfactorily help employees overcome specific difficulties they encounter, without being able to teach the best way of performing the job as clearly and skillfully as another person might. Supervisors are not ordinarily selected primarily for their ability to teach an untrained person from scratch. A special group of people extensively used to conduct instruction in their departments can be so selected; therefore they are generally likely to do a better job of it. There is usually an advantageous order in which a trainee should learn the functions required in his job, and a clear way, as well as many confusing ways, of explaining those functions to him. The instructor spending a considerable proportion of his time in perfecting an optimum way of teaching trainees is likely to develop greater skill in training than that possessed by the supervisor, to whom the training of new employees is an incidental part of his work. If a supervisor is unusually gifted in training new employees, he will probably achieve as good results as would a formal training program. In such an event, it may be economical to let this gifted supervisor devote his efforts to training all new employees in his department so that all, not merely his portion, will benefit from his unusual capability to turn out highly competent workers in the shortest period of time. It is usually economical to substitute training for continued close supervision where other circumstances render this practical.

4. The more limited the supervisory personnel, the less time available, and the scarcer the equipment or material required for training, the greater the need for a formal training program. Few jobs cannot be learned through on-the-job experience and coaching if personal tutoring facilities, expendable learning time, and the amount of semiskilled use of equipment and material available for the work are unlimited. At the beginning of the chapter training was referred to as a process of condensing the time required for a person's growth to a specified level of skill, knowledge, or attitude. The greater the pressure for achieving a high level of employee proficiency in a short period of time with a minimum waste of manpower, the greater the value of a training program.

Checking the circumstances of a particular organization against Table 4 will provide a rough estimate of the possible economy of different types of training programs. If the answers predominantly fall on the left side of the chart, the organization probably has little need of a formal training program. If the answers tend to run down the middle, a carefully designed on-the-job training program involving apprentice training or close supervision should meet the company's needs. If the answers tend to fall on the right, a training course of a length appropriate to the skill level will probably save the company money. (There are three exceptions to this general interpretation: If either Item 2 or 7 falls on the right, some sort of training course is likely to be in the best interests of economy. If both Items 4 and 5 fall on the extreme left, an on-the-job training program is likely to give better results, although it will not necessarily be most economical.)

TABLE 4. CHART FOR DETERMINING TRAINING NEEDS

1. The skills and knowledges required by employees are:
    (*a*) simple? (*b*) moderate? (*c*) complex? (*d*) very complex?
2. The number of trainees ordinarily being trained at the same time is:
    (*a*) 1–2? (*b*) 3–4? (*c*) 5–6? (*d*) 7–8? (*e*) 9–10? (*f*) 10+?
3. There would be such a group to train:
    (*a*) yearly? (*b*) quarterly? (*c*) monthly? (*d*) weekly?
4. Normal supervision of work is:
    (*a*) close? (*b*) fairly close? (*c*) loose? (*d*) perfunctory or nominal?
5. The degree of training and skill of supervisors is:
    (*a*) high? (*b*) average? (*c*) low? (*d*) very low?
6. Learning by watching or being helped by other workers is:
    (*a*) effective and   (*b*) effective but in-   (*c*) ineffective or
    inexpensive?   terferes with work?   difficult?
7. Use of workers of comparatively low skill is:
    (*a*) all right for a   (*b*) possible but dif-   (*c*) quite unsatis-
    short time?   ficult or undesirable?   factory?

Organizing and Administering a Training Program

Should a training program be organized and administered on a departmental or companywide basis? Should each department be responsible for the training of its personnel, or can the job be done better and more economically through one highly specialized department responsible for training?

A mixture of the plans usually gives better results and is certainly adaptable to more companies than either one alone. No one outside the department is likely to know its particular needs, resources, taboos, and operating conditions as well as the department head and his staff. At the same time, directing a training program is, itself, fully as highly specialized a skill as running a department, and excellent knowledge of the department's circumstances cannot substitute for professional knowledge of training principles and practices, any more than plenty of lubricating oil in an engine can substitute for a lack of gasoline.

The most satisfactory plan seems to be to have a director of training on a company's central staff (commonly under the department of personnel, although he may be elsewhere). His full-time responsibility is to advise, assist, stimulate, encourage, criticize, and otherwise promote the quantity and quality of training conducted in the various departments. Just having someone whose primary job is to keep training going on is important, because in every department training is *not* the primary job, with the result that it often gets neglected. Often every other phase of departmental work has a department member who has that phase as his primary responsibility. Each is alert to see that his area of responsibility is accorded its full recognition. Training, being a service activity rather than an operational activity, often has no one in the department primarily responsible for it, holds the lowest priority on personnel's time and attention, and is left out.

The director of training is ordinarily a staff man, as contrasted with line personnel. This means that the director of training cannot *require* department heads to conduct training programs nor dictate to them the sort of programs they should conduct. However, as the chief expert in a highly complex field, his opinions should carry considerable weight, and if he is given proper support by a company's executive branch, his advice and recommendations will be sought and taken very seriously by the line officials.

Whether responsible to the personnel department or directly to the president, the director of training should have direct access, without having to clear through any person or agency, to all employees and work of the company. Such direct observations and personal interviews, devoid of any official red tape, are one of his most valid tools for evaluating the quality of training being conducted in a company and for identifying areas where more or different training is necessary. Of course this direct access is essential in helping him estimate the type of training which would be most effective in a particular situation. His findings, being those of a trained analyst not involved in the current operation of a section or department, will be a valuable supplement to the views of the department officials. Together they present a much more accurate picture of a department's training needs than do the introspective observations of the department personnel alone.

Where differences of opinion arise between the training director and department heads, they should (as in the case of all disputes) be settled on a basis of mutual conciliation and compromise. When this is impossible, recourse must be made to executive authority for a settlement. Such conflicts will very often involve matters where the long-range training-program benefits envisioned by the training director seem to the department head to interfere with the immediate operation of the department, because it is the very nature of the job of the training director that his work pays off in the future, while the department head's pay-off is in the current quarterly operating records.

As a rule, the training director should be extremely cautious about taking a strong stand on the subject matter of a training program for personnel of a department. The department personnel are in a better position to know their needs. He may, however, have an obligation to point out that there is too much of something, too little of something, or too much detail in the proposed curriculum or that the subject matter does not support the professed objectives.

In the matter of methods, the preparation of instructors, the control of instructors for purposes of the program, and the adequacy of lesson plans, presentations, and similar educational matters, the opinion of the training director should usually prevail. A company policy leaving the department head final say-so on content of a training program and the training director on its conduct (and with strong advisory influence on selection of departmental personnel as instructors, as well as control of them when they function as instructors) will usually afford the best training program.

Setting Up a Supervisor-conducted On-the-job Training Program

A supervisor-conducted on-the-job training program is the first step away from the completely informal "show them their job and drop by occasionally" type of training. It involves a supervisor's giving a trainee or trainees a demonstration of the job to be done and an explanation of how to do it, observing the trainee doing it and suggesting how he might do it better, and subsequently checking up to note progress and give help where needed. It is an economical and effective method of teaching common or simple skills if the quality of the supervisors is high and if they know something of instructional methods. It is woefully wasteful if supervisors are merely somewhat more highly skilled workers, without special skill in teaching.

If a training director and a department head agree that an on-the-job type of training program meets the needs of a situation —as it may be the most advantageous plan in training certain sales personnel, tenders of semiautomatic machines, workers on simple assembly or production jobs, or common and routine clerical jobs—they should study carefully the available supervisors and select those who would be best adapted to this work. Then the training director or his representative should conduct the selected supervisors through a training course, the exact length and composition of which would be determined by the quality of the supervisors and the nature of the activity they will be teaching. Such a course should include lecture, demonstration, and drill on the demonstration-performance method of instruction, as applied to manual and procedural skills. Particular attention should be given to teaching the supervisors how to make their explanations clear and plain because this is the area in which they are most frequently weak. In this connection, many companies have found it advantageous to develop packaged explanations (really short lectures) of various operations and as a part of the training course have the supervisors practice giving the substance of these explanations in their own words.

Some attention to human relations should usually be included in a supervisory training program of this type, emphasizing ways of correcting in a manner that leaves the trainee hopeful of improving rather than sullen and resentful. Role-playing is a good device for this.

If a supervisor has many trainees to instruct by the close-supervision process, it becomes very time-consuming, and provision for it must be made in other aspects of his work load. Some supervisors are simply temperamentally unsuited to conducting on-the-job training because of impatience, brusqueness, or mere lack of interest in helping others improve. This is not a training method that can be implemented satisfactorily by parceling out trainees among all supervisors. It requires selection and preparation of a skilled staff to prevent waste of time and ineffectiveness of results all around.

These supervisors should be given a work load reduced in other areas to make it possible for them to give the constructive supervision required by the supervisor-conducted on-the-job training. The training director should exercise initial close supervision over the instructional performance of the supervisors, often accompanying one as he gives on-the-job guidance to a trainee. During such follow-up activities the training director can observe the success of both his own instructor training program and the supervisor-conducted training, and accumulate ideas for the improvement of each.

A supervisor-conducted on-the-job training program designed and conducted according to these principles will save many times its cost every year in lowering the time required to bring trainees up to a full-production level and increasing their ultimate productivity. Also, and far from least, it will give trainees a respect for the competence and consideration shown in training new workers which will lower the high rate of resignation or absenteeism often encountered among employees in a trainee status.

Setting Up an Apprentice Training Program

Jobs where two employees work together, especially if they are of a nature that one employee can do predominantly higher-skilled and the other lower-skilled work, are particularly suitable for apprentice training. Jobs which involve more than two men working as a team are often adaptable to this type of training, too, but discussion here will be largely in terms of the two man team, and the individual instructor can make appropriate adaptations of the general method to suit his own conditions.

The bricklayer's helper is a common example of an apprentice-trained job. So is helper to a machine operator, stenographer to a legal secretary, and credit reporter for a credit rater. Obviously, one would not learn to become a stenographer by being a file clerk for a stenographer, or a lawyer by being a legal secretary. The critical point in determining the applicability of this type of training in a company is: *Are the knowledges and skills required in the particular job complex enough that simple observation and practice would scarcely suffice to produce them, yet simple enough that they can be directly explained and understood without a broad background of theoretical knowledge or specialized physical skills?*

The chief virtue of the apprentice training program is that it costs next to nothing to conduct. Trainees are performing necessary work virtually all the time and can pick up the up-grading knowledges and skills more or less as bonus effects, on the side. Furthermore, they are acquiring these up-grading knowledges and skills in the exact situation in which they will subsequently use them. Such supervision as they receive usually has the effect of helping them get more work done, and so entails minimum expense. All things considered, it can be a highly satisfactory training method!

As in all other training methods, a few things can be done to make it even better. Virtually every job nicely adaptable to this type of training requires some explanation to orient the trainee to the department, office, or section. The jobs are complex enough so that there usually exists a body of fundamental knowledge which, when mastered, improves the immediate efficiency of the trainee's work and provides a better basis for future learning. It will be observed that trainees under certain masters consistently learn faster and better than those working under others. This is clear indication that the way the work is divided between the team members and the way the trainee is supervised are influential in determining his rate of progress.

If the director of training and the department head agree that an apprentice training program best meets the needs of a particular situation, the next step should usually be an analysis of what trainees need to be able to do—a job analysis of the positions they are being trained for. Then the knowledges and skills required to do these things should be determined through observing skilled workers at work and through logical reasoning and deduction based on the knowledge and experience of departmental personnel and the training director. (Ways of expressing this information in usable form and putting it in a teachable pattern were discussed in Chapter 4.) The body of information thus developed constitutes the content of the training program.

The training director and department personnel should then study the different skills and knowledges to see how they can be most quickly and economically produced in trainees. Will several trainees simultaneously require some hours of explanation on basically similar matters? Perhaps an hour of lecture to the group each morning and afternoon for a few days would be more effective than having each one individually told it all by his other team member. Are some human-relations skills involved? Letting the trainees practice on each other a few times, after observing a role-playing episode, instead of on clients or customers, might save money in the long run.

When it has been agreed which objectives and learning outcomes can be most easily achieved by some form of group instruction and which can be done most satisfactorily by strict apprenticeship procedures, pick the employees best qualified to supervise the apprentices and develop their programs of supervision in the same manner that was discussed in the section on supervisor-conducted on-the-job training.

At this point it may be well to emphasize that it is imperative that both trainees and their tutors understand clearly that they are not just two employees working together. It must be clearly and unequivocally understood that the tutor is a boss (at least for the purpose and duration of the training program) and that the trainee is under him. The full benefits of the apprentice type of instruction are often unrealized because, through unwillingness to delegate authority or oversensitivity about a trainee's feelings, the department head does not make clear to all concerned that the trainee is working for his tutor. Trainees have a way of refusing to recognize this unless told it lucidly, concisely, and unmistakably, and chaos results if they are actually and officially in a learner status, but are permitted to act as if on the same level of decision making and self-determination as those being held responsible for their development.

The other portion of the instructional program for the apprentice-trainee, that consisting of more formal group instruction, should be developed along the lines discussed in the next section of this chapter, dealing with setting up a training course.

Setting Up a Training Course

Where a position involves many technical, complex, specialized skills or knowledges, there is seldom an adequate substitute for a full-fledged, formal training course. The course offers an opportunity to depend only on specially qualified instructors, teach a standardized curriculum, employ the whole range of instructional methods as needed, and get a maximum of trainee learning through reading assignments to an extent quite impossible in other types of programs. This is not to say the training course is better than the supervisor-conducted on-the-job training program or apprentice training. It is merely adaptable to more complex and higher-level skills and knowledges than can be taught economically by the other methods.

Training programs for supervisors, with the great mass of information desirable for supervisors to learn, are likely to give better results per hour spent when conducted as fairly formalized courses. So are programs training insurance underwriters in the intricacies of their subjects. Telephone operators are likely to do best if they are given a short course before going into some form of on-the-job training, as are workers in manual skills where a broad foundation of special knowledge and judgment is needed for best use of the skills they are to develop.

Company officials should see to it that when a decision is made to conduct a training course for a group of employees, the simultaneous decision is made that the course will take precedence on their time over any other duties. Unless this policy is supported from top management, the training director will be well advised to avoid organizing and conducting a course and concentrate on one of the other types of training programs. Morale, spirit, desire to learn, interest, all go out the window of a training course when trainees are excused because of other demands made on their time. Everyone recognizes that, whatever may be said, in actuality the training course is of second-rate importance, and the chance of getting high motivation, holding close attention, or inspiring the work that leads to comprehension is gone. Perhaps worst of all, in such a case no one beside the training director is likely to realize that outside forces have wrecked any chance the program might have had for success, and he will be held accountable for its failure. So many training directors have been caught in this trap that a special warning regarding it is justified.

Having received reasonable assurance that the first prerequisite of a training course, i.e., unchallenged possession of the trainees for an agreed period of time, has been met, the training director logically proceeds to establish the nature and content of the course (in conference with the department heads involved, of course). The first step is to survey the jobs the trainees will be doing and set as objectives of the course developing those abilities which the jobs require, then to identify the knowledges, skills, and attitudes which must be developed to achieve those abilities, and *then* to determine the materials which must be studied and the exercises performed to develop these knowledges and skills. (Look back to Chapter 4 for details on developing a course of instruction.)

Then instructors are selected. It is likely to be impossible to find ready at hand company personnel who meet fully the characteristics of a competent instructor unless the director of training is fortunate enough to have a full-time staff composed of people picked to meet those standards. If such a staff is not available, the training director, in conference with the department head of the trainees who will be in the course, selects from the department concerned the necessary personnel to serve as instructors of the course.

It is usually wise to assign as few instructors as possible. Unless the course is so long that an instructor will get seriously out of touch with his regular job, a few full-time instructors for the duration of the training course are usually preferable to several part-time ones. Not only will they do better work by concentrating exclusively on instructing, but they also will develop high instructional proficiency just twice as fast from teaching two hours a day as from teaching one. Of course, in many instances an instructor working full time cannot gather data and prepare lesson plans for more than one hour of instruction per day, and the staff has to be enlarged proportionately. It is "wasteful economy" to give an instructor a teaching load that is too heavy to permit thorough preparation. But up to that point, the fewer instructors, the better. The training director can give more personalized attention and help to each one, and the quality of instructor he gets is likely to be better if he asks for the *one* best man than if he requests the *four* best from a department!

With his instructors, the training director goes over the material tentatively identified in conference with department representatives as important for the course. There is a three-fold purpose in identifying this material *before* the instructors are selected:

1. It is desirable for the department officials to have a direct hand in determining the actual content of the course.

2. It gets more minds at work on the problem of what should be included.

3. Knowledge of what is to be taught permits more discriminating selection of who will be best qualified to do the teaching.

Assignments of material are made to the different instructors and the methods of instruction which will be employed are determined. A tentative schedule of the course can then be made.

The instructors selected will in all likelihood themselves require instruction on how to use the different methods. If at all possible, each should have a rehearsal with the training director or other instructors as his class. His audience should try to make suggestions which will enable him to improve his presentation before he actually gives it to the trainees.

The longer an instructor stays with a training course, the higher his proficiency is likely to become, and the more economical it is, since he can use his basic preparation of a period over and over again, needing only revisions and additional rehearsals. The lesson plan prepared by one instructor is, regrettably, seldom usable by another. So if a training director gets a good instructor, he should make every effort to hang onto him.

Follow-up of Training

No matter how well designed they may be, few if any training courses (or other training programs either, for that matter!) will produce desired results if they do not provide for follow-up— visiting trainees after the official training program is over, seeing how they are doing, giving them constructive suggestions when possible, and getting ideas as to where the training was weak or might be improved. So in planning any type of training program, and in discussing it with department heads, the wise training director provides for follow-up. Hour for hour spent, it will probably pay the training course bigger dividends than any other expenditure of training time.

SUMMARY

The simplest form of training involves a short introduction of the trainee to his job and incidental advice and direction in the normal course of his work. Where work is at all difficult or complex, additional training in the form of supervisor-conducted on-the-job training, apprentice training, or a training course is needed.

How highly systematized a training program will be profitable in a particular situation varies directly with the complexity of the skills and knowledges to be mastered, the number of employees to be trained at a time, the freedom from supervision under which work is normally conducted, and the time pressure for fully prepared workers.

It will probably pay any sizable company to employ a director of training who is competent to advise line officers of the company on training needs and how they can best be met. He usually has no direct authority over the operating personnel, but his advice and recommendations should be given strong support by the executives of the company.

Training needs for lower-level skills may be met economically by putting trainees on actual jobs under close watch and assistance by supervisors, following brief preliminary explanations. Where more complex skills and knowledges are required, more extensive study or an apprentice assignment under the immediate personal direction of an experienced worker is preferable before a trainee goes on the job alone.

At the highest levels of knowledge and skill, the training course is usually most satisfactory and economical in the long run. Such courses should take precedence over other demands on the people assigned to them. The instructors should be selected with care and trained as thoroughly as is feasible. The course must be carefully planned and rehearsed.

For best results all training programs should contain provision for follow-up observation and guidance of trainees who have completed them.

SUGGESTED READINGS

HAIRE, J.: *Psychology in Management,* McGraw-Hill Book Company, Inc., New York, 1956.

HODGES, H. G.: *Management: Principles, Practices, Problems,* Houghton Mifflin Company, The Riverside Press, Cambridge, Mass., 1956.

HOLDEN, P. E., L. S. FISH, and H. L. SMITH: *Top-management Organization and Control,* McGraw-Hill Book Company, Inc., New York, 1951.

JUCIUS, M. J.: *Personnel Management,* Richard D. Irwin, Inc., Homewood, Ill., 1955.

SCOTT, W. D., R. C. CLOTHIER, and W. R. SPRIEGEL: *Personnel Management,* 5th ed., McGraw-Hill Book Company, Inc., New York, 1954.

WHITEHILL, A. M.: *Personnel Relations: The Human Aspects of Administration,* McGraw-Hill Book Company, Inc., New York, 1955.

YODER, D.: *Personnel Management and Industrial Relations,* Prentice-Hall, Inc., Englewood Cliffs, N.J., 1956.

Index